Longman Handbooks for Language Teachers

Jeremy Harmer

The Practice of English Language Teaching

New Edition

 LONGMAN

London and New York

Addison Wesley Longman Limited
Edinburgh Gate, Harlow
Essex CM20 2JE, England
and Associated Companies throughout the world.

Distributed in the United States of America
by Longman Publishing, New York

© Longman Group UK Limited 1991

First published 1991
Twelfth impression 1998
ISBN 0582 04656 4

British Library Cataloguing in Publication Data
Harmer, Jeremy *1950–*
    The practice of English language teaching. – (Longman
handbooks for language teachers).
    1. Non-English speaking students. Curriculum subjects:
English language. Teaching
    I. Title
    428.2407

Library of Congress Cataloging in Publication Data
Harmer, Jeremy.
    The practice of English language teaching/Jeremy Harmer. — New
ed.
        p. cm. – (Longman Handbooks for Language Teachers)
    Includes bibliographical references (p. 285) and index.
    ISBN 0-582-04656-4
    1. English language—Study and teaching—Foreign speakers.
    I. Title. II. Series.
    PE1128.A2H34 1991
    428'.007—dc20   90-48696

Set in 10/12 pt Times

Produced through Longman Malaysia, VVP

Contents

For Philip

Preface

Since the publication of *The Practice of English Language Teaching* in 1983 much has happened in the world of language teaching: new concerns have occupied the minds of methodologists and applied linguists; new textbooks have been written; new techniques have become fashionable. We must be grateful for all this flux and change since without it teaching would be a grey and ultimately depressing experience. But of course it isn't (except sometimes!). It's a constantly interesting and exciting occupation and the new discoveries and insights that we come across or which are put before us make it more challenging and keep us on our toes where otherwise we might become stifled by the routine of it all.

With all these things going on it became clear that a new edition of *The Practice of English Language Teaching* was necessary. In the first place the textbook examples in the first edition were quite simply out of date. A new generation of materials is in use and this needs to be reflected in the book. Then there is the issue of methodology. In the last few years we have seen an awakening of interest in task-based learning, self-directed learning, learner training, and discovery techniques to name but a few of the many concerns that have excited us all. There has also been a renaissance of interest in vocabulary and vocabulary teaching.

These, then are some of the considerations which have prompted this new edition. Readers who are familiar with the original will find here a completely new chapter on teaching vocabulary (Chapter 9). Discovery techniques appear (especially in Chapters 6 and 9); there is an extended discussion on language learning theory and approaches in Chapter 4 (including new sections on Task-based learning and Humanistic approaches) and a recognition of the change in perception about what communicative competence might be in Chapters 2 and 3. Dictation makes an appearance in Chapter 7 and the chapter on communicative activities (Chapter 8) includes new categories for oral and written exercises and sections on learner training and projects. In Chapter 11 the discussion of teacher roles has been expanded and clarified; there is a new section on the use of the mother tongue. Chapter 12 has a new specimen lesson plan.

Overall the many examples of textbook materials have been updated to reflect the current style and content of such materials and mention is made of both video and computers – both of which are considerably more commonplace than they were when the first edition of this book was written.

Despite all these additions and changes, however, the structure of *The Practice of English Language Teaching* remains essentially the same. In Part A: Background Issues, we look at some of the theoretical concerns which influence the teaching of English as a Foreign Language. In Part B: Practice, we study materials and techniques for teaching, and in Part C: Management and Planning, we look at how classrooms and students can be organised and what is the best way to prepare for a lesson. The appendix on materials evaluation should help anyone who is in a position to select the textbook which their students are going to use.

The Practice of English Language Teaching deals specifically with the teaching of English as a Foreign Language (EFL). It is not focused especially on English as a Second Language (ESL) although much of the content of the book can be applied to that slightly different teaching situation. The book is directed at the teaching of 'general' English: the teaching of English for Specific Purposes (ESP) is of course mentioned, but does not form a major part of the work.

In the first edition of this book I acknowledged the help and example that I had received from a number of people, especially Richard Rossner, Walter Plumb and Jean Pender, to say nothing of the exceptional reader's comments from Donn Byrne and Jane Willis, Tim Hunt's encouragement at Longman and the support and professional advice which I received from Anita Harmer. Their influence remains in this new edition, especially that of Richard Rossner with whom I have been able to discuss many of the issues that a handbook like this raises and who has read some of the new version, offering constructive comment and criticism in the most positive and encouraging fashion.

Both Anita Harmer and (at Longman) Damien Tunnacliffe have provided encouragement and incentive for me to get on and complete this new version. In their different ways their enthusiasm for the project has helped me to tackle what turned out to be a bigger job than at first anticipated. As editor, Helena Gomm has helped to make the whole process bearable and Alyson Lee has cheerfully steered the book through its final stages.

I have been extremely fortunate in the comments I have received from Julian Edge which have been stimulating and often amusing. More than once he has been able to suggest ways out of certain problems, for which I am very grateful. I also had useful comments from Nick Dawson.

Since *The Practice of English Language Teaching* was published I have had the good fortune to work with a large number of language teachers in many different countries. The comments they have made and the feedback I have received about methodology in general (and this book in particular) have been immensely helpful during this period.

To all these people, many thanks. I can only hope that they will look upon the results of their influence and endeavours with pleasure.

Jeremy Harmer
Cambridge 1991

1 Why do people learn languages?

In this chapter we are going to look at the reasons people have for learning languages (especially English), and the reasons for their success as language learners.

1.1 Reasons for learning languages

Why do people want to learn foreign languages? Why do people want to study English? Is it for pleasure? Is it because they want to understand Shakespeare? Maybe they want to get a better job. There are a number of different reasons for language study and the following list (which is not exhaustive) will give an idea of the great variety of such reasons.

(a) School curriculum

Probably the greatest number of language students in the world do it because it is on the school curriculum whether they like it or not! For many of these students English, in particular, is something that both they and their parents want to have taught. For others, however, the study of languages is something they feel neutral (or sometimes negative) about.

(b) Advancement

Some people want to study English (or another foreign language) because they think it offers a chance for advancement in their professional lives. They will get a better job with two languages than if they only know their mother tongue. English has a special position here since it has become the international language of communication.

(c) Target language community

Some language students find themselves living in a target language community (either temporarily or permanently). A target language community (TLC) is one where the inhabitants speak the language which

1

the student is learning; for students of English an English-speaking country would be a TLC. The students would need to learn English to survive in that community.

(d) English for Specific Purposes[1]

The term *English for Special* or *Specific Purposes* has been applied to situations where students have some specific reason for wanting to learn the language. For example, air traffic controllers need English primarily to guide aircraft through the skies. They may not use the language at all apart from this. Business executives need English for international trade. Waiters may need English to serve their customers. These needs have often been referred to as EOP (*English for Occupational Purposes*).

Students who are going to study at a university in the USA, Great Britain, Australia or Canada, on the other hand, may need English so that they can write reports or essays and function in seminars. This is often called EAP (*English for Academic Purposes*). Students of medicine or nuclear physics – or other scientific disciplines – (studying in their own countries) need to be able to read articles and textbooks about those subjects in English. This is often referred to as EST (or *English for Science and Technology*). We can summarise these differences in the following way:

Figure 1 English for Specific Purposes

What is interesting about all these examples is that the type of English the students want to learn may be different: waiters may want to talk and listen, whereas scientists may want to read and write.[2]

(e) Culture

Some students study a foreign language because they are attracted to the culture of one of the TLCs (see (c) above). They learn the language because they want to know more about the people who speak it, the places where it is spoken and (in some cases) the writings which it has produced.

(f) Miscellaneous

There are of course many other possible reasons for learning a language. Some people do it just for fun – because they like the activity of going to class. Some people do it because they want to be tourists in a country where that language is spoken. Some people do it just because all their friends are learning the language.

It will be clear from this list that there are many possible reasons for studying a language. What will also be clear is that not all the students mentioned above will necessarily be treated in the same way. Students who are only interested in one of the forms of ESP mentioned above may be taught very differently from students who are learning English 'for fun'. Students who study English because it is on the curriculum need to be handled in a different way from those who go to a language institute out of choice.

Most students who make that decision – to study in their own time – do so for a mixture of the reasons mentioned above. We will be focusing on them in this book. We will also be dealing with students for whom English is part of the curriculum. We will not concentrate specifically on students of ESP although we will be mentioning them at various stages throughout the book.

1.2 Success in language learning

Why are some students successful at language learning whilst others are not? If we knew the answer to that question the job of teaching and learning a language would be easy. We don't, of course, but we can point to a number of factors which seem to have a strong effect on a student's success or failure.

1.2.1 Motivation

People involved in language teaching often say that students who really want to learn will succeed whatever the circumstances in which they study. All teachers can think of situations in which certain 'motivated' students do significantly better than their peers; students frequently succeed in what appear to be unfavourable conditions; they succeed despite using methods which experts consider unsatisfactory. In the face of such phenomena it seems reasonable to suggest that the motivation that students bring to class is the biggest single factor affecting their success.

Motivation is some kind of *internal drive* that encourages somebody to pursue a course of action. If we perceive a goal (that is, something we wish to achieve) and if that goal is sufficiently attractive, we will be strongly motivated to do whatever is necessary to reach that goal. Goals can be of different types; for example if we are determined to own a new compact disc player, a bike or a horse we may work overtime in order to earn the necessary money. If we want to win a TV general knowledge quiz we may put in incredibly long hours of fact-learning activity.

Language learners who are motivated perceive goals of various kinds. We can make a useful distinction between *short-term goals* and *long-term goals*. Long-term goals might have something to do with a wish to get a better job at some future date, or a desire to be able to communicate with members of a target language community. Short-term goals might include such things as wanting to pass an end-of-semester test or wanting to finish a unit in a book.

In general strongly motivated students with long-term goals are probably easier to teach than those who have no such goals (and therefore no real drive). For such students short-term goals will often provide the only motivation they feel.

What kind of motivation do students have? Is it always the same? We will separate it into two main categories: *extrinsic motivation*, which is concerned with factors outside the classroom, and *intrinsic motivation*, which is concerned with what takes place inside the classroom.

**1.2.2
Extrinsic
motivation**

We have said that some students study a language because they have an idea of something which they wish to achieve. It has been suggested that there are two main types of such motivation, *integrative motivation* and *instrumental motivation*.[3]

(a) Integrative motivation

For this kind of motivation students need to be attracted by the culture of the target language community, and in the strong form of integrative motivation they wish to integrate themselves into that culture. A weaker form of such motivation would be the desire to know as much as possible about the culture of the TLC.

(b) Instrumental motivation

This term describes a situation in which students believe that mastery of the target language will be instrumental in getting them a better job, position or status. The language is an instrument in their attainment of such a goal.

Many other factors have an impact upon a student's level of extrinsic motivation and most of these have to do with his or her attitude to the language. This in turn will be affected by the attitude of those who have influence with that student; if the parents are very much against the (culture of the) language this will probably affect his or her motivation in a negative way. If they are very much in favour of the language this might have the opposite effect. The student's peers (his or her equals) will also be in a powerful position to affect his or her attitude as will other members of the student's community.

Another factor affecting the attitude of students is their previous experiences as language learners. If they were successful then they may be pre-disposed to success now. Failure then may mean that they expect failure now.

What can teachers do about extrinsic motivation and student attitude?[4] It is clear that we cannot create it since it comes into the classroom from outside. It is clear, too, that students have to be prepared to take some responsibility for their own learning. But with that in mind we can still do our best to ensure that students view the language and the learning experience in a positive light. We can do this by creating a positive attitude to the language and its speakers, and we can try to be certain that we are supportive and encouraging to our students rather than critical and destructive.

**1.2.3
Intrinsic
motivation**

While it is reasonable to suppose that many adult learners have some degree of extrinsic motivation, and while it is clear that the attitude of students can be affected by members of their communities, there can be no doubt that intrinsic motivation plays a vital part in most students' success or failure as language learners. Many students bring no extrinsic motivation to the classroom. They may even have negative feelings about language learning. For them what happens in the classroom will be of vital importance in determining their attitude to the language, and in supplying motivation, which we have suggested is a vital component in successful language learning. As we have also suggested above, what happens in the classroom will have an important effect on students who are already in some way extrinsically motivated. We can consider factors affecting intrinsic motivation under the headings of *physical conditions, method, the teacher* and *success.*

(a) Physical conditions

It is clearly the case that physical conditions have a great effect on learning and can alter a student's motivation either positively or negatively. Classrooms that are badly lit and overcrowded can be excessively de-motivating, but unfortunately many of them exist in schools. Vitally important will be the board: is it easily visible? Is the surface in good condition?, etc. In general, teachers should presumably try to make their classrooms as pleasant as possible. Even where conditions are bad it may be possible to improve the atmosphere with posters, students' work, etc. on the walls.

We can say, then, that the atmosphere in which a language is learnt is vitally important: the cold greyness of much institutionalised education must be compensated for in some way if it is not to have a negative effect on motivation.

(b) Method

The method by which students are taught must have some effect on their motivation. If they find it deadly boring they will probably become de-motivated, whereas if they have confidence in the method they will find it motivating. But perhaps this is the most difficult area of all to be certain of. We said earlier that a really motivated student will probably succeed whatever method (within reason) is used. It is also true that different students are more or less sympathetic to any particular method depending upon their expectations. Teachers can easily recall students who felt that there was not enough grammar or enough conversation (depending on the students' taste at the time)! Despite various attempts there is unfortunately no research which clearly shows the success of one method over another. What we do know, however, is that if the student loses confidence in the method he or she will become de-motivated. And the student's confidence in the method is largely in the hands of the most important factor affecting intrinsic motivation, *the teacher.*

(c) The teacher

Whether the student likes the teacher or not may not be very significant. What can be said, though, is that two teachers using the same method can have vastly different results. How then can we assess the qualities a teacher needs to help in providing intrinsic motivation?

In 1970 a study done by Denis Girard attempted to answer this question.[5] A thousand children between the ages of twelve and seventeen were asked to put a list of teacher 'qualities' in order of preference. The children showed what their learning priorities were by putting these qualities in the following order (1 = most important, 10 = least important):

 1 He makes his course interesting.
 2 He teaches good pronunciation.
 3 He explains clearly.
 4 He speaks good English.
 5 He shows the same interest in all his students.
 6 He makes all the students participate.
 7 He shows great patience.
 8 He insists on the spoken language.
 9 He makes his pupils work.
10 He uses an audio-lingual method.

Interestingly, the main point of the study – to see if the audio-lingual method was popular – only comes tenth. Students were more concerned that classes should be interesting, and three of the top ten qualities (5, 6 and 7) are concerned with the relationship between teacher and student. We can speculate that these qualities would emerge whatever subject was being taught.

The students were also asked to list any additional qualities they thought were important. The most popular were:
– He shows sympathy for his pupils.
– He is fair to all his students (whether good or bad at English).
– He inspires confidence.

In a less formal study[6] I asked both teachers and students what they thought 'makes a good teacher'. The teachers were English language teachers in Britain, Finland and Spain. The students were half EFL students and half British secondary school children. The two areas that most of the people mentioned were the teacher's rapport with the students and the teacher's personality. People wanted a teacher who was 'fun' or one who 'understands children'. But many people also mentioned the need for teachers to motivate students through enjoyable and interesting classes; and quite a few wanted their teachers to be 'well prepared' and to be teachers they could have confidence in.

Neither Girard's students nor the small survey mentioned in the previous paragraph prove anything about good teachers; other methodologists have failed to provide us with a definitive answer either. But we can make some generalisations with confidence.

In the first place the teacher's personality matters a lot (and yet this is the most difficult area to quantify or to train for). But beyond that it is clear that teachers need to do everything possible to create a good rapport with their students. Partly this happens by providing interesting and motivating classes: partly this comes from such things as treating all the students the same (one of the secondary students I questioned said 'a good teacher is ... someone who asks the people who don't always put their hands up') and acting upon their hopes and aspirations. Most of all it depends on paying more attention to the students than to the teacher!

Lastly teachers clearly need to be able to show that they know their subject – or in the words of an experienced EFL teacher 'If you don't know what you're talking about they soon see through you!' They should be able to give clear instructions and examples and as far as possible have answers to the students' questions.

(d) Success

Success or lack of it plays a vital part in the motivational drive of a student. Both complete failure and complete success may be de-motivating. It will be the teacher's job to set goals and tasks at which most of his or her students can be successful – or rather tasks which he or she could realistically expect the students to be able to achieve. To give students very *high challenge* activities (high, because the level of difficulty for the students is extreme) where this is not appropriate may have a negative effect on motivation. It will also be the case that *low challenge* activities are equally de-motivating. If the students can achieve all the tasks with no difficulty at all they may lose the motivation that they have when faced with the right level of challenge.

Much of the teacher's work in the classroom concerns getting the level of challenge right: this involves the type of tasks set, the speed expected from the student, etc.

Ultimately the students' success or failure is in their own hands, but the teacher can influence the course of events in the students' favour.

**1.3
Motivational
differences**

To know exactly how or why your students are motivated will mean finding out how they feel about learning English at the beginning of a course (this would anyway be a good idea since it would give the teacher valuable information about the students). It is unlikely that everyone in the class will have the same motivation, and we have already said that motivation is a mixture of different factors. Nevertheless it is possible to make some general statements about motivational factors for different age groups and different levels. We will look at *children, adolescents, adult beginners*, *adult intermediate students* and *adult advanced students*.

1.3.1
Children[7]

More than anything else, children are curious, and this in itself is motivating. At the same time their span of attention or concentration is less than that of an adult. Children will often seek teacher approval: the fact that the\teacher notices them and shows appreciation for what they are doing is of vital importance.

Children need frequent changes of activity: they need activities which are exciting and stimulate their curiosity: they need to be involved in something active (they will usually not sit and listen!), and they need to be appreciated by the teacher, an important figure for them. It is unlikely that they will have any motivation outside these considerations, and so almost everything for them will depend on the attitude and behaviour of the teacher.

1.3.2
Adolescents

Adolescents are perhaps the most interesting students to teach, but they can also present the teacher with more problems than any other age group.

We can certainly not expect any extrinsic motivation from the majority of our students – particularly the younger ones. We may hope, however, that the students' attitude has been positively influenced by those around them. We have to remember that adolescents are often brittle! They will probably not be inspired by mere curiosity, and teacher approval is no longer of vital importance. Indeed, the teacher may not be the leader, but rather the potential enemy. *Peer approval* will, however, be important.

The teacher should never, then, forget that adolescents need to be seen in a good light by their peers, and that with the changes taking place at that age they are easily prone to humiliation if the teacher is careless with criticism. But adolescents also can be highly intelligent if stimulated, and dedicated if involved. At this age, getting the level of challenge right (see 1.2.3(d)) is vital. Where this level is too low the students may simply 'switch off': where it is too high they may become discouraged and de-motivated. It is the teacher's task, too, to put language teaching into an interesting context for the students. More than anything else they have to be involved in the task and eager to accomplish it.

1.3.3
Adult beginners

Adult beginners are in some ways the easiest people to teach! Firstly they may well come to the classroom with a high degree of extrinsic motivation. Secondly they will often succeed very quickly. Goals within the class (learning a certain piece of language or finishing a unit) are easy to perceive and relatively easy to achieve.

But it is still difficult to start learning a foreign language, and unrealistic challenge coupled with a negative teacher attitude can have disastrous effects on students' motivation.

1.3.4
Adult intermediate students[8]

Adult intermediate students may well be motivated extrinsically. They may well have very positive feelings about the way they are treated in the classrooms in which they are studying. Success may be motivating, and the perception of having 'more advanced English' may be a primary goal.

It is for the latter reason that problems often arise. Beginners, as we have said, easily perceive success; since everything is new, anything learnt is a success. But intermediate students already know a lot and may not perceive any progress. Alternatively they may be overwhelmed by the new complexity of the language.

Our job would seem to be that of showing the students that there is still a lot to learn (without making this fact demoralising) and then setting realistic goals for them to achieve. Once again, a major factor seems to be getting the level of challenge right.

1.3.5
Adult advanced students[9]

These students are often highly motivated. If they were not they would not see the need to continue with language study when they have already achieved so much. Like some intermediate students (but even more so) they will find progress more difficult to perceive. Much of the time they may not be learning anything 'new' but learning better how to use what they already know.

The teacher has a responsibility to point this fact out and to show the students what it is they will achieve at this level: it is a different kind of achievement. Many advanced teachers expect too much from their students, feeling that the setting of tasks and goals is in some way demeaning. But just because advanced students have difficulty in perceiving progress and success they may well need the clarity that the setting of short-term goals, tasks, etc. can give them.

**1.4
Conclusions**

We have seen, then, that there are many different reasons for learning a language, and we have said that we are mainly concerned with a classroom situation in which 'general' English is being studied. We have included both those students who have themselves made the decision to study and also those for whom the study of a language is a compulsory part of their education.

We have suggested many different factors that may affect a student's motivation, stressing that a strongly motivated student is in a far better position as a learner than a student who is not motivated.

Most importantly we have said that both positively motivated students and those who do not have this motivation can be strongly affected by what happens in the classroom. Thus, for example, the student with no long-term goals (such as a strong instrumental motivation) may nevertheless be highly motivated by realistic short-term goals within the learning process.

We have seen that the teacher's personality and the rapport he or she is able to establish with the students are of vital importance: so too is the ability to provide motivating and interesting classes which are based both on a knowledge of techniques and activities and upon our ability to inspire confidence in our students and have answers to their questions.

Teachers, too, must realise the important effect success has on motivation. They must be able to assess the students' ability so that the latter are faced with the right degree of challenge: success, in other words, should not be too easy or too difficult.

Discussion

1 Can you think of any other reasons why people learn languages apart from those given in 1.1?
2 Why are your students learning English?
3 What is a 'good method'? (See 1.2.3 (b).)
4 Which of the different types of student in 1.3 would you like to teach? Why?

Exercises

1 Design a questionnaire which will tell you:
   a) Why your students are learning English.
   b) If they are intrinsically motivated.
   Give it to the students. Discuss the results with colleagues and students.
2 In consultation with a colleague decide on three more qualities a teacher needs apart from those mentioned in 1.2.3 (c).
3 With a colleague choose one of the levels/age groups mentioned in 1.3 and make a list of things you could do with them which would not be suitable for the other ages/levels mentioned.

References

1 For more on ESP see R Mackay and A Mountford (1978), T Hutchinson and A Waters (1984) and C Kennedy and R Bolitho (1984).
2 Of course it is not as simple as that, and many ESP students may also want to do other things with the language rather than just restricting themselves to the specific purpose they are studying for.
3 Gardner and Lambert were largely responsible for this division – and for discussing the importance of motivation. The results of their research, in

which they suggested that the most successful students were integratively motivated, can be found in R Gardner and W Lambert (1972). See also E Hamp-Lyons (1983) and E Hoadley-Maidment (1977).

4 See R Allwright (1977a) who argues that teachers cannot be responsible for all of the student's motivation: in the end that must be the responsibility of the student.

5 This study is described in D Girard (1977).

6 The study was carried out in preparation for a paper called 'What makes a good teacher?' first given at the 1990 JALT (Japanese Association of Language Teachers) conference.

7 For more on teaching children see W Scott and L Ytreberg (1990) and T Doble (1984).

8 For a discussion of motivation problems and their solutions at the intermediate level see M Pujals (1986).

9 On teaching advanced learners see, for example, L Munro and S Parker (1985) and H Thomas (1984). See also the section on projects in 8.4.

2

What a native speaker knows

In this chapter[1] we will analyse what it is that native speakers know about their language which enables them to use that language effectively. Our description of what native speakers know is obviously idealised, but they all share the characteristics we will be talking about to some extent. (It should be said that this is true not just of native speakers, but also of any competent users of that language – people who use it as a second, third or fourth means of communication, for example.[2]) We will look at the following areas of native speaker knowledge: *pronunciation, grammar, vocabulary, appropriacy, discourse and language skills.*

2.1 Pronunciation[3]

Native speakers (or competent users of the language) know how to say a word – that is how to pronounce it. This knowledge is made up of three areas, *sounds, stress* and *intonation*.

2.1.1 Sounds

On their own the sounds of a language may well be meaningless. If you say /t/ (the lines show that this is phonetic script) a few times, e.g. '*tu, tu, tu*' it will not mean very much in English. Neither will the sounds /k/, /a/, or /s/. But if we put all these sounds together in a certain order we end up with the word 'cats' – and that does mean something.

All words are made up of sounds like this, and speakers of a language need to know these sounds if they are to understand what is said to them and be understood in their turn. Some of the problems that speakers of English as a foreign language have are precisely because they have difficulty with individual sounds – for example the Spanish speaker who says 'bery' instead of 'very' or the Japanese speaker who says a word which sounds like 'light' instead of the intended 'right'.

2.1.2 Stress

When they use a word native speakers know which part of that word should receive the heaviest emphasis. For example, in the word 'photograph' not all the parts are of equal importance. We can divide the word into three parts: '*pho*', '*to*', and '*graph*'. Competent speakers of the language will say the

11

word like this, '*PHOtograph*', stressing the first syllable. The situation changes with the word 'photographer' where the stress shifts to the second syllable, i.e. '*phoTOgrapher*'. Stress in words also changes depending upon a word's grammatical function: '*perMIT*' is a verb, but '*PERmit*' is a noun, and the same is true of the words '*imPORT*' and '*IMport*', for example.

The changing use of stress in sentences is also one of the areas of knowledge that competent language speakers have. For example if I say '*I can RUN*' I am probably only talking about my ability to run. But if I say '*I CAN run*' I am probably stressing the word *can* because somebody is suggesting that I am not able to run and I am vehemently denying it. In the same way if someone said to you ' *Is this your PENcil?*' it might well be a simple question with no hidden meaning, but if the question was '*Is this YOUR pencil?*' this might suggest that there was something very surprising about your ownership of the pencil.

Native speakers of a language unconsciously know about stress and how it works. They know which syllables of words are stressed and they know how to use stress to change the meaning of phrases, sentences and questions.

2.1.3
Intonation[4]

Closely connected with stress is intonation, which means the tune you use when you are speaking, the music of speech.

Intonation means the pitch you use and the music you use to change that pitch. Do you use a high pitch when you say a word? Does your voice fall or rise at the end of a sentence? For example, if I say 'You're from Australia, aren't you?' starting my question at the medium pitch of my voice range and dropping the pitch at the end of the sentence (on 'aren't you') this will indicate to other competent speakers of English that I am merely seeking confirmation of a fact about which I am almost completely certain. If, on the other hand, I say the same question with my voice rising at the end, i.e.

You're from Australia, aren't you?

this might well indicate that the question is a genuine one and I am asking the listener to satisfy my doubts about their nationality.

Intonation is a big indicator of involvement as well. If I tell what I think is a fascinating story and my listener says 'How interesting', starting at a low pitch and dropping their voice on the '*int*' of 'interesting' I will be fairly despondent since by their use of pitch and intonation they will have plainly told me that they didn't think much of my story. High pitch and a small fall, on the other hand would be much nicer, since that would indicate that my audience was fascinated by what I had to say.

Intonation is clearly important then, and competent users of the language recognise what meaning it has and can change the meaning of what they say through using it in different ways.

2.2
Grammar[5]

If you ask the average speaker of a language what they know about grammar they may remember the odd lesson from school, but beyond that they will say that they have forgotten what grammar they once knew. The same speaker, however, can say a sentence like 'If I had known, I'd have come earlier' without thinking, even though it is grammatically complex. How is this possible?

Linguists have been investigating the native speaker's knowledge for years, just as they have been trying to think of the best way of describing that knowledge and the grammatical system. What they have found is that the grammatical system is rule-based and that competent users of the language 'know' these rules in some way.

An example will show both a method of description and how grammar rules allow us to generate language. If we take a simple sentence 'The boy kicked the dog' we can represent it with a tree diagram like this:

Figure 2

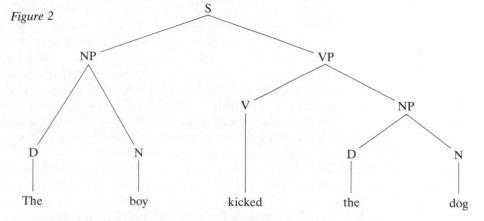

This formulation tells us that the sentences (S) contains a noun phrase (NP) and a verb phrase (VP). The noun phrase contains a determiner (D) and a noun (N) and the verb phrase contains a verb (V) and another noun phrase.

What is important here is not the particular way in which this diagram is presented, but the fact that it does demonstrate the grammar of one sentence. It is the grammar that allows us to make completely different sentences (which nevertheless have the same relationship between subjects and objects) if we use different words, e.g. 'The girl loved the man', 'The American ate the hamburger', 'The artist painted the boy'. In other words the sentence has changed, but the rule has stayed the same.

We can go further than this. Competent English speakers also know that these active sentences can easily be transformed into passive ones to give us 'The dog was kicked by the boy', for example.

What seems to be the case is that all competent language users know these rules – although the majority of us would find it difficult to articulate them. This largely subconscious knowledge consists of a finite number of rules with which it is possible to create an infinite number of sentences. Our one example alone could generate literally thousands of sentences and a moment's reflection will convince us that we will never be able to say all the possible sentences of the language. We will not even approach that number for, with the huge range of vocabulary at our disposal, it would just not be possible. And yet we all subconsciously know the grammar of our language otherwise we wouldn't be able to string any sentences together at all.

A distinction has to be drawn, therefore, between what we know and how that knowledge is used to construct sentences. The linguist Noam Chomsky called these concepts *competence* (knowledge) and *performance* (the realisation of this knowledge as sentences).

So our average native speakers who say they do not know grammar are both right and wrong. They do not consciously know any grammar and could not produce any rules of grammar without study and thought. But they do have a language competence which is subconscious and which allows them to generate grammatically correct sentences.

2.3 Vocabulary[6]

Of course competent speakers of the language also know the *lexis* (or vocabulary) of a language – although that knowledge will vary depending, for example, on their education and occupation. They know what words mean and they also know the subtleties of some of those meanings. Competent speakers of English know what a heart is but they do not get confused by sentences like 'He wears his heart on his sleeve.'

Competent speakers of a language also know the connotations of a word: for example, would you tell your best friend that they were 'thin', 'slim', 'skinny' or 'emaciated'?

Competent speakers of a language also know how to change words – how to make 'possible' 'impossible', how to make 'interesting' 'interested' and so on.

Competent speakers of a language follow what is happening to their language and how words change their meaning – and sometimes cross grammatical borders. For example the word 'awesome' used to mean something that filled people with a mixture of respect and fear. Now it means simply 'good' or 'great' (especially in American English (see 3.7)). Some nouns are now used frequently as verbs (e.g. 'to input' or 'access' data).

Competent language users, in other words, know what words mean both literally and metaphorically. They know how words operate grammatically and they are sensitive to changes in word value. Without this lexical knowledge they would not be able to use the grammar to generate sentences with meaning.

2.4 Discourse

Even armed with language competence and lexical knowledge, however, language users may not be able to operate efficiently unless they appreciate how language is used. Grammatical competence is not enough: native speakers also have *communicative competence*[7] – that is a subconscious knowledge of language use, and of language as discourse. Communicative competence involves not just language competence (grammar, vocabulary, etc.) but also a knowledge of how language is used appropriately and how language is organised as discourse. We will look at *appropriacy* and *structuring discourse.*

2.4.1
Appropriacy

A knowledge of language use is the knowledge of how to use language appropriately – how to get it to do what we want it to do in the right circumstances. Thus a British speaker of English would be unlikely to invite a high status superior to dinner by saying 'Hey, d'you fancy a bite to eat?' since such language would be inappropriately informal in such circumstances. Equally they would be unlikely to say 'I was wondering if you would be interested in partaking of a hamburger' to their best friend. We can think of many more examples: doctors speaking to doctors about an illness use different language from doctors talking to patients; adults do not speak to children in the same way as they speak to each other; lecturers do not talk to 2,000 students in a big hall in the same way as they talk to two of them over a cup of coffee.

What governs appropriacy? What factors can affect how we choose what words we use? The following variables would seem to provide some of the answer:

(a) Setting

Where are we when we use language? What situation are we in?

(b) Participants

Who is taking part in the language exchange?

(c) Purpose

What is the purpose of the speaker or writer? Is it to invite or to complain? To apologise or disagree? To explain or to demand?

(d) Channel

Is the communication face to face? Does it take place over the telephone? Is it contained in a letter or a fax or a novel?

(e) Topic

What are the words about? A wedding or particle physics? Childbirth or the latest film?

All these factors influence language users in their choice of words. For example, if the setting is a church and you are trying to talk to someone three seats away without attracting too much attention you may use as few words as possible. If your purpose is to enquire about your friend's father you might say (in a whisper) 'Your father?' Outside the church you might say 'How's your father these days?'. If you want to disagree with a close friend you might say 'Rubbish!' but you would probably not disagree in the same way with someone you had just invited to your house for the first time. You would not use the same language, either, in written communication (in a letter for example). With that channel of communication it would simply not be appropriate.

Of course the choice of language will depend crucially on what your purpose is. If you want to apologise, you choose apologising language (though here again you will have to choose between 'I'm sorry I've broken a glass' and 'I'm afraid this glass seems to have broken'). If you want to ask someone a favour you may well say something like 'Could you possibly . . .?'

Much of what we say, then, is conditioned by the purposes we have, e.g. apologising, greeting, denying, warning, offering etc.

Using language appropriately is one of the factors that differentiates native speakers from non-native speakers or competent language users from incompetent ones! But it should not be forgotten that native/competent speakers are perfectly capable of both intentional and unintentional uses of language which are completely inappropriate.

2.4.2 Structuring discourse	We have described how competent language users need to know how to use the grammar and vocabulary of the language appropriately. But there is another kind of knowledge too and that is the skill of *structuring discourse*.[8] We may know how to say things in the language but do we know how to string them together? How do we organise the points we wish to make? What do we say first?

In writing, for example, we tend to organise paragraphs in predictable ways such as starting with a topic sentence, continuing with example sentences and going on, sometimes, with contrary points of view before reaching a conclusion. In speech we use intonation and the restatement of points together with a range of speech phenomena (see page 212) to structure what we say.

All the 'knowledges' we have talked about so far concern the knowing *of/about* certain things (grammar, appropriacy, discourse structure etc.). We have been able to describe this knowledge as competence or communicative competence. But perhaps there is also another type of competence – the knowledge of *how* to use the language, the knowledge of *how* to access and use all those other knowledges. Together with (communicative) competence, in other words, we may also have a *strategic competence*[9] which is not knowledge *about* anything but rather knowledge of *how* to evaluate what is said to us and of *how* to plan and execute what we want to say back. It is the knowledge of what to do with the language competence that we have, and it is this dynamic processing mechanism which puts all the other knowledges we have to real use.

2.5
Language skills

We have said that our choice of language may depend upon the channel of communication. If we examine this concept more fully we can identify certain language skills that native speakers and competent language users possess.

Literate people who use language have a number of different abilities. They will be able to speak on the telephone, write letters, listen to the radio or read books. In other words they possess the four basic language skills of *speaking, writing, listening* and *reading*.

Speaking and writing involve language production and are therefore often referred to as *productive skills*. Listening and reading, on the other hand, involve receiving messages and are therefore often referred to as *receptive skills*.

Very often, of course, language users employ a combination of skills at the same time. Speaking and listening usually happen simultaneously, and people may well read and write at the same time when they make notes or write something based on what they are reading.

We can summarise the four major language skills in the following way:

MEDIUM SKILL	SPEECH	WRITTEN WORD
RECEPTIVE	Listening and understanding	Reading and understanding
PRODUCTIVE	Speaking	Writing

Figure 3 The Four Language Skills

Of course this is a very general picture of language skills. We should also identify a number of categories (or *genres*). The skill of writing will provide a good example of this, since clearly there are many different kinds of writing. Writing an informal letter is very different from writing a scientific report. Writing a poem means using skills that are different from writing a (travel) brochure – which is again very different from taking notes. These various categories can be summarised in the following way:

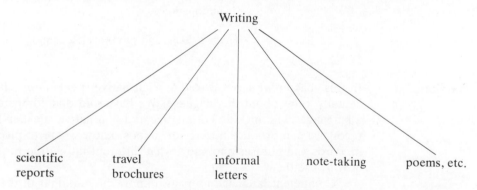

Figure 4 Writing – genres

Different language users will obviously have different skills.[10] In the first place a large number of people cannot read and write. Secondly, education, training and occupation often determine the set of (writing) genres that any one person can operate in. The type of speaking skill that dealers on a stock exchange need is completely different from that of a teacher since they are dealing in different speaking genres. But whatever kind of category of skill language users deal with, they still need to possess both the main skill and a number of sub-skills which we will look at next.

2.5.1
Skills and
sub-skills

In order to use language skills competent users of a language need a number of *sub-skills* for processing the language that they use and are faced with.

If we look at the receptive skills (reading and listening) we can see that there are many sub-skills which we can call upon. The way we listen for general understanding will be different from the way we listen in order to extract specific bits of information. The same is true for reading, of course. Sometimes we read in order to interpret, sometimes we read in order to transfer the information to another medium, e.g. a chart.

People who use language skills and the sub-skills that go with them are able to select those sub-skills that are most appropriate to their task. If they only want a certain piece of information from a radio programme they will select a way of listening which is different from the way they listen to a radio play; if they read a text for the purposes of literary criticism they will select different sub-skills from those they would select if they were 'reading' a dictionary to look for a word. It is because they have these sub-skills that they are able to process the language that they use and receive. We can summarise the difference between skills (sometimes called *macro skills*) and sub-skills (sometimes called *micro skills*) in the following way:

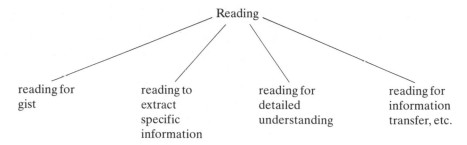

reading for gist

reading to extract specific information

reading for detailed understanding

reading for information transfer, etc.

Figure 5 Skills and sub-skills (Reading)

2.6 Conclusions

In this chapter we have looked at what native speakers of a language actually know about the language. We have said that competent users of a language (who include both native and non-native speakers) know how to recognise and produce a range of sounds, know where to place the stress in words and phrases and know what different intonation tunes mean and how to use them.

Competent language users also know the grammar of the language in the sense that this (largely) subconscious knowledge of the rules allows them to produce an infinite number of sentences. And of course they have lexical knowledge too – they know words in the language and how they operate and change.

Knowing a language is not just a matter of having grammatical 'competence', however. We have seen that we also need to add communicative competence – that is the understanding of what language is appropriate in certain situations. We also discussed the ability to structure discourse – our knowledge of organisational sequence which enables us to order what we say and write.

We considered one other competence that native speakers have – strategic competence. This is our ability to access and process our language/communicative competence; knowing how to use language rather than just knowing about language.

We discussed the four major language skills and looked at different genres within each skill – e.g. different kinds of writing or listening. And finally we said that in order to use a language skill the native speaker needs a set of sub-skills (such as the skill of listening for specific information or the skill of reading for gist).

Discussion	1 Do you know any grammar rules, either in your own language or in English (if it is not your first language)? 2 Can you think of situations in your language where it would be inappropriate to say certain things? Do you address different people in different ways in your language? How? Why? 3 How important is it for the 'average citizen' to be able to write well? What categories of writing are the most important?
Exercises	1 Take any word in English and say how many sounds it has. 2 Take any vocabulary item and see how much you can change it by adding to it or taking something away. How does this process change the meaning of the word? 3 Take any sentence in English and see if you can change its meaning by changing stress and intonation. 4 Take a simple English sentence and see how many more sentences you can make which have a different meaning but the same grammar. 5 Select one of the four skills (apart from reading) and see how many strategic sub-skills you can think of.
References	1 I am especially grateful to Julian Edge whose comments on the original Chapters 2 and 3 of this book suggested which directions I might want to follow. 2 M Rampton (1990) argues persuasively that the notions of 'native speaker' and 'mother tongue' are no longer relevant in a multi-lingual world. He prefers to talk about language *expertise*, language *inheritance* and language *affiliation*. In this chapter I use the term 'competent language user' to mean any speaker of the language who is an expert, whatever language they inherited. 3 An excellent book on sounds, stress and intonation (and issues of pronunciation teaching generally) is J Kenworthy (1987). See also P Tench (1981) and E Stevick (1982) Chapters 17–19. There is now a new dictionary devoted to the pronunciation of English words (see J C Wells 1989)) and practice books to go with it (see, for example, C Fletcher (1990)). 4 For more on intonation see M Coulthard (1985) and D Brazil et al. (1980). 5 This brief discussion of grammar relies heavily on the conclusions drawn by linguists and applied linguists from the work of Noam Chomsky. Readers who wish to investigate further can consult J Lyons (1970). 6 For a more detailed discussion on the range of vocabulary knowledge see Chapter 9 and the references quoted there.

7 The concept of communicative competence is based to a large extent on the work of the sociolinguist Dell Hymes. See, for example, extracts quoted in C Brumfit and K Johnson (1979). M Coulthard (1985) Chapter 3 summarises Hymes' work. For those interested in following the development of communicative competence as a way of describing language ability (and some of the re-evaluation that has taken place since the 1970s), the June 1989 edition of the journal *Applied Linguistics* (10/2) is worth reading.

8 On the analysis of discourse see M Coulthard (1985).

9 The issue of strategic competence was raised notably by M Canale and M Swain (1980). In his book on testing L Bachman explains the concept clearly (Bachman 1990, Chapter 4).

10 For a discussion of language skills and how native speakers use them see H Widdowson (1978) Chapter 3 – and see 5.5 and 5.6.

3

What a language student should learn

In this chapter we will use the information from Chapter 2 (about native/competent speakers) to decide what language students should learn. Should students of English sound like native English speakers, for example? How appropriate does their language use need to be and in what contexts? What coverage of language skills and sub-skills do they need?

We will examine *pronunciation, grammar, vocabulary, discourse, skills* and *the syllabus.*

3.1 Pronunciation

When we teach English we need to be sure that our students can be understood when they speak. They need to be able to say what they want to say. This means that their pronunciation should be at least adequate for that purpose.

In our teaching we will want to be sure that the students can make the various sounds that occur in the English language. We will help them to differentiate between these sounds, especially where such distinctions change meaning ('live'/ɪ/and 'leave'/i:/ for example), and we will also help them to understand and use certain sound rules – for example the different pronunciations of the *-ed* past tense endings.

Students need to use rhythm and stress correctly if they are to be understood. We will make sure that when they learn new words they know where they are stressed (see 9.3.3), we will make sure that they are able to say sentences, etc. with appropriate stress (see 6.3) and we will show them how stress can be used to change the meaning of questions, sentences and phrases.

Students need to be able to recognise intonation – at the very least they need to recognise whether the tune of someone's voice suggests that the speaker is sure or uncertain. They need to understand the relationship between pitch and intonation. When we teach language we will try and ensure that students use it with intonation which is appropriate.

One issue that confronts us in the teaching of pronunciation is that of accent. In other words, how important is it for our students to sound like native speakers of the language? Should they have perfect British accents – or sound like Texans or residents of New Zealand, for example?

Some teachers seem to think that students should aim for this ideal. It is worth pointing out, however, that some learners seem more inclined to native-speaker-like pronunciation than others. A lot depends, too, on their contact with native speakers. If they live in target language communities they are more likely to acquire the accent of that community than if they do not.

So although a lot of time is spent on pursuing the elusive goal of getting students to have perfect pronunciation, to some extent this goal is in the students' own hands.[1] But anyway it may be an unrealistic and inappropriate one. Much more important, perhaps, is the goal of intelligibility and efficiency. In other words our aim should be to make sure that students can always be understood to say what they want to say. They will need good pronunciation for this, though they may not need to have perfect accents. The teaching of pronunciation should, therefore, aim to give students *communicative efficiency*.[2]

3.1.1
The importance
of listening

In order to develop communicative efficiency in pronunciation the students need to understand how sounds are made and how stress is used. This is something the teacher can tell them through explanation and example. They also need to hear the language used so that they can both imitate the pronunciation and also subconsciously acquire some of its sounds and patterns (see 4.1.3).

One source of language they can listen to is the teacher, of course, and this source will be absolutely vital since, in so many ways, the teacher will be the language model for the students to aim at. But it is also important for students to be exposed to other voices and that is why listening to tapes is so important. Of course, if students are living in a target language community they should be able to find unlimited access to native-speaker speech through personal contact and radio and television. Outside such communities it may be more difficult, however, and that is why teachers must ensure that they give students as much listening material (on tape or video) as possible. The first answer to the question about how to teach pronunciation is that students should be given as much exposure to people speaking the language correctly as possible (see 10.5).

3.2
Grammar

Since a knowledge of grammar is essential for competent users of a language (see 2.2) it is clearly necessary for our students. Obviously, for example, they need to know that verbs in the third person singular have an 's' ending in the present simple (e.g. 'he swims', 'she runs', 'it takes'). They also need to know that modal auxiliaries are followed by bare infinitives without 'to' so that they can eventually avoid making mistakes like * *He must to go*'. At some stage they also need to know that if phrases like 'No sooner' are put at the front of sentences they affect word order, e.g. 'No sooner had I arrived . . .' and not * *'No sooner I had arrived . . .'*.

Luckily there is a consensus about what grammar should be taught at what level. Any experienced teacher will know that the use of 'No sooner' and other similar phrases at the beginning of sentences is a matter for advanced students whereas the correct use of 'must' is something that an elementary student should know. While there may be variations in the actual order of grammatical items taught (teachers tend to teach past tenses – especially 'was' and 'were' – earlier than they used to, for example) a glance through the majority of currently available teaching materials will show how strong the consensus is.

Our aim in teaching grammar should be to ensure that students are *communicatively efficient* with the grammar they have at their level. We may not teach them the finer points of style at the intermediate level, but we should make sure that they can use what they know.

3.2.1 The importance of language awareness

When we present grammar through structural patterns we tend to give students tidy pieces of language to work with. We introduce grammar which can easily be explained and presented. There are many different ways of doing this which do not (only) involve the transmission of grammar rules (see Chapter 6 for the presentation of grammar).

It is certainly possible to teach aspects of grammar – indeed that is what language teachers have been doing for centuries – but language is a difficult business and it is often used very inventively by its speakers. In other words real language use is often very untidy and cannot be automatically reduced to simple grammar patterns. Students need to be aware of this, just as they need to be aware of all language possibilities. Such awareness does not mean that they have to be taught each variation and linguistic twist, however. It just means that they have to be aware of language and how it is used. That is why reading and listening are so important, and that is why discovery activities are so valuable (see 6.4) since by asking students to discover ways in which language is used we help to raise their awareness about the creative use of grammar – amongst other things.

As teachers we should be prepared to use a variety of techniques to help our students learn and acquire grammar. Sometimes this involves teaching grammar rules; sometimes it means allowing students to discover the rules for themselves.

3.3 Vocabulary

Language students need to learn the lexis of the language. They need to learn what words mean and how they are used. Whilst this obviously involves giving them the names for things (e.g. 'table', 'chair', etc.) it also involves showing them how words are stretched and twisted (e.g. 'to table a motion', 'to chair a meeting'). Clearly some words are more likely to be taught at lower levels than others, and some uses of words may be more sophisticated than others – and, therefore, more appropriate for advanced students.

We should ensure that our students are aware of the vocabulary they need for their level and that they can use the words which they want to use – and/or the words we have selected for them to use. Vocabulary, what it means and how it should be taught, is dealt with in detail in Chapter 9.

3.3.1
Vocabulary
in context

There is a way of looking at vocabulary learning which suggests that students should go home every evening and learn a list of fifty words 'by heart'. Such a practice may have beneficial results, of course, but it avoids one of the central features of vocabulary use, namely that words occur in context. If we are really to teach students what words mean and how they are used, we need to show them being used, together with other words, in context. Words do not just exist on their own: they live with other words and they depend upon each other. We need our students to be aware of this. That is why, once again, reading and listening will play such a part in the acquisition of vocabulary.

When students learn words in context they are far more likely to remember them than if they learn them as single items.[3] And even if this were not true they would at least get a much better picture of what the words mean.

3.4
Discourse

When we discussed discourse in Chapter 2 (2.4) we saw how what we say depends on a number of variables such as where we are, what we want to say and who we are talking to. It also involves our ability to structure discourse – to organise what we say into a coherent whole.

Clearly students need to be aware of the different ways language is used in different situations. They need to know the difference between formal and informal language use. They need to know when they can get away with 'sorry' and when it would be better to say 'I really must apologise' for example. Such knowledge involves learning language functions.

3.4.1
Language
functions[4]

One of the variables which governs appropriacy is purpose. We decide what we want to say on the basis of what purpose we wish to achieve. Do we wish to invite? To agree? To congratulate? All these purposes have been called language functions, since to say 'Congratulations' to someone actually performs the function of congratulating as soon as the word is out of your mouth. 'I promise' performs the function of promising. With such words the relationship between word and function is easy. It is more complex when a superior says pointedly to someone else in the room 'It's very hot in here' in such a way that he or she is clearly requesting the other person to open the window.

The realisation of many functions can often fall between these two extremes, however, since 'Would you like to come to the cinema?' is a transparent way of inviting, and 'Could you open the window?' is clearly performing a request function.

We will want to teach our students how to perform language functions (but see 3.6.1), and we may well decide which ones are more important for which levels. A problem arises, though, with the actual language used for these functions. We have already seen the request function performed in two ways ('It's very hot in here', and 'Could you open the window?'), but we could also say 'Please open the window.'; 'How about opening the window?'; 'I was wondering if you could open the window?'; 'Would it be possible for you to open that window?' and so on.

In deciding what language to teach when working with functions we need to bear in mind the level of difficulty, the level of transparency (is the meaning clear) and the level of formality. In general it seems safe to say that easy, transparent and neutral realisations of a language function are better for students at lower levels whereas difficulty, lack of transparency and extremes of formality (and informality) are more suitable for more advanced students. In other words, we would teach 'Could you open the window?' before 'Would it be possible for you to open the window?'

**3.4.2
Discourse
organisation**

At the same time as students are studying grammar, vocabulary and language functions we can encourage them to work on the way they organise what they say and write. We can help them to see how other speakers and writers structure their discourse and thus help them to understand better.

For students of English organising written discourse is extremely important and we will study this in a section on cohesion (see 7.2.3). In the chapter on receptive skills we will look at ways of training students to recognise discourse structure (see 10.4.6 and 10.5.6).

**3.5
Skills**

As we saw in 2.5, competent users of a language are proficient in a range of language skills, though not all of them have the same range of sub-skills.

It will be our responsibility to see that the students' language skills are transferred to the use of English. In other words, we may not be teaching them to read, but we are teaching them to read in English. And because they are dealing with a foreign language we will need to help them with the skills that they are already (subconsciously) familiar with. We will emphasise reading for gist, for example, or listening for detailed comprehension. If we concentrate on these skills and sub-skills it will help the students to approach the foreign language with more confidence and a greater expectation of success.

Of course it is possible that some students may not be proficient at all the skills in their own languages. Then our task will be twofold: to give them confidence in English and to equip them with hitherto unknown skills in either their own mother tongue or English.

At lower levels our teaching of skills will be general, becoming more refined as the students become more advanced. A lot will depend on student need and the syllabus, however (see 3.6).

**3.6
The syllabus**

We know what students need to know about the language they are learning but before we start to teach them we will have to decide which parts of this knowledge we want them to have and when. How is the language to be organised and what skills should we concentrate on? This organisation is called a syllabus.

Some syllabuses are fairly short lists of grammatical structures or functions. Some are much more detailed, containing lists not only of language, but also of topic and subject matter or activities and tasks. We need to consider these various types.[5]

3.6.1
Structures and
functions

In the nineteen-seventies a major debate centred around what the focus of a language syllabus should be. Some methodologists advocated abandoning the older grammatical syllabuses (with lists like *verb to be*, *there is/there are*, *present continuous*, *present simple*) in favour of functional syllabuses (with lists like *introductions*, *invitations*, *apologies*, *requests*, etc.). The argument was that studying grammar failed to show what people actually did with language. It was suggested that we should teach functions first and the grammar would come later.[6]

It soon became clear, however, that language functions alone were not a satisfactory organising principle. In the first place some realisations of functions are in fact little more than fixed phrases (e.g. 'You must be joking!' 'Come off it!'). It may be important to learn them, but that is all you learn! In other words, some functional exponents are just single items – you cannot use them to generate more language as you can with grammatical structure (see 2.2). Another problem lies in how to grade functions. Which should come first? What order should the grammar be taught in for students to be able to apply it to functions? A purely functional organisation meant that notions of difficulty which had informed earlier grammatical syllabuses could not be used since the grammar used to perform one function might be more or less difficult than the grammar used to perform the other. And the teaching of functions raised many problems that grammatical teaching had not previously done.[7] (One contentious argument was that by teaching people how British people apologise, for example, you were imposing a cultural stereotype on them.[8])

The consensus that seemed to emerge from the debate was that in language terms grammar was still the best organising principle for a syllabus, but that functional uses could be developed from such syllabuses. A unit on the past simple might end with a lesson about apologising ('I'm sorry I'm late ... I missed the bus', etc.); a unit on *have to* and *would like to* might include a functional exchange such as 'Would you like to come for dinner?' 'I can't, I'm afraid. I have to do my homework.'

Students need to be taught functions, but they also need to learn grammar. It is around grammar that functional items can hang on a syllabus.

3.6.2
Vocabulary

One way of organising a syllabus would be in terms of vocabulary rather than grammatical structures or functions. This would certainly have the advantage of giving students words in an organised and sequenced way, and indeed with the advent of computer-based vocabulary studies such a syllabus has become a real possibility (see 9.2 and the references quoted there). Vocabulary-based syllabuses obviously need to mesh in with grammatical syllabuses, but the way in which such connections could be made is not yet clearly established – although attempts have been made.[9]

The idea of vocabulary as an organising feature of a syllabus – rather than as an afterthought – is closely connected with situation and topic-based syllabuses (see below) for it is with situations and topics that lexical items cluster together.

3.6.3
Situation,
topic and task

Language may not be the only way to organise a syllabus. We could also organise our teaching based round a number of situations – *at the bank*, *at the railway station*, for example. This certainly looks like a good idea especially if students are likely to be in those situations. But for the general language student we may find that situational organisation is a bit restrictive since it limits the amount of vocabulary available and may produce language use which only works in that situation.

Topic-based syllabuses take a subject or topic as their organising principle. Thus unit 1 might well deal with *health*, unit 2 with *fashion*, unit 3 with *families*, etc. Such organisation allows for a wide range of language and activities. Within the topic of *health*, for example, students can talk about the body, illnesses, sickness and cure, healthy living, environmental dangers to health, etc.

Topic-based syllabuses are certainly suitable for vocabulary material. They may also be more useful at more advanced levels since with limited language (for beginner and elementary students) it is difficult to sustain a topic over a length of time.

In general the danger with topic-based syllabuses is that they demand the students' continuing interest in the topic – something which we cannot take for granted. Nevertheless they provide a way of organising the syllabus which many teachers and students find attractive precisely because they do not insist on the teaching of language for its own sake, but use it in the service of interesting subjects.

Task-based syllabuses, on the other hand, take activities or tasks as the main organising principle (see 4.1.4). The syllabus becomes a list of tasks, rather than language or topics, etc. Task-based syllabuses are especially useful for skill-based courses where the students can run through a range of sub-skills in a variety of carefully sequenced tasks. For general courses however they may well be limiting in terms of language.

3.6.4
The syllabus and student needs

The final shape of a syllabus may depend to a large extent on the needs of the students who are going to be taught. The syllabus for a group of agronomists might look very different from the syllabus for a group of waiters. The level of the students will be vital too since we would expect a beginners' syllabus to be very different from one for advanced students. The age of the students may have a lot to do with it as well – especially where the selection of themes and topics is concerned.

Other factors will also play a part. How often do students study? What is the cultural and educational background of the students? What kind of institution are they studying in? How many of them are there likely to be in the classroom?

Depending upon our students' needs we may wish to restrict the syllabus in some way. For beginners we restrict the language in the syllabus. For science students doing post-graduate studies we may restrict the skills in the syllabus to (mainly) reading – although this is by no means certain. For waiters we may restrict the tasks and we may place especial emphasis on others – e.g. simulation and role play.

This book deals especially with *general* English, however, and in that context we must treat the issue of restriction with great care. Certainly, as we have already said, language may be restricted according to level. We may want to restrict our choice of topics and activities based on the kind of students we are going to teach, but this would only be in terms of suitability according to age and class size, etc. Teaching general English classes means that syllabus designers, materials writers and teachers have a wide range of possibilities at their disposal.

One area in which we would not expect to impose restrictions is the area of language skills – we would want to include work on all four skills in our syllabus, in other words. Certainly we might exclude some genres (e.g. writing technical reports, reading scientific articles) from our list and we might restrict our sub-skills based on level, but a general English course should be a four-skills course.

What then of the competing claims of the different kinds of syllabus? The truth is that syllabus designers need to be able to organise all the elements we have talked about into a coherent whole. Any programme of language study should have a list of language to be taught (and in what order), a list of functions, a list of vocabulary, a list of themes and topics to be dealt with (and the situations they are to be dealt with in) and a list of tasks and activities that are to be included. Whether you are designing the syllabus for a national education system or simply for your own class these are the issues that confront you (as we shall see when we look at lesson planning in Chapter 12). The manner in which these lists are written (or not written if teachers have them 'in their heads') may vary. The issue of which part of the syllabus is the main organising principle may not be an important one, therefore, since it is in the interrelationship of all the elements that we plan for our students' needs most adequately.

3.7 Language varieties

One last issue needs to be dealt with in this chapter on what students need to learn and that is the issue of language variety. Crudely, we can ask whether we should teach American or British English? What about Jamaican English or Nigerian English or Indian English? What about Northern British English and Southern British English?

The situation is very complex. We cannot say that English is one language. It is many languages, or rather there are many varieties of English used all over the world.[10]

There are some people who would suggest that some of these varieties of English are 'better' than others, but that is not an attitude which has any place here. What we can discuss is whether students should learn one particular variety or whether it matters which variety or varieties they are exposed to.

Three factors are important in this discussion. The first is the variety of English which the teacher uses. That will surely be the one which the students become most accustomed to. The second is which variety is most appropriate for the students. If they are going to study in the United States, for example, American English may be preferable to other varieties. The third factor concerns what variety of English is dealt with by the materials which the teacher and students are using.

For students at lower levels it is probably advisable to stick with one variety of English. As students go through the intermediate area, however, they can be exposed to other accents and varieties. Indeed with the status of English as an international language it is vital that any competent user of the language is able to understand as many varieties and accents as possible.

3.8
Conclusions

In this chapter we have discussed what language students need to learn.

We looked at the need to teach students how to produce and recognise the sounds, stress and intonation of the language. We said that for many the goal of native-speaker pronunciation was not important (or appropriate), but communicative efficiency (being intelligible in the foreign language) was. We emphasised the importance of listening as a way of acquiring pronunciation.

We discussed the grammar that students need to learn, noting that some grammar was necessary for lower level students while some was more stylistically appropriate to advanced levels. We emphasised the need for students to have language awareness and as part of this to use discovery activities.

We discussed the need for students to learn the vocabulary which was appropriate for their level and we stressed the importance of learning vocabulary in context.

We saw how students need to learn ways of performing functions in English and how we clearly need to train them in the use of language skills insofar as they apply to the foreign language and we emphasised the need for work on discourse organisation.

We discussed the basis on which syllabuses are organised and we measured the relative merits of grammar, vocabulary, functions, situations, topics and tasks as the main organising principle round which a syllabus could be designed. We concluded that the job of the syllabus designer was to combine all these elements to a greater or lesser degree depending upon the needs of the students.

Finally we discussed the many varieties of English. We said that at lower levels the teacher's variety of English might be the main one for the students whereas for more advanced students knowledge of many varieties is a definite advantage.

Discussion

1 How important is good pronunciation in a foreign language to you? How important is it for your students? What is good pronunciation?

2 How important is it to teach grammar? What is the best way of doing it?

3 Would you teach the four skills equally on a general English course? Would the level of the students matter?

4 In what ways (if at all) would you restrict the syllabus if your students were:
a) taxi drivers?
b) travel agents?

Exercises

1 Find any authentic piece of English writing. What language would you make your students especially aware of when they read it? What level would the students need to be to understand it?

2 List as many functions as you can. Choose one and say how many ways there are of performing it.

29

3 Make a list of ten words you would teach beginners and ten words you would definitely not teach beginners. What is different about the words in the two lists?

4 Make a list of the varieties of language spoken in your country. Which variety would you teach a foreigner? Why?

References

1 It may be that some speakers of foreign languages do not actually want to sound like native speakers: they may be happy with the aim of being intelligible without sounding awkward.

2 For more on pronunciation goals see J Kenworthy (1987) Chapter 1. Chapter 2 of the same book discusses the concept of intelligibility in great detail.

3 See for example P Nation and J Coady (1988).

4 For more on language functions see especially D A Wilkins (1976) and K Morrow (1977). See also J Roberts (1980) and a response to it (K Johnson (1980)). Both are reprinted in K Johnson (1982). K Johnson and K Morrow (eds.) (1978) is a good collection of articles on functional teaching.

5 K Johnson (1982) discusses a number of different approaches to syllabus design and issues related to them in a series of articles.

6 For more on the structural/functional debate see K Johnson (1981) and (1982), Chapter 8, C Brumfit (1980) and (1981) and H Widdowson (1979). Much of this discussion stemmed from reactions to D A Wilkins (1976), although it must be emphasised that Wilkins never advocated a purely functional approach to language teaching.

7 See J Roberts (1980) and (1983) and M Varela (1980).

8 This argument is put forward by C Brumfit in the articles 'Notional syllabuses: a reassessment' and 'The English language, ideology and international communication' in Brumfit (1980).

9 See D Willis and J Willis (1988).

10 For more on language varieties see P Strevens (1977) Chapter 11, and especially B Kachru (ed.) (1983).

4

Language learning and language teaching

In this chapter[1] we will look at some of the main theories and trends that have informed the practice of English language teaching over the last decades. From this overview we will draw up a language learning and teaching methodology which will be exemplified in Part B of this book.

**4.1
Learning
theories and
approaches**

No one knows exactly how people learn languages although a great deal of research has been done into the subject. Certain theories have, however, had a profound effect upon the practice of language teaching (and continue to do so) despite the fact that they have often originated in studies of how people learn their first language. It is only comparatively recently that the study of *second* language acquisition has achieved the importance that it now has.

4.1.1
Behaviourism[2]

In an article published in 1920,[3] two psychologists, Watson and Raynor, reported the results of experiments they had carried out with a young baby called Albert. When Albert was nine months old they discovered that the easiest way to frighten him was to make a loud noise (by striking a steel bar with a hammer). At various intervals over the next three months they frightened Albert in this way while he was in the presence of various animals (a rat, a rabbit, and a dog). The result of these experiments was that after three months Albert showed fear when confronted with these animals even when the noise was not made, and even showed unease when a fur coat was put in front of him. The psychologists suggested that they would be able to cure Albert's fear but were unable to do so because he was no longer available (his parents had withdrawn him from the experiment). Watson and Raynor even discussed the possibility of Albert's fear of fur coats when he reached the age of twenty!

The ethics of this experiment are, of course, highly questionable, but Albert's experiences are an early example of the idea of *conditioning*. Watson and Raynor had managed to condition Albert to be afraid of the rat, rabbit, dog (and fur coat) where before he had a neutral emotional reaction to them.

The idea of conditioning is based on the theory that you can train an animal to do anything (within reason); to do this you need to follow a three-stage procedure where the stages are *stimulus*, *response* and *reinforcement*. For example, a signal light is operated (*the stimulus*), the rat goes up to a bar and presses it (*the response*) and a tasty food pellet drops at its feet (*the reinforcement*). If the rat's behaviour is reinforced a sufficient number of times it will always press the bar when the light comes on.

Reinforcement in this example took the form of a reward and was therefore positive. But you could also train the rat not to do something by giving him negative reinforcement, maybe in the form of a small electric shock.

In a book called *Verbal Behaviour*,[4] the psychologist Skinner applied this theory of conditioning to the way humans acquire their first language. Language, he suggested, is a form of behaviour in much the same way as the rat pressing the bar exhibits a form of behaviour. (It is because we are concerned with a form of behaviour that this theory is called *behaviourism*.) The same model of stimulus–response–reinforcement, he argued, accounts for how a human baby learns a language. An internal stimulus such as hunger prompts crying as a response, and this crying is reinforced by the milk that is subsequently made available to the baby. Our performance as language learners is largely the result of such positive (or negative) reinforcement.

Behaviourism, which was after all a psychological theory, was adopted for some time by language teaching methodologists, particularly in America, and the result was the *audio-lingual method* still used in many parts of the world.[5] This method made constant drilling of the students followed by positive or negative reinforcement a major focus of classroom activity. Of course the approach wasn't exclusively devoted to repetition, but the stimulus–response–reinforcement model formed the basis of the methodology. The language 'habit' was formed by constant repetition and the reinforcement of the teacher. Mistakes were immediately criticised, and correct utterances were immediately praised. It should be said that audio-lingualism was thought to be highly successful in some contexts – particularly the foreign-language training of military personnel.

4.1.2
Cognitivism

The term *cognitivism* (sometimes referred to as *mentalism*) refers to a group of psychological theories which draw heavily on the work in linguistics of Noam Chomsky (see 2.2).

In 1959 Chomsky published a strong attack on Skinner's *Verbal Behaviour* which became justifiably famous.[6] In his review of Skinner's book he explained his rejection of the behaviourist view of language acquisition (how a baby learns a language) on the basis of his model of competence and performance.

We can appreciate the rejection of the behaviourist view by the asking of questions: if all language is learnt behaviour, how is it that young children can say things that they have never said before? How is it possible that adults all through their lives say things they have never said before? How is it possible that a new sentence in the mouth of a four-year-old is the result of conditioning?

Language is not a form of behaviour, Chomsky maintained. On the contrary, it is an intricate rule-based system and a large part of language acquisition is the learning of the system. There are a finite number of grammatical rules in the system and with a knowledge of these an infinite number of sentences can be performed in the language (see 2.2). It is competence that a child gradually acquires, and it is this language competence (or knowledge of the grammar rules) that allows children to be creative as language users (e.g. experimenting and saying things they have not said before). We looked at a simple example of what the concept of competence and performance involved in 2.2.

Language teaching has never adopted a methodology based on Chomsky's work or strictly upon cognitivist theories in general. Chomsky's theorising was never directed at adult language learning and he has repeatedly made this clear. But the idea that language is not a set of habits – that what matters is for learners to internalise a rule and that this will allow for creative performance – has informed many teaching techniques and methodologies. Thus students are often encouraged to use rules to create sentences of their own. We could summarise this as: show them the underlying structure and then let them have a go on their own. Creating new sentences is the objective.

4.1.3 Acquisition and learning[7]

More recent investigations of how people become language users have centred on the distinction between *acquisition* and *learning*. In particular Stephen Krashen[8] characterised the former as a subconscious process which results in the knowledge of a language whereas the latter results only in 'knowing about' the language. Acquiring a language is more successful and longer lasting than learning.

The suggestion Krashen made is that second (or foreign) language learning needs to be more like the child's acquisition of its native language. But how do children become competent users of their language? Although there may be some limits on the language that they hear (see below), they are never consciously 'taught it', nor do they consciously set out to learn it. Instead they hear and experience a considerable amount of the language in situations where they are involved in communicating with an adult – usually a parent. Their gradual ability to use language is the result of many subconscious processes. They have not consciously set out to learn a language; it happens as a result of the input they receive and the experiences which accompany this input. Much foreign language teaching, on the other hand, seems to concentrate on getting the adult student to consciously learn items of language in isolation – the exact opposite of this process.

Krashen saw successful acquisition as being very bound up with the nature of the language *input* which the students receive.[9] Input is a term used to mean the language that the students hear or read. This input should contain language that the students already 'know' as well as language that they have not previously seen: i.e. the input should be at a slightly higher level than the students are capable of using, but at a level that they are capable of understanding. Krashen called the use of such language to students 'rough tuning' and compared it to the way adults talk to children.

Mothers and fathers tend to simplify the language they use so that the children can more or less understand it. They do not simplify their language in any precise way, however, using only certain structures; rather they get the level of their language more or less right for the child's level of understanding: there are similarities in the way people talk to 'foreigners'. Perhaps if language students constantly receive input that is *roughly-tuned* – that is, slightly above their level – they will acquire those items of language that they did not previously know without making a conscious effort to do so.

The suggestion made by Krashen, then, is that students can acquire language on their own provided that they get a great deal of *comprehensible input* (that is roughly-tuned in the way we have described). This is in marked contrast to conscious learning where students receive *finely-tuned input* – that is language chosen to be precisely at their level. This finely-tuned input is then made the object of conscious learning. According to Krashen, such language is not acquired and can only be used to *monitor* what someone is going to say. In other words, whereas language which is acquired is part of the language store we use when we want to communicate, the only use for consciously learned language is to check that acquired language just as we are about to use it. Consciously learned language, in other words, is only available in highly restricted circumstances, as a monitor. Learning does not directly help acquisition.[10]

<table>
<tr><td>

4.1.4
Task-based
learning
</td><td>

Many methodologists have concentrated not so much on the nature of language input, but on the learning tasks that students are involved in. There has been an agreement that rather than pure rote learning or de-contextualised practice, language has to be acquired as a result of some deeper experience[11] than the concentration on a grammar point.
</td></tr>
</table>

In the 1970s the British applied linguist Allwright[12] conducted an experiment which challenged traditional notions of language teaching. He theorised that:

> ... if the 'language teacher's' management activities are directed exclusively at involving the learners in solving communication problems in the target language, then language learning will take care of itself ... (1977b:5)

In other words there is no need for formal instruction (e.g. the teaching of a grammatical point). Instead students are simply asked to perform communicative activities in which they have to use the foreign language. The more they do this the better they become at using the language.

Allwright's experiment took place at the University of Essex where a number of foreign students were about to take postgraduate courses (where the language used would, of course, be English). They were given activities which forced them to use English, but at no time did their teachers help them with the language or tell them anything about English grammar, etc. They refused to correct errors, too. Thus the students played communication games (see 8.1.4) or were sent to the library to find out how to use the card index system; in another example they had to interview one of the professors (who was unconnected with language teaching in any way) to find out certain information. The students were all at roughly intermediate level before they arrived at the University of Essex, and the results were, apparently, extremely satisfactory.

In 1979 in Bangalore, Southern India, N S Prabhu originated a long-running project which used task-based learning in a very different context.[13] He and his colleagues working in secondary schools were dissatisfied with traditional methodology and with syllabuses which consisted of grammatical items (see 3.6). Like Allwright he theorised that students were just as likely to learn structures if they were thinking of something else as they were if they were only concentrating on the structures themselves. In other words Prabhu suggested that if the emphasis in class was on meaning, the language would be learnt incidentally. The way this was to come about was through a series of tasks which had a problem-solving element: in solving the problems the students naturally came into contact with language, but this contact happened because the students were actively involved in reaching solutions to tasks.

Prabhu called the tasks which he and his colleagues prepared a *procedural syllabus*. Unlike other syllabuses, for example those based on lists of structures or functions, the Bangalore Project's syllabuses comprised a list of tasks which consisted of things like finding your way on maps, interpreting timetables or answering questions about dialogues in which the students have to solve problems.

The main interaction in the clasroom took place between the teacher and the students (generally between forty-five and sixty in number). The class performed pre-tasks which involved questions and vocabulary checking and then they answered the questions with which they solved the problems that were set, for example[14] students looked at a train timetable and discussed questions such as 'When does the Brindavan Express leave Madras/arrive in Bangalore?' and the teacher helped them through their difficulties. Next the teacher handed out another timetable and after asking a few more questions left the students to do the task individually.

The Bangalore Project is important not just because its originator had the courage to put his theories into (large-scale) practice, but also because it is based on quite radical theories of language learning. Like Krashen, Prabhu believes in the importance of the development of comprehension before production (Prabhu 1987: 78–81) and like Allwright he sees meaning (and tasks) as the focus where language learning can take care of itself.

4.1.5
Humanistic
approaches

Another perspective which has gained increasing prominence in language teaching is that of the student as a 'whole person'. In other words, language teaching is not just about teaching language, it is also about helping students to develop themselves as people.

These beliefs have led to a number of teaching methodologies and techniques which have stressed the *humanistic* aspects of learning. In such methodologies the experience of the student is what counts and the development of their personality and the encouragement of positive feelings are seen to be as important as their learning of a language.[15] In a book aptly titled *Caring and Sharing in the Foreign Language Classroom*[16] Getrude

Moscowitz provides a number of interactive activities designed to make students feel good and (often) remember happy times and events whilst at the same time practising language. Other writers have used similar student-centred activities (where the topic is frequently the students themselves, their lives and their relationships) to practise grammar or vocabulary.[17]

Others go further,[18] providing whole methodologies. *Community Language Learning*, based on the educational movement of counselling learning,[19] attempts to give students only the language they need. Ideally students sit in a circle outside of which is a 'knower' who will help them with the language they want to use. When they have decided what they want to say they do it in their language and the knower translates it for them so that they can then use the target language instead. In this way students acquire the language they want to acquire. In a variation of the procedure students say what they want to into a tape-recorder, only speaking when they feel the urge. The tape is transcribed by the teacher who can then offer personal feedback.[20]

Suggestopaedia is a methodology developed by Lozanov in which students must be comfortably relaxed. This frequently means comfortable furniture and (baroque) music. In this setting students are given new names and listen to extended dialogues. The contention is that the general ease of the situation, the adoption of a new identity and the dependence on listening to the dialogues will help the students to acquire the language.[21]

The Silent Way[22] developed by Caleb Gattegno is marked by the fact that the teacher gives a very limited amount of input, modelling the language to be learnt once only and then indicating what the students should do through pointing and other silent means. The teacher will not criticise or praise but simply keeps indicating that the student should try again until success is achieved. Teachers can deploy *Cuisenaire rods* (little rods of different lengths and colours) which can be used to signify grammatical units, stressed and non-stressed parts of words, and even whole stories.[23]

Total Physical Response,[24] developed by James Asher, is a method which finds favour with Krashen's view of roughly-tuned or comprehensible input. In TPR (as it is known) the teacher gives students instructions. The students don't have to speak, they simply have to carry out the teacher's commands. When they are ready for it they can give commands to other students. The students thus learn language through actions, through a physical response rather than through drills.

Despite the controlling role of the teacher in many of these methodologies (see 11.1), they have all been called humanistic in some circles. Certainly Community Language Learning and Suggestopaedia concentrate heavily on the students and their state of mind, seeing in their wants and their relaxation the key to successful learning. TPR allows a pre-speaking phase where students are not forced to speak until they feel confident to do so. The Silent Way forces students to rely heavily on their own resources even when under the teacher's direction.

4.1.6
Self-directed
learning

Focus on the student has also led to the development of learner training and self-directed learning programmes. Methodologists have turned their attention not just to the teaching of the language but also to training students how to be good learners.[25] If students make the most of their own resources and if they can take their own decisions about what to do next and how best to study, so the argument goes, their learning is better and they achieve more. Ideally, therefore, a language programme would be a mixture of classwork and self-study (or self-directed learning). Giblin and Spalding[26] describe a course where their aim was to encourage self-directed learning. As the weeks went by they gradually decreased the number of 'input' classes where they taught in the conventional way and they increased sessions where students could 'opt out' of the regular class and work on their own (under teacher supervision). Coupled with this were exercises and advice on how to approach learning tasks such as reading, writing reports, etc. Lastly the students were encouraged to keep a diary of their experiences (see 8.2.5).

The main thrust of such work is to encourage students to take charge of their own learning:[27] we cannot teach students everything so we have to train them to teach themselves. (See 8.5 for examples of learner training materials.)

4.2 Foreign language learning

What conclusions can we draw from this discussion of various theories and techniques for foreign language learning? Is the idea of conscious learning absurd or, if there is some merit in it, should it be based solely on the students' cognitive abilities and exclude all conditioning? Is a programme based exclusively on acquisition theory necessarily the most effective way of teaching? How much, in fact, does teaching get in the way of learning?

There can be no doubt of the value of comprehensible input: the fact that students are hearing or reading language that they more or less understand must help them to acquire that language. If they are exposed to language enough they will almost certainly be able to use some (or all) of it themselves. It may be that one of the teacher's main functions when talking informally to the class is to provide just that kind of comprehensible input.[28]

It also seems to make sense that people can acquire languages while they are doing something else (the basic philosophy followed by Allwright, Prabhu and methodologies such as TPR). It also seems unexceptional to suggest that we should try to involve students' personalities through the use of humanistic exercises and a genuine exchange of ideas (although it is worth pointing out that all teachers are in a sense 'humanistic' and there may be dangers in taking quasi-psychoanalytic techniques too far). Finally, if we can get students to really concentrate on their own learning strategies and if we can persuade them to take charge of their own learning as far as possible, so much the better.

If we look more closely at some of the theories and solutions proposed, however, the situation becomes less clear. Krashen, for example, suggests that comprehensible input means that language is acquired and is therefore available for use (in other words the student can produce the language spontaneously) whereas consciously studied language is only learnt (and is therefore much more difficult to produce spontaneously). Acquired language is somehow 'better' than learnt language because you would have to concentrate to produce the latter, thus interrupting the flow of language production.

This kind of division, however, just doesn't make sense:[29] in the first place it will be almost impossible to say whether someone has learnt or acquired a certain piece of language. If two people are exposed to the same roughly-tuned input how will we know whether one makes conscious attempts to learn it or not? It is almost impossible, in other words, to test this hypothesis since to do so we would have to be able to see into the minds of all the people who had been exposed to the same input and record their thought processes! Neither does it make sense that learnt language cannot become part of the acquired language store, as Krashen seems to suggest. It is clear that language that has been learnt does 'sink in' at some stage: maybe students will not be able to produce it immediately in spontaneous conversation, but it will eventually come out, given time. Learnt language which is practised does seem to become part of the acquired store[30] even though it may be the case that only certain grammatical features are susceptible to such treatment.[31] It has been suggested[32] that freer practice activities (Communicative activities, especially – see Chapter 8) may act as a *switch* which allows consciously learnt language to transfer to the acquired store.

Another problem about acquisition is that it takes a long time. In fact, time is a crucial issue. The vast majority of students in the world study languages for about two and a half hours a week, for about thirty weeks a year, which is not much time when compared to the time taken by children to acquire their first languages. A key question for us must be whether we use our time well. Is our teaching 'cost-effective'? It is almost certainly the case that the conscious learning of certain items does speed the process up, even if its main function is to raise the student's grammatical awareness. Not only that but many of our students want and expect this type of learning: we would need to be very sure we were right before we told them that it was in some way bad for them.

Time is not the only crucial issue here. We must also look at the conditions under which language learning takes place and who the students are. Allwright's students at Essex, for example, were all intermediate before they started his course. Since they were all going on to study at postgraduate level in the UK we can safely assume that they were fairly intelligent and also highly motivated. And on top of these facts we must remember that they were studying in Great Britain where they had regular access to English-speaking people and other resources.

Other methodologies make considerable demands, too, on time, conditions and resources. For example, Suggestopaedia needs small groups and comfortable rooms, but most teachers handle large classes in uncomfortable surroundings. Transcribing the students' tape-recorded English after a Community Language Learning class is not such a good idea with a class of thirty students. And while it may be possible to train students to take charge of their own learning over a period of weeks in a well-equipped school in the UK, with small classes (fifteen students) and with the students attending classes for a minimum of six hours a day, it will be more difficult in other less convenient locations and conditions.

It is precisely because of the limitations that many teachers have to face that the Bangalore Project (which we mentioned in 4.1.4) is so impressive.

The classes were large and the conditions less than ideal, but despite this the results which have so far been published have been encouraging.[33] Maybe here is proof that conscious learning does not really have a place in the classroom after all. And yet three worries about this position emerge: in the first place many of Prabhu's tasks give rise to very concentrated examples of particular grammar patterns and structures (as our example in 4.1.4 shows) even if the students do not have to take part in actual production drills. This often looks very much like the conscious learning the project aims to replace. Secondly, Prabhu does not encourage groupwork, citing the conditions which his teachers work in and the size of classes etc., and yet this makes the use of humanistic and cooperative techniques very difficult, and thirdly it is by no means certain that the approach adopted in the Bangalore project is the best and only way of teaching English (as opposed to a good way – one of many). As Johnson writes in his article on the study:

> It is . . . . . important that ultimate evaluation of the project should consider not only whether it works, but also whether it is the most cost-effective solution available. (1982:143)

Where does this leave us and our attitude to conscious learning? It certainly seems that the use of tasks and the provision of a lot of comprehensible input will help our students in a lot of ways. The former will allow students to activate their knowledge and the latter will help to provide them with a rich language store. But it is also true that (especially) adults will gain great benefit from clearly explained language work which they can then use to 'create' new sentences: as they find that they are getting the language right they can internalise it correctly so that it gradually becomes part of their acquired store. And the concentration on particular items of language in various practice contexts can help that internalisation process whilst at the same time giving many students a strong feeling of security, especially at beginner and elementary levels.

What is being suggested, then, is that roughly-tuned input and the use of the foreign language in communicative tasks and situations can satisfactorily exist side by side with work which concentrates on conscious learning where new language is being introduced and practised. At the same time we will be looking to see how we can incorporate the language learning into the performance of motivating tasks and how we can begin to train students to become good learners. And the content of our language classes can be designed in a way that does not exclude the kind of humanistic approach and techniques that we talked about in 4.1.5.

The major difference between what we are suggesting here and less recent approaches to language teaching is that we will place much more importance on roughly-tuned input and communicative tasks and activities than some other methodologies have tended to do. Conscious learning is thus seen as only one part of the methodological approach which also encourages language acquisition through a large amount of input and a significant emphasis on the use of language in communicative tasks and activities.

**4.3
Input and
output**

In deciding how to approach the teaching and learning of English we can divide classroom activities into two broad categories: those that give students language *input*, and those which encourage them to produce language *output*. Whether acquisition or conscious learning is taking place there will be stages at which the student is receiving language – language is in some way being 'put into' the students (though they will decide whether or not they want to receive it). But exposing students to language input is not enough: we also need to provide opportunities for them to activate this knowledge, for it is only when students are producing language that they can select from the input they have received. Language production allows students to rehearse language use in classroom conditions whilst receiving feedback (from the teachers, from other students and from themselves) which allows them to adjust their perceptions of the language input they have received.

This production of language, or language output, can be divided into two distinct sub-categories. In the first, *practice*, students are asked to use new items of language in different contexts. Activities are designed which promote the use of specific language or tasks. The aim is to give students a chance to rehearse language structures and functions so that they may focus on items that they wish to internalise more completely than before, whilst at the same time being engaged in meaningful and motivating activities. Practice output marks some kind of a half-way stage between input and communicative output. We will look at practice in Chapter 7.

Communicative output, on the other hand, refers to activities in which students use language as a vehicle for communication because their main purpose is to complete some kind of communicative task. Because the task in a communicative activity is of paramount importance the language used to perform it takes, as it were, second place. It becomes an instrument of communication rather than being an end in itself. In most communicative activities (which we will examine in detail in Chapter 8) the students will be using any and/or all the language that they know: they will be forced to access the language they have in their language store, and they will gradually develop strategies for communication (see 2.4) that over-concentration on presentation and practice would almost certainly inhibit.

A further distinction has to be made, however, between two different kinds of input: *roughly-tuned input* and *finely-tuned input*.[34] The former, as we have already said, is language which the students can more or less understand even though it is above their own productive level. The teacher is a major source of roughly tuned input, and so are the reading and listening texts which we provide for our students. At lower levels such material is likely to be roughly-tuned in the way we have suggested and so whilst we are training students in the skills necessary for reading and listening in English (see Chapter 10) we are also exposing them to language, some of which may form part of their acquired language store. Finely-tuned input, on the other hand, is language which has been very precisely selected to be at exactly the students' level. For our purposes finely-tuned input can be taken to mean that language which we select for conscious learning and teaching (see Chapter 6). Such language is often the focus of the *presentation* of new language where repetition, teacher correction, discussion and/or discovery techniques are frequently used to promote the cognitive strategies we mentioned in 4.1.2. We will look at the introduction of new language in Chapter 6.

During the presentation stage teachers tend to act as controllers, both selecting the language the students are to use and asking for the accurate reproduction of new language items. They will want to correct the mistakes they hear and see at this stage fairly rigorously – in marked contrast to the kind of correction that is generally offered in practice and communicative activities.[35] (See 6.3.3 and 5.3.)

We can summarise the components of input and output in the following way:

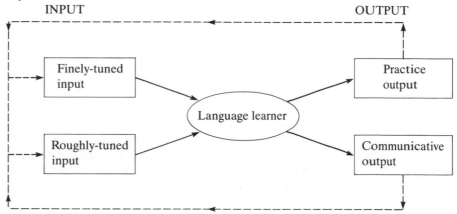

Figure 6 Input and output

The dotted lines show how output – and the learner's (and teacher's) reaction to it – may feed back into input. Even during a communicative activity a student's output and the degree of success that output achieves may provide valuable information about that language which is then internalised. Teacher correction during a practice activity may give the student more input information about the language in question.

Our methodological approach in 4.4 will use these input and output characteristics, paying special attention to the need for roughly-tuned input and communicative output whilst not ignoring the need for finely-tuned input and language practice.

4.4 A balanced activities approach

We can now sum up a methodological approach to the learning of languages which takes account of categories of input and output. Because of the focus on communicative activities and the concentration on language as a means of communication such an approach has been called the *communicative approach*.[36] This is because its aims are overtly communicative and great emphasis is placed on training students to use language for communication. At various stages writers have also included the teaching of language functions (see 3.4.1), task-based learning and humanistic approaches under this umbrella term, making them – apparently – integral parts of the approach.

Certainly the aim of all our teaching is to train students for communicative efficiency, but we have already seen components of the approach we are advocating here which are not in themselves communicative – for example finely-tuned input when presentation takes place, and practice activities.[37] And we have also suggested that concentration on communication only may not be in the best interests of the students. The importance of stages where there is an emphasis on (problem-solving) tasks and the students' own personalities and responsibility for their own learning has to go together with more formal language work, and that is where the status of a 'communicative' approach is called into question. An approach that includes controlled language work (which is not at all communicative (see 5.3)) cannot really be given such a misleading name. And after all, most language teaching is designed to teach students to communicate, however the learning is organised. Rather than worry about these apparent contradictions, it is perhaps better to see the methodology in terms of the activities which we involve students in and to assemble a balanced programme of such activities.

A *balanced activities approach* sees the job of the teacher as that of ensuring that students get a variety of activities which foster acquisition and which foster learning. The programme will be planned on the basis of achieving a balance between the different categories of input and output where roughly-tuned input and communicative activities will tend to predominate over (but not by any means exclude) controlled language presentation and practice output. It is on this basis that we will effect part of our balance.

A balanced activities approach has a more human aspect, however, which is bound up with the concerns of intrinsic motivation (see 1.2.3). By presenting students with a variety of activities we can ensure their continuing interest and involvement in the language programme. Classes which continually have the same activities are not likely to sustain interest, particularly where the students have no extrinsic motivation and do not perceive any clear long-term goal. A programme that presents a variety of activities, on the other hand, is far more likely to continually engage the students' interest. The concern with a balanced activities approach will be reflected when we discuss planning in Chapter 12.

A final, but important, component of the balanced activities approach is the teacher's willingness to be both *adaptable* and *flexible*. Adaptability refers to the teacher's ability to adapt the programme (and the balance) on the basis of the different groups that are being taught. We talked at length in 1.3 about motivational differences, and these should have a powerful influence on the teacher's use and choice of activities and materials. Flexibility, on the other hand, refers to the behaviour of teachers in class and their ability to be sensitive to the changing needs of the group as the lesson progresses. In simple terms it means that decisions taken before the lesson about what is going to happen are not in some way sacred. Good teachers must be prepared to adapt and alter their plans if this proves necessary.

The balanced activities approach, then, sees the methodology as being a balance between the components we wish to include in that approach, and it is an approach that sees the students' continuing interest and involvement in the learning process as being the necessary dominant factor in language teaching.

**4.5
Conclusions**

In this chapter we have studied some theories of language learning and some approaches to language teaching in order to come to conclusions about a methodological approach to the subject. We have not been exhaustive by any means, but we have discussed those issues which have most closely influenced the methodology in Parts B and C of this book.

We have seen that behaviourist philosophy saw the acquisition of language as the result of conditioning; cognitivism, on the other hand, led to language learning being seen as the ability to be creative on the basis of acquired rules.

We studied more recent methodological implications of approaches that stress the need for acquisition (rather than conscious learning) and communicative activities in the classroom. We discussed approaches that depended on task-based learning and humanistic techniques. We looked at the students' ability to take charge of their own learning. The suggestion was that the involvement of the students through task-based activities and the acquisition of language through comprehensible input would be more effective than the conscious learning of language items.

We concluded that while students need a lot of input which is roughly-tuned, and while there must be an emphasis on communicative activities which improve the students' ability to communicate, there is also a place for controlled presentation of finely-tuned input and semi-controlled language practice.

Finally we advocated a balanced activities approach which sees the methodology as being a balance between the components of input and output. Both for pedagogical reasons and for our students' continuing interest in the language programme this balance is the essential ingredient of the methodology.

Discussion

1 If you were learning a foreign language would you expect the teacher to involve you in conscious learning? If so, why?
2 We have said that it is a good idea to offer students input that is roughly-tuned. Do you roughly-tune your input when you are speaking to any other type of person?
3 In your opinion, is conditioning an important part of learning either a first or a second language?
4 Think back to your own experience as a school language learner. Can you identify moments when you received roughly-tuned input or finely-tuned input? How much communicative output was there in the classroom?

Exercises

1 Make a list of activities which you think could be used for communication output in the classroom.
2 Look at an English language textbook and see if you can identify

what activities it suggests. Say whether the activities/exercises give input or are designed for output practice. Decide if the input is roughly- or finely-tuned, and say whether the output activities are for practice or communication.

3 Think of a problem-solving task similar to the kind mentioned in our discussion of Prabhu's procedural syllabus (e.g. reading timetables, map-reading etc.). What language would such a task be most likely to provoke?

References

1 I am especially grateful to Richard Rossner for his comments on an earlier draft of this re-written chapter.

2 For more on the relative merits of behaviourism and cognitivism see J Lyons (1970) Chapter 3 and D A Wilkins (1972) Chapter 6.

3 See J B Watson and R Raynor (1920). I am grateful to Arthur Hughes for drawing this research to my attention.

4 See B Skinner (1957).

5 For more on audio-lingualism and the techniques it uses see E Stevick (1982) Chapters 6–8.

6 See N Chomsky (1959).

7 For a comprehensive account of second language acquisition research and the questions it poses see R Ellis (1985).

8 For a comprehensive view of his work see S Krashen (1981) and the later S Krashen (1984) which expands his views and answers some of his critics. R Ellis (1985) Chapter 10 sets Krashen's work in the general context of other second language acquisition studies.

9 See S Krashen (1982).

10 It should be said that Krashen has backed off such a definite statement as this, but it was where he started and where much of the controversy originated.

11 E Stevick (1976) offers a version of the concept of deep experience.

12 See R Allwright (1977b).

13 For a concise description of the Bangalore Project see C Brumfit (1984). For a detailed account of the reasoning behind the work and the project itself see N S Prabhu (1987).

14 This example comes from N S Prabhu (1987) page 32.

15 Some people feel, however, that attention to humanistic techniques sometimes takes place at the expense of teaching language. See, for example, D Atkinson (1989).

16 See G Moscowitz (1978).

17 See, for example, M Rinvolucri (1985) and J Morgan and M Rinvolucri (1986).

18 For an excellently concise description of these methodologies see M Celce-Murcia (1981). E Stevick (1976) Part 3 is also very useful.

19 See C Curran (1976).

20 See R Bolitho (1983).

21 See J Cureau (1982) and M Lawlor (1986).

22 For more on the Silent Way see C Bartoli (1981) and C Gattegno (1976) and (1982).

23 See S Norman (1981).

24 See J Asher (1969 and 1987), J Mooijam and J Van den Bos (1984) and (1986), T Tomscha (1984) and M Sano (1986).

25 See E Bertoldi, J Kollar and E Ricard (1988) and G Ellis and B Sinclair (1989) for materials that specifically aim to train students to be better learners.

26 See K Giblin and E Spalding (1988).

27 See Allwright's description of a course he organised in Poland (R Allwright (1981)).

28 See T Lowe (1985).

29 Many people have been critical of Krashen's distinction between acquisition and learning. Among the more academic writings are M Sharwood-Smith (1981) and K Gregg (1984). A usefully short account is R Ellis (1983). See also E Stevick (1982) Chapter 3 and J Harmer (1983).

30 See M Sharwood-Smith (1981).

31 See R Ellis (1988).

32 See R Ellis (1982).

33 See A Beretta and A Davies (1985).

34 These terms are borrowed from S Krashen (1981). In other articles (see, for example, S Krashen 1982) he prefers to refer to *comprehensible input* (i.e. input that students can comprehend without too much difficulty). One the factors necessary for successful comprehensible input is that students should feel free from anxiety and this is of primary importance in the natural approach (see S Krashen and T Terell (1982)). The natural approach places heavy emphasis on a pre-speaking phase where students receive roughly-tuned input and react to it, but are not forced into immediate production (see also reference 25 for TPR).

35 For more on errors and mistakes and what to do with them see J Norrish (1983) and J Edge (1989).

36 For more on the communicative approach see C Brumfit and K Johnson (1979) and K Morrow (1981). The communicative approach is not without controversy, however. The most notable clash was between M Swan (1985) and H Widdowson (1985). P Medgyes (1986) has also worried about the implications of a communicative approach for many non-native-speaker teachers. The three articles are reprinted in R Rossner and R Bolitho (1990).

37 For more on the internal contradictions of the concept of a communicative *approach* (as opposed to communicative *activities*) see J Harmer (1982).

5 Teaching the productive skills

PART B: PRACTICE

In this chapter we will discuss the nature of communication and its relevance to various stages of learning. We will emphasise the importance of integrating skills and we will also discuss the differences and similarities in learning to speak and write.

The main aim of this chapter is to preface Chapters 6–9 which deal with specific techniques for the major stages of learning the productive skills.

5.1 The nature of communication

Communication between humans is an extremely complex and ever-changing phenomenon, and it is not my intention to examine all the many variables that are involved. But there are certain generalisations that we can make about the majority of communicative events and these will have particular relevance for the learning and teaching of languages.

When two people are engaged in talking to each other we can be fairly sure that they are doing so for good reasons. What are these reasons?

1 *They want to say something.* 'Want' is used here in a general way to suggest that speakers make definite decisions to address other people. Speaking may, of course, be forced upon them, but we can still say that they feel the need to speak, otherwise they would keep silent.
2 *They have some communicative purpose.* Speakers say things because they want something to happen as a result of what they say. They may want to charm their listeners; they may want to give some information or express pleasure. They may decide to be rude or to flatter, to agree or complain. In each of these cases they are interested in achieving this communicative purpose – what is important is the message they wish to convey and the effect they want it to have.

3 *They select from their language store.* Speakers have an infinite capacity to create new sentences (especially if they are native speakers – see 2.2). In order to achieve this communicative purpose they will select (from the 'store' of language they possess) the language they think is appropriate for this purpose.

These three generalisations apply equally to someone having a private conversation and to the politician giving a speech to thousands. They apply to the schoolteacher and the radio announcer, the judge and the shop assistant.

It is important, too, to realise that these generalisations do not only apply to the spoken word: they characterise written communication as well, and although a difference may be that the writer is not in immediate contact with the reader (whereas in a conversation two or more people are together), the same also applies to the example of the radio announcer, and, to some extent, the academic giving a lecture in a packed hall (although there is of course much greater contact here).

Assuming an effective piece of communication, we can also make some generalisations about a listener (or reader) of language. By effective communication we mean that there is a desire for the communication to be effective both from the point of view of the speaker and the listener. Of course there are many other characteristics that are necessary for effective communication (for example some communicative efficiency/competence on the part of the speakers), and there are many possible reasons for breakdown in communication, but once again three points can be made about the listeners:

4 *They want to listen to 'something'.* Once again 'want' is used in a general way. But in order for someone to understand what they are listening to (or reading) they must have some desire to do so.
5 *They are interested in the communicative purpose of what is being said.* In general people listen to language because they want to find out what the speaker is trying to say – in other words what ideas they are conveying, and what effect they wish the communication to have.
6 *They process a variety of language.* Although the listener may have a good idea of what the speaker is going to say next, in general terms, he or she has to be prepared to process a great variety of grammar and vocabulary to understand exactly what is being said.

Once again these comments apply generally to all listeners, and are equally true of readers.

Whenever communication takes place, of course, there is a speaker (and/or writer) and a listener (and/or reader). This is the case even where a novelist writes a manuscript, for here the writer assumes that there will be a reader one day and that that reader will be performing a communicative act when reading the book.

In conversation and, for example, the exchange of letters, the speaker or writer quickly becomes a listener or reader as the communication progresses. We can summarise our generalisations about the nature of communication in Figure 7 on page 48:

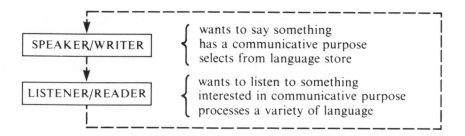

Figure 7 The nature of communication

When organising communicative activities (see Chapter 8) we will try to ensure that these activities share the characteristics we have mentioned here. We will discuss this further in 5.3.

5.2
The information gap

We have said that speakers normally have a communicative purpose and that listeners are interested in discovering what that purpose is. However, even if listeners have some idea about the purpose, they must listen in order to be sure. They cannot be sure, in other words, what it is before they hear what the speaker says. We can illustrate this with a simple example. Consider the following example in which a man (*A*) speaks to a woman (*B*) at a bus stop:

A: Excuse me.
B: Yes?
A: Do you have a watch?
B: Yes ... why?
A: I wonder if you could tell me what the time is?
B: Certainly ... it's three o'clock.
A: Thank you.
B: Don't mention it.

The man who starts the conversation may have many reasons for speaking: he may want to get into conversation with the woman because he thinks she looks interesting, and the question about the time may simply be a pretext for this. On the other hand he may genuinely want to know the time. In both cases there exists an *information gap* between what *A* and *B* know. If the question about the time is a genuine one we can say that *B* has information that *A* doesn't have (the time) and *A* wants that information. In other words there is a gap between the two in the information they possess, and the conversation helps to close that gap so that now both speakers have the same information. But even if this were not the real purpose of the conversation there is still a gap between the speakers where *B* does not know what *A*'s purpose is before he speaks.

In the classroom we will want to create the same kind of information gap if we are to encourage real communication. Many of the activities in Chapters 7 and 8 will be designed so that there is an information gap between the participants, thus ensuring lifelike communication to some extent.

**5.3
The
communication
continuum[1]**

In 4.3 we considered the concepts of input and output and we said that there were stages where communication was more important than accuracy. Having discussed the nature of communication we can now suggest characteristics that are necessary for input and output stages.

Where students are working on an output stage with an emphasis on communication we can use our generalisations about the nature of communication to come to a number of conclusions. Whatever activity the students are involved in, if it is to be genuinely communicative and if it is really promoting language use, the students should have a desire to communicate (see points 1 and 4 in 5.1). If they do not want to be involved in communication then that communication will probably not be effective. The students should have some kind of communicative purpose (see points 2 and 5 in 5.1): in other words they should be using language in some way to achieve an objective, and this objective (or purpose) should be the most important part of the communication. If students do have a purpose of this kind then their attention should be centred on the content of what is being said or written and not the language form that is being used. The students, however, will have to deal with a variety of language (either receptively or productively) rather than just one grammatical construction, for example. While the students are engaged in the communicative activity the teacher should not intervene. By 'intervene' we mean telling students that they are making mistakes, insisting on accuracy and asking for repetition, etc. This would undermine the communicative purpose of the activity. The teacher may of course be involved in the activity as a participant, and will also be watching and listening very carefully in order to be able to conduct feedback. To these five characteristics of genuinely communicative activities we can add a sixth; no materials control (see Figure 8 on page 50). Often students work with materials which force the use of certain language, or at least restrict the students' choice of what to say and how to say it (we will see examples of this in Chapter 7). But by restricting the students' options the materials are denying the language variety characteristic which we have said is important for genuine communication.

The six characteristics for communicative activities can be seen as forming one end of a continuum of classroom activity in language teaching, and they can be matched by opposite points at the other end of the continuum.

Thus for non-communicative activities there will be no desire to communicate on the part of the students and they will have no communicative purpose. In other words, where students are involved in a drill or in repetition, they will be motivated not by a desire to reach a communicative objective, but by the need to reach the objective of accuracy. The emphasis is on the form of the language, not its content. Often only one language item will be the focus of attention and the teacher will often intervene to correct mistakes, nominate students, and generally ensure accuracy. And of course the materials will be specially designed to focus on a restricted amount of language. A lot of language presentation techniques (see Chapter 6) have these characteristics.

We can summarise the points we have made in Figure 8 on page 50:

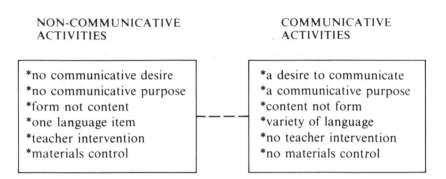

NON-COMMUNICATIVE ACTIVITIES	COMMUNICATIVE ACTIVITIES
*no communicative desire *no communicative purpose *form not content *one language item *teacher intervention *materials control	*a desire to communicate *a communicative purpose *content not form *variety of language *no teacher intervention *no materials control

Figure 8 The communication continuum

Of course not all classroom activities are either 'communicative' or 'non-communicative'. As we shall see in 5.4 there are many techniques that fall somewhere between our two extremes.

**5.4
Stages in language learning/ teaching[2]**

5.4.1
Introducing new language

Based on the continuum in 5.3 we will divide work on the productive skills into three major stages, *introducing new language*, *practice*, and *communicative activities*.

The introduction of new language is frequently an activity that falls at the 'non-communicative' end of our continuum. Often, here, the teacher will work with controlled techniques, asking students to repeat and perform in drills (though the use of 'discovery techniques' – see 6.4 – may differ from this). At the same time we will insist on accuracy, correcting where students make mistakes. Although these introduction stages (often called *presentation*) should be kept short, and the drilling abandoned as soon as possible, they are nevertheless important in helping the students to assimilate facts about new language and in enabling them to produce the new language for the first time. We will concentrate on the introduction of new language in Chapter 6.

5.4.2
Practice

Practice activities are those which fall somewhere between the two extremes of our continuum. While students performing them may have a communicative purpose, and while they may be working in pairs, there may also be a lack of language variety, and the materials may determine what the students do or say. During practice stages the teacher may intervene slightly to help guide and to point out inaccuracy (see the concept of gentle correction in 6.3.3 and 11.1.2).

Practice activities, then, often have some features of both non-communicative and communicative activities and we will concentrate on such activities in Chapter 7.

5.4.3
Communicative activities

Communicative activities are those which exhibit the characteristics at the communicative end of our continuum. Students are somehow involved in activities that give them both the desire to communicate and a purpose which involves them in a varied use of language. Such activities are vital in a language classroom since here the students can do their best to use the language as individuals, arriving at a degree of language autonomy. We will look at activities of this kind in Chapter 8.

A point can be made here about the use of the students' own language (rather than English) during practice and communicative activities. Particularly where students working in pairs and groups share the same native language there is a tendency for them to revert to that language when they find a task hard. To some extent it will be their responsibility to make sure this does not happen, and the teacher will have to explain the importance of the activities (and the use of English) to the students (see 11.2.4 for a fuller discussion of this point).

5.4.4
The relationship between the different stages

There is a clear relationship between the introduction and practice stages whereas the relationship between communicative activities and the introduction and practice stages is not so clear.

If teachers introduce new language they will often want to practise it in a controlled way. After an introduction stage, therefore, they may use one of the practice techniques we will look at in Chapter 7 to give the students a chance to use the new language in a controlled environment. However, the practice stage will often not follow the introduction stage immediately; other activities might intervene before students again work on the same language.

By the nature of communicative activities, they are not tied to the other stages since they are designed to elicit all and any language from the students. Two points can be made, though. Firstly, teachers listening to a communicative activity may notice that a majority of students find it difficult to use the same language. By noting this fact the teacher is in a position to design a subsequent class in which the language the students could not use is focused on.[3] There is, therefore, a natural progression from communicative activity to the introduction of new language.

Sometimes, of course, the teacher may have been working on a certain area of language which will be useful for a future communicative activity. Thus if students have been looking at ways of inviting, for example, they will then be able to use that knowledge in a communicative activity that asks them to write each other letters of invitation.

It will of course be the case that while not all presentation activities fall exclusively at the 'non-communicative' end of the continuum, neither will all the activities in Chapter 8 have exactly the characteristics of communicative activities, although in general they will be followed.

It is probably true that at the very early stages of language learning there is more introduction of new language and practice than there are communicative activities. This balance should change dramatically, however, as the standard of students' English rises. Here one would expect there to be a heavier emphasis on practice and communicative activities than on presentation. However, this balance is often more the result of decisions about what the students need on a particular day in a particular situation (as we shall see when we discuss planning in Chapter 12) than it is a decision about the interrelation of stages. It should be remembered, too, that beginners should receive a large amount of roughly-tuned input (see 4.3).

5.5
Integrating skills

In 2.5 we discussed briefly the four main language 'skills' and it would seem clear that in a general class it is the teacher's responsibility to see that all the skills are practised. We have made a division between productive and receptive skills (see 2.5) so that Chapters 6, 7, 8 deal with the former and Chapter 10 with the latter.

This suggests that in some way the skills are separate and should be treated as such; on one day students will concentrate on reading, and reading only, on the next speaking and *only* speaking, etc. In fact this position is clearly ridiculous for two reasons. Firstly it is very often true that one skill cannot be performed without another. It is impossible to speak in a conversation if you do not listen as well, and people seldom write without reading – even if they only read what they have just written. Secondly, though, people use different skills when dealing with the same subject for all sorts of reasons. Someone who listens to a lecture may take notes and then write a report of the lecture. The same person might also describe the lecture to friends or colleagues, and follow it up by reading an article that the lecturer suggested. Another case would be that of a person who reads about a concert or play in the paper and invites a friend to go to it. The same person will probably read the programme for the concert/play and talk with his or her guest. Later he or she may well write a letter to someone telling of the experience.

In these cases, and in many more, the same experience or topic leads to the use of many different skills, and in our teaching we will try to reflect this. Where students practise reading we will use that reading as the basis for practising other skills. Students involved in an oral communicative activity will have to do some writing or reading in order to accomplish the task which the activity asks them to perform. Students will be asked to write, but on the basis of reading, listening or discussing.

Often our activities will have a focus on one particular skill, it is true, so that at a certain stage the students will concentrate on reading abilities. But the focus can later shift to one or more of the other skills.

In many of the examples in the next four chapters the principle of integrating skills – where focus on one skill leads to practice in another – will be followed, and although there are cases where individual skills may be treated individually the principle of integration is thought to be important.

5.6
Speaking and writing

The next three chapters in this book are concerned with focusing activities on speaking or writing – although promoting skill integration at the same time. In each chapter (Introducing new language structure, Practice, and Communicative activities) there will be sections on oral production and on written production, although in Chapter 6 there is less emphasis on writing as a separate skill since its function is often to reinforce new language learnt orally. This does not mean, however, that writing is considered in some ways to be a 'lesser' skill, and both Chapters 7 and 8 contain large sections on the learning of writing skills.

At this point it might be a good idea to make some comparisons between written and spoken English, since the differences imply different types of exercises which focus on different aspects of language and demand different levels of correctness, for example.

Speakers have a great range of expressive possibilities at their command. Apart from the actual words they use they can vary their intonation and stress (see 2.1) which helps them to show which part of what they are saying is most important. By varying the pitch and intonation in their voice they can clearly convey their attitude to what they are saying, too; they can indicate interest or lack of it, for example, and they can show whether they wish to be taken seriously.

At any point in a speech event speakers can rephrase what they are saying; they can speed up or slow down. This will often be done in response to the feedback they are getting from their listeners who will show through a variety of gestures, expressions and interruptions that they do not understand. And in a face to face interaction the speaker can use a whole range of facial expressions, gestures and general body language to help to convey the message.

Not all speakers have the benefit of such immediate listener feedback, however. Whilst even speech makers may be able to discern through the expressions and atmosphere of an audience how their message is getting across, speakers on the telephone, for example, have to rely on the words and the use of intonation, pitch and stress only, without being able to see all the visual clues that would help them to know what the other person was thinking.

Perhaps the single most important difference between writing and speaking, however, concerns the need for accuracy. Native speakers constantly make 'mistakes' when they are speaking. They hesitate and say the same thing in different ways and they often change the subject of what they are saying in mid-sentence. Clear examples of this are provided on page 212. Except in extremely formal situations this is considered normal and acceptable behaviour. A piece of writing, however, with mistakes and half-finished sentences, etc. would be judged by many native speakers as illiterate since it is expected that writing should be 'correct'. From the point of view of language teaching, therefore, there is often far greater pressure for written accuracy than there is for accuracy in speaking.

The writer also suffers from the disadvantage of not getting immediate feedback from the reader – and sometimes getting no feedback at all. Writers cannot use intonation or stress, and facial expression, gesture and body movement are denied them. These disadvantages have to be compensated for by greater clarity and by the use of grammatical and stylistic techniques for focusing attention on main points, etc. Perhaps most importantly there is a greater need for logical organisation in a piece of writing than there is in a conversation, for the reader has to understand what has been written without asking for clarification or relying on the writer's tone of voice or expression.

Lastly there are the twin problems of spelling and handwriting.[4] English spelling is notoriously difficult for speakers of other languages, and handwriting is particularly problematic for speakers of languages such as Arabic, Farsi, Chinese and Bengali which do not have Roman script.

When teaching writing, therefore, there are special considerations to be taken into account which include the organising of sentences into paragraphs, how paragraphs are joined together, and the general organisation of ideas into a coherent piece of discourse. We will be looking at these areas in Chapter 7. There is also, of course, a need for communicative writing activities and we will look at these in Chapter 8.

Students need to see the difference between spoken and written English. In part this will happen as a result of exposure to listening and reading material, but it will also be necessary to provide exercises that deal specifically with features of spoken and written discourse.

5.7
Level

The three chapters dealing with the productive skills will give exercises at various levels. In general the emphasis will be on beginner and elementary materials, activities and techniques, but there will also be examples of more intermediate and advanced material.

5.8
Conclusions

In this chapter we have studied the nature of communication in order to come to some conclusions about the type of activities our students should be involved in.

We have seen a need for activities that involve the students in having a communicative purpose, using language freely with no teacher intervention. We have also said, however, that students will need controlled exposure and practice of new language.

We have stressed the need for the integration of skills, showing how in real life people seldom work with one skill only when dealing with a topic, and we have shown how speaking and writing have some major differences which must be dealt with in a teaching programme.

Discussion

1 Which do you think are more important in a language learning programme; practice activities or communicative activities? Why?
2 Do you think that all speaking and writing has a 'purpose'?
3 If you were learning a foreign language would you like to work with your classmates with no teacher supervision? What advantages and disadvantages would there be in such an activity?
4 How important is the written skill for your students? How important would it be for you if you were learning a foreign language?
5 In what ways is writing 'more difficult' than speaking? Do all students find writing more difficult?

Exercises

1 Think of any conversation you have had in the last two days. What was your purpose in that conversation, and what purpose did the other participant in the conversation have?
2 Take an exercise from an English language textbook and say where it would occur on the communication continuum.
3 Take any piece of reading material from an English textbook and think of how it could be used for integrated practice of other skills.
4 Try and write down some English you have heard used by a native speaker exactly as he or she said it. Then note the number of 'mistakes', hesitations, re-phrasings, changes of subject, etc. that occur.

5 Take any piece of written English that explains how something works and then write down how you might explain the same thing orally to a friend. What differences would there be?

References

1 I am grateful to Jane Willis for her comments on an earlier version of this part of the chapter. I also found a transcript of a talk by John Sinclair entitled 'The Teaching of Oral Communication' (given in Singapore in April 1980) extremely useful. See also C Manual Cuenca (1990) who has a different list of characteristics that make up a communicative activity, although the activities she describes could equally well be described by the 'communication continuum' in this chapter.

2 W Littlewood (1981) divides the stages of learning into *pre-communicative* and *communicative* activities. Under *pre-communicative* he has *structural activities* (similar to 'introducing new language' in this chapter) and *quasi-communicative* activities (similar to the practice stage in 5.4.2).

3 This procedure as a general approach to language teaching is advocated by C Brumfit (1978) and K Johnson (1980).

4 For comments on handwriting see D Byrne (1988), Chapter 12 and the references quoted there.

6 Introducing new language structure

In this chapter we will consider ways in which students can be introduced to new language – in particular language structures. For the most part this is the conscious learning mentioned in 4.1.3 and which we called 'finely-tuned input' in 4.3. By 'new' language we mean language we think students are not yet able to use (although we will need to check that this is the case – see 6.3). The stage of the lesson when new language is introduced is often called *presentation.*

6.1 What do we introduce?

Our job at this stage of the lesson (aided by the materials we are using) is to present the students with clear information about the language they are learning. We must show them what the language means and how it is used; we must also show them what the grammatical form of the new language is, and how it is said and/or written.

6.1.1 The presentation of meaning and use

We do not only have to show students what language means, we also have to show them how it is used. An example will explain the difference between these two concepts.

    We all know that the present continuous tense (*is doing*) is used to describe actions that are taking place now. However, native speakers do not use this tense to describe people's actions all the time. We don't spend our time saying 'Look. I'm opening the door. I'm drinking a cup of tea ... etc.' That's not how we use the present continuous. We actually use it when there is some point, some value in commenting on people's actions. So we might ring home and say 'Oh, what's John doing at the moment?' It's a reasonable question since we can't see him and don't know the answer to our question. If we are demonstrating a recipe to a TV audience we might then describe what we are doing, e.g. '... So now I'm mixing the butter and the flour ...'[1]

What we are suggesting here is that students need to get an idea of how the new language is used by native speakers and the best way of doing this is to present language in *context*.

The context for introducing new language should have a number of characteristics. It should show what the new language means and how it is used, for example. That is why many useful contexts have the new language being used in a written text or a dialogue.

A good context should be interesting for the students. This doesn't mean that all the subject matter we use for presentation should be wildly funny or inventive all of the time. But the students should at least want to see or hear the information.

Lastly, a good context will provide the background for a lot of language use so that students can use the information not only for the repetition of model sentences but also for making their own sentences (see *immediate creativity* on pages 60 and 62).

Often the textbook will have all the characteristics mentioned here and the teacher can confidently rely on the material for the presentation. But the textbook is not always so appropriate (see 12.1): for a number of reasons the information in the book may not be right for our students. In such cases we will want to create our own contexts for language use.

6.1.2	
Types of context	*Context* means the situation or body of information which causes language to be used. There are a number of different context types, but for our purposes we will concentrate on three; *the students' world*, *the outside world* and *formulated information*.

The students' world can be a major source of contexts for language presentation. There are two kinds of students' world. Clearly we can use the *physical surroundings* that the students are in – the classroom, school or institution. But classrooms and their physical properties (tables, chairs, windows, etc.) are limited. The *students' lives* are not constrained in the same way, however, and we can use facts about them, their families, friends and experiences.

The outside world provides us with rich contexts for presentation. For example, there is an almost infinite number of *stories* we can use to present different tenses. We can also create *situations* where people speak because they are in those situations, or where the writer describes some special information. This is especially useful for the practice of functional language, for example.

We can ask students to look at *examples of language* which show the new language in operation, though this last category can sometimes have no context. These three sub-categories, story, situation or language, can be *simulated* or *real*. Most teachers are familiar with 'made-up' stories which are often useful for classwork: real stories work well too, of course. In the same way we can create the simulation of an invitation dialogue, for example. But here again we could also show students a real invitation dialogue. In general we can say that real contexts are better simply because they are real, but they may have complexities of language and comprehensibility which can be avoided by simulated contexts – life-like but clearly made-up to some extent.

Formulated information refers to all that information which is presented in the form of timetables, notes, charts etc. Once again we can use real charts and timetables, growth statistics, etc. or we can design our own which will be just right for our students.

There are variations on these different kinds of context, of course, but we can broadly summarise what we have said so far in the following way:

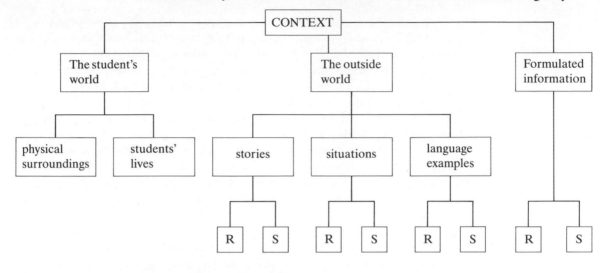

[R = real/S = simulated]

Figure 9 Contexts for introducing new language

The context we choose will depend on the type of language being introduced. If we are creating our own contexts we will have to decide what is right for our students. Will they find that an invented story is not motivating enough? Would they rather have some real information in chart form to play around with? Perhaps our students are in the right mood for a light-hearted simulated situation, however. It is difficult to generalise, and teachers should be sensitive to the varying degrees of motivation that different contexts provide.

Finally it is worth pointing out that language can be presented in one context (e.g. a dialogue) but then the context may change for accurate reproduction or immediate creativity.

6.2
The presentation of structural form

One of the teacher's jobs is to show how the new language is formed – how the grammar works and how it is put together. One way of doing this is to explain the grammar in detail, using grammatical terminology and giving a mini-lecture on the subject. This seems problematical, though, for two reasons; firstly many students may find grammatical concepts difficult, and secondly it will only be possible in a monolingual group at lower levels if the teacher conducts the explanation in the students' mother tongue. In a multi-lingual group such as those found in Britain, America, Australia, etc. such explanations for beginners will be almost impossible.

A more effective – and less frightening – way of presenting form is to let the students see and/or hear the new language, drawing their attention in a number of different ways to the grammatical elements of which it is made. For whilst advanced students may profit from grammatical explanations to a certain extent, at lower levels we must usually find simpler and more transparent ways of giving students grammatical information.

6.2.1
Forms and patterns

Before we introduce any new language we should have analysed the form we are going to teach (how the verb is formed, how certain nouns become plural, for example) and also the grammatical *pattern* we are going to teach it in.

Suppose, for example, that the new language to be introduced is the third person singular of the present simple tense (e.g. 'The President gets up at six o'clock'); the grammar point we wish to teach is clearly the occurrence of the 's' on the verb stem. But we can use the third person singular of the present simple in all sorts of different constructions (e.g. 'He loves his wife', 'It never rains but it pours', 'She lives in Guadalajara', 'She goes to work by bus on Wednesdays', etc.). In the first sentence we have a subject + verb + object construction. The second sentence, on the other hand, has two clauses; the first has an adverb of frequency, the second doesn't. The third sentence has a subject, a verb, and an adverbial ('in Guadalajara'). The last sentence has three adverbials ('to work', 'by bus', and 'on Wednesdays').

As teachers and materials writers we will make a choice about the grammatical pattern in which we will introduce the new grammar point. In other words, we might decide to concentrate on a pattern of subject + verb + adverbial. This would produce such sentences as 'He lives in Cambridge', etc. The point about such a pattern is that it is made up of *changeable units*. In 2.2 we saw an interpretation of a sentence, and we saw how we could create different sentences with the same syntax simply by changing the words. That is what we are doing here.

We can demonstrate the principle of pattern and changeable units using our **S**(ubject) + **V**(erb) + **A**(dverbial) pattern in the following way:

PATTERN	SUBJECT	VERB	ADVERBIAL
Examples	He She It John	lives stays happens works	in London at home in the town at the airport

Figure 10

If, when we introduce the present simple (third person singular) for the first time, we stick to a pattern such as the one shown above it will help students to focus on the new grammar point (e.g. the 's' on the verb). Students will very soon, however, be able to use the new verb tense in different patterns. This can be tried at the immediate creativity stage (see 6.3), or even before with a good class.

The idea of changeable units is that they allow us to create *models* for the students to work with. A model is an example of the pattern. Thus the teacher who is introducing the present simple (third person singular) will ask the students to work with a number of sentences all of which conform to a pattern such as the subject + verb + adverbial sequence above. This will be during the accurate reproduction stage (see pages 61 and 65). As soon as possible, however, students will be encouraged to use the present simple with other grammatical patterns.

So far we have considered the changeable units for a grammatical structure. Functional language, too, will often contain the same kind of units. If we are teaching students how to invite, for example, we might introduce the form '*Would you like to*' + *verb*. The latter part of this pattern is clearly changeable, so that we can introduce models such as 'Would you like to come to the cinema/have lunch/play tennis?', etc.

Certain phrases which teachers introduce, or which appear in the textbook, however, may not have such changeable units – or at least the choices may be very restricted. For the function of agreeing, for example, we can say 'I'd agree with you there'. The only real possibility for substitution would be to say 'I'd go along with you there'.

The teacher needs to be clear about how the language to be presented is said and written. Thus the 's' of our present simple ending sometimes sounds like 's' (e.g. works, laughs, writes, etc.); sometimes it sounds like a 'z' (e.g. plays, says, lives, etc.) and sometimes it sounds like 'iz' (e.g. watches, closes, catches, etc.). We may decide to introduce these verbs in a definite order depending on the different sounds of the ending. We will not do so, of course, if we think the different sounds will not cause problems.

We must also work out how the models we are going to introduce are normally stressed so that in saying them to the students we will give a clear idea of correct spoken English.

6.3 A general model for introducing new language

We can now look at a general model for introducing new language which gives an overall picture of the procedure. All the examples we are going to show in 6.6 follow this model to some degree.

The model has five components: *lead-in*, *elicitation*, *explanation*, *accurate reproduction*, and *immediate creativity*.

During the *lead-in* the context is introduced and the meaning or use of the new language is demonstrated. This is the stage at which students may hear or see some language (including the new language) and during which students may become aware of certain *key concepts*. The key concepts are those pieces of information about the context that are vital if students are to understand the context and thus the meaning and use of the new language. If we are introducing a dialogue in which a visitor to a town is asking for directions from a local resident it will be necessary for the students to understand that:

1 The speaker is a stranger.
2 He or she doesn't know where something is.
3 He or she is talking to someone who lives in the town.

With this knowledge the students will understand what the speaker is saying (and why) in the following dialogue:

VISITOR: Excuse me!
RESIDENT: Yes?
VISITOR: Where's the station?
RESIDENT: It's opposite the hospital at the end of this street.
VISITOR: Thank you very much.
RESIDENT: Don't mention it.

In the case of formulated information (such as the airline timetable in 6.6.5 (a)) it will be necessary for students to understand the concepts of *destination*, *via*, *departure* and *arrival*, for without these they will not understand the meaning of such sentences as 'Flight 309 goes to Paris'. During the lead-in stage the teacher can also demonstrate the probable course of an interaction (particularly at more advanced levels). An example of this is 6.6.3 (a). During the lead-in stage, then, we introduce our context (making sure that key concepts are understood) and show the new language in use.

During the *elicitation* stage the teacher tries to see if the students can produce the new language. If they can it would clearly be wasteful and de-motivating for them if a lot of time was spent practising the language that they already know. At the elicitation stage – depending on how well (and if) the students can produce the new language – the teacher can decide which of the stages to go to next. If the students can't produce the new language at all, for example, we will move to the explanation stage. If they can, but with minor mistakes, we may move to the accurate reproduction stage to clear up those problems. If they know the new language but need a bit more controlled practice in producing it we may move directly to the immediate creativity stage (this is indicated by the dotted lines in Figure 11). Elicitation is vitally important for it gives the teacher information upon which to act: it is also motivating for the students and actively involves their learning abilities. Elicitation techniques will be detailed in our examples in 6.6.

During the *explanation* stage the teacher shows how the new language is formed. It is here that we may give a listening drill or explain something in the students' own language; we may demonstrate grammatical form on the blackboard. In other words, this is where the students learn how the new language is constructed; we will look at explanation techniques in more detail in 6.3.1.

During the *accurate reproduction* stage students are asked to repeat and practise a certain number of models. The emphasis here will be on the accuracy of what the students say rather than meaning or use. Here the teacher makes sure that the students can form the new language correctly, getting the grammar right and perfecting their pronunciation as far as is necessary. We will look at accurate reproduction techniques in detail in 6.3.2.

When the students and teacher are confident that the students can form the new language correctly they will move to *immediate creativity*. Here they try to use what they have just learned to make sentences of their own, rather than sentences which the teacher or book has introduced as models. It is at this stage that both teacher and student can see if the students have really understood the meaning, use and form of the new language. If they are able to produce their own sentences they can feel confident that the presentation was a success. We will see many examples of immediate creativity in 6.6.

We can represent the model for introducing new language in diagram form:

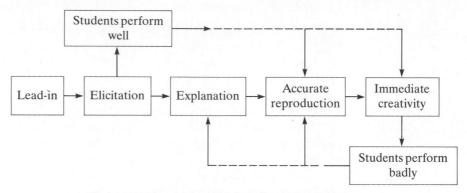

Figure 11 A general model for introducing new language

Notice again that if the students perform well during elicitation the teacher can move straight to immediate creativity. If at that stage they perform badly the teacher may find it necessary either to return to a short accurate reproduction stage or, in extreme cases, to re-explain the new language.

In 6.6 we will show how the model can be applied to a number of presentation situations, many of which are taken from published textbooks. The model can also be used for discovery activities (see 6.4) though elicitation will take a slightly different form.

6.3.1 Explanation techniques

We will look at two procedures for explaining the form of the new language. In both cases the intention is to demonstrate to the student what the grammar of the construction is.

(a) Explaining statements

In this case the teacher wishes to explain the first model based on the flight timetable on page 87. The model is:

Flight 309 goes to Paris.

Here is a procedure we can follow:

Stage 1 The teacher says the sentence in a normal way with a clear voice using correct stress and intonation. This may be done two or three times.

Stage 2 The teacher isolates a particular feature of the model.

Stage 3 The teacher distorts this feature showing how it is constructed.

Stage 4 The teacher returns to the isolated element.

Stage 5 The teacher gives the normal model again.

We can represent this procedure in Figure 12:

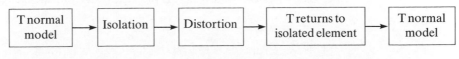

Figure 12

Sometimes, however, the teacher may not have to distort the isolated feature (where it is only a one syllable word).

Where there is more than one item that needs isolating the teacher goes through the procedure in Figure 12 with the first item to be isolated and then repeats the sequence with the second item.

The following example clearly shows the procedure in action. The teacher wishes to isolate both the verb form and the pronunciation of the flight number:

T:　Listen ... Flight 309 goes to Paris ... flight 309 goes to Paris ... listen ... goes ... goes ... go ... /z/ ... go ... /z/ ... goes ... flight 309 goes to Paris ... listen ... three-oh-nine ... flight 309 goes to Paris ... flight 309 goes to Paris.

The teacher may back up this oral explanation by writing the following on the blackboard:

Flight 309 go⟨es⟩ to Paris.

The use of a box to highlight the main grammar points helps to focus the students' attention on that point.

(b) Explaining question forms

When we have to do the same kind of explanation for a question form we may follow the same procedure as for (a) above. However, particularly where a question form is taught after the affirmative version of the same grammar point has already been the subject of practice, some extra techniques may help the students to understand the form of the question.

Unlike many languages English uses inversion to signal a question. Thus if we take an affirmative sentence such as 'He is running' we find that the equivalent question form has the subject and the auxiliary in a different order, e.g. 'Is he running?'. Even where we put a question word (such as 'which', 'what', 'how', 'when', etc.) at the beginning of the question this inversion is still used. Students of English frequently find this confusing.

When introducing a question teachers will follow the same procedure as for (a) above. They will, however, isolate and distort in a slightly different way, and it will be advisable to use the blackboard and/or gesture to make the inversion clear.

Suppose we wished to 'explain' the question model 'Is he running?' We might do it in the following way:

T: Listen ... Is he running? Is he running? ... listen ... he is running? ... no (*teacher shakes head and crosses arms in an 'inversion' gesture*) ... Is he running? ... Is he running?

We can write the following on the blackboard at the same time:

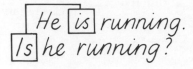

If we wished to present the question 'Does flight 309 go to London?' we would follow the same procedure as for the previous example. On the blackboard, however, we might write the following:

Flight 309 goes to London.
Does Flight 309 go to London?

The importance of visual demonstration for grammar cannot be exaggerated. Many students react far better to written stimuli, and in the examples we have shown the teacher's use of the blackboard (to highlight important features) helps students to understand the new point being taught.

Once the teacher has gone through an explanation phase he or she will then move to accurate reproduction.

(c) Using hands and gestures

Teachers can use their hands and various gestures to make grammatical form clearer.

One of the things we often need to do is to show how a full grammatical form is contracted in speech. Two examples show this happening: 'they are leaving' becomes 'they're leaving'; 'I would have come earlier' becomes 'I'd've come earlier'.

One way of explaining this to beginning students is to use the fingers of one hand to represent the different parts of the sentence, e.g.

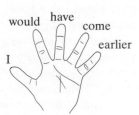

Figure 13

As we say the words we point to the fingers of the hand which represent those words.

Now we can show how 'I would have' becomes 'I'd've':

I'd've

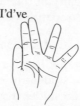

Figure 14

The use of the fingers has given a graphic description to the class.

We can also use fingers to hold imaginary words, rather like a magician. For example we can pretend to hold the word 'do' in one hand and 'not' in the other. By bringing the hands together we show how 'don't' is formed.

Some teachers use gesturing over their shoulders to indicate the past and pointing ahead of them to indicate future tenses.

Finally, arms can be used to indicate intonation patterns (rising and falling) and stress patterns, beating time rather like a conductor in an orchestra. This is especially useful for choral repetition.

6.3.2 Accurate reproduction[2]

As we said on page 61, the purpose of an accurate reproduction stage is to give students controlled practice in the form of the new language. We will look at three stages of this part of the lesson, *choral repetition*, *individual repetition* and *cue-response drills*.

(a) Choral repetition

When we have explained a model as in 6.3.1 we ask the whole class to repeat the model together. This is choral repetition. The technique is useful because it gives all the students a chance to say the new language immediately, with the teacher controlling the speed and the stress. It gives students confidence (where immediate individual repetition might cause anxiety) and it gives the teacher a general idea of whether the students have grasped the model.

There are three things to remember about choral repetition:

1 Clearly indicate (by conducting) when the students should start the chorus.
2 Clearly indicate the correct stress during the chorus.
3 Stay silent during the chorus so that you can hear how well the students are performing.

If we take our model sentence from 6.3.1(a) the chorus might go something like this:

T: (*finishing the explanation*) Flight 309 goes to Paris . . . flight 309 goes to Paris . . . everybody. (*T makes a gesture*).
SS: Flight 309 goes to Paris.
T: Again. (*gesture*)
SS: Flight 309 goes to Paris.

We will have to decide how many choruses we need based on such factors as the difficulty of the model, the students, etc.

Choral repetition can also be used during correction (see 6.3.3(b)).

(b) Individual repetition

Individual repetition is conducted in three stages. The teacher nominates a student, the student responds, and the teacher gives feedback. Nomination (selecting the student) can be done by calling the student's name or by pointing, although the latter should be done with care so as to avoid causing offence.

We can summarise the procedure for individual repetition in Figure 15:

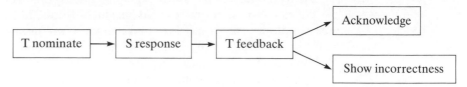

Figure 15 Individual repetition

If we continue with our sentence about flight 309 individual repetition might be something like this:

T: (*finishing choral repetition*) Again.
SS: Flight 309 goes to Paris.
T: Good . . . now Juan.
S1: Flight 309 goes to Paris.
T: Good . . . Myra.
S2: Flight 309 goes to Paris.
T: Yeah . . . (*T points to S3*)
S3: Flight 309 go to Paris.
T: Flight 309 go?
S3: Oh . . . flight 309 goes to Paris.   *etc.*

With the first two sentences the teacher gave feedback by acknowledging that the student's response was correct. This was done by saying 'good' and 'yeah'. The teacher might also say 'yes' or just nod. Some teachers say nothing at all, but pass on to another student. A lot depends on the individual students and the teacher. The main thing is that the students should be quite clear that the response was correct.

S3, however, made a mistake and so the teacher did not acknowledge a correct response, but rather showed incorrectness. We will discuss correction in more detail in 6.3.3.

When conducting individual repetition we should be sure that we do not nominate students in a clearly discernible order, for this has the effect of making the drill less exciting. The students always know who is going to be nominated and when. A random order, however, keeps the interest level high since anyone could be nominated at any minute.

(c) Cue-response drills

Cue-response drilling takes place when the students are working with more than one model. When we have presented the first model and organised choral and individual repetition we will elicit the second model. If the students can produce the model we might go straight to choral and individual repetition. If they cannot we may go through an explanation stage again. When there has been adequate repetition of the second model we start a cue-response drill in which we ask students to choose one of the two models based on a cue.

We can summarise this procedure in Figure 16:

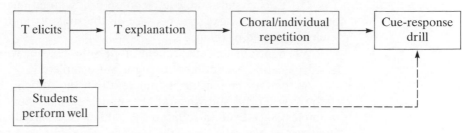

Figure 16 Introducing second and subsequent models

A cue-response drill is conducted in three stages:

Stage 1 Instruct: Tell the students what you want them to do. You might say 'tell me' to indicate that you want a statement or 'question' to indicate that you want a question. Often the instruction is not actually said, but is understood by the class.

Stage 2 Cue: Indicate which model you wish the student to say. You might do this by giving a cue word. Thus you could say 'Paris' to get the response 'Flight 309 goes to Paris.' You might mime an action. Thus you could mime 'smoking' to get the student response 'John smokes three packets a day'. You can also point to a particular picture or give a number (where you have previously assigned numbers to your models).

Stage 3 Nominate: Select the student you wish to give the response (see (b) above).

We can now see the whole process described so far in operation:

T: (*conducting individual repetition*) Juan.
S1: Flight 309 stops in Miami.
T: Good . . . now can anyone tell me about flight 309 and Miami (*indicating the wallchart*) . . . anyone?
S2: Flight 309 stop in Miami.
T: Yes . . . good . . . but listen . . . flight 309 stops in Miami . . . flight 309 stops in Miami . . . stops . . . stops . . . flight 309 stops in Miami . . . everybody.
SS: Flight 309 stops in Miami.
T: Good . . . Myra.
S2: Flight 309 stops in Miami.
T: OK . . . Keiko.
S4: Flight 309 stops in Miami.
(*The teacher continues to conduct individual repetition and then says . . .*)

> *T*: OK ... tell me ... Paris ... Juan.
> *S1*: Er ... flight 309 goes to Paris.
> *T*: Good ... Miami ... Myra.
> *S2*: Flight 309 stops in Miami.   *etc.*

Notice how the teacher does not distort the word 'stops' in the explanation, presumably because he or she thinks it is not necessary this time. Notice, too, how the second model is elicited.

The teacher starts the cue-response drill with an instruction (tell me) but drops this the next time because all the students understand that this is what is required of them.

When introducing subsequent models the teacher will do less and less explanation, sometimes cutting it out completely.

As soon as the teacher is confident that the students can manage the cue-response drill, and when all the models (usually between four and six examples) have been introduced the students can be put in pairs.
One student can now act as the teacher, giving the cue, and the other can give the response. Then the second student gives the cue and the first one responds, etc. We would include this stage so that as many students as possible get a chance to practise.

The teacher should make sure that this pairwork stage does not last too long, for if it does the students will probably lose interest.

In general it must be emphasised that the accurate reproduction stage should be dealt with as quickly as possible. If it goes on for too long the students start to get bored and start making more and more mistakes: the drill is then completely counter-productive. The length of time will depend largely on the size of the class and the difficulty and number of models, but it is rarely advisable to continue the accurate reproduction stage for more than ten minutes, and even that will often be excessive. After all, the accurate reproduction stage is only there to enable students to get to more creative parts of the lesson.

6.3.3
Correction

During the accurate reproduction phase there are two basic correction stages: showing incorrectness (indicating to the student that something is wrong – see 6.3.2 (b)) and using correction techniques.

(a) Showing incorrectness

This means that we will indicate to the student that a mistake has been made. If the student understands this feedback he or she will be able to correct the mistake and this self-correction will be helpful to him or her as part of the learning process.

There are a number of techniques for showing incorrectness:

1 *Repeating*: Here we simply ask the student to repeat what he or she has just said by using the word 'again'. This, said with a questioning intonation, will usually indicate that the response was unsatisfactory (although it could be misunderstood as only indicating that the teacher has not heard the student's response).

2 *Echoing*: We will be even clearer if we repeat what the student has just said, using a questioning intonation since this will clearly indicate that we are doubting the accuracy or content of what is being said.

Sometimes we can echo the complete student response, probably stressing the part of the utterance that was incorrect, for example:

Flight 309 GO to Paris?

Another possibility is to echo the student's response, but only up to the point where the mistake was made, for example:

Flight 309 GO?

This was the technique used in our example on page 66. Echoing, in its various forms, is probably the most efficient way of showing incorrectness.

3 *Denial*: We can simply tell the student that the response was unsatisfactory and ask for it to be repeated. This seems somewhat drier than the techniques so far discussed; it may be a bit more discouraging.

4 *Questioning*: We can say 'Is that correct?' asking any student in the class to answer our question. This has the advantage of focusing everybody's mind on the problem, though it may make the student who made the mistake seem somewhat exposed.

5 *Expression*: Many teachers indicate that a response was incorrect by their expression or by some gesture. This is very economical (and can be quite funny) but can be dangerous if the student thinks that the expression or gesture is a form of mockery.

In general, showing incorrectness should be handled with tact and consideration. The process of student self-correction which it provokes is an important and useful part of the learning process. Showing incorrectness should be seen as a positive act, in other words, not as a reprimand.

Frequently, however, we find that showing incorrectness is not enough for the correction of a mistake or an error and the teacher may therefore have to use some correction techniques.

(b) Using correction techniques

If students are unable to correct themselves we can resort to one of the following techniques.

1 *Student corrects student*: we can ask if anyone else can give the correct response. We can ask if anyone can 'help' the student who has made the mistake. If another student can supply the correct information it will be good for that student's self-esteem. However, the student who originally made the mistake may feel humiliated if this technique is used insensitively.

2 *Teacher corrects student(s)*: Sometimes we may feel that we should take charge of correction because the students are extremely mixed-up about what the correct response should be. In that case we can re-explain the item of language which is causing the trouble. This will be especially

appropriate when we see that a majority of the class are having the same problem. After the re-explanation we can move to choral and individual repetition (if necessary) before moving on.

The object of using correction techniques, of course, is to give the student(s) a chance to (know how to) get the new language right. It is important, therefore, that when we have used one of the techniques suggested above, we ask the student who originally made the mistake to give us a correct response.

The stages of correction we have shown here are especially useful for accuracy work, where the main focus is grammatical correctness. Another possibility, however, for the immediate creativity stage and for practice activities (see Chapter 7) is *gentle* correction. This involves showing the student that something is wrong, but not asking for repetition (see 11.1.2 for a more detailed account of correction at different stages and for different activities).

6.3.4
The importance of meaning

It is undoubtedly important for the students to understand the meaning of the new language they are learning. This is conveyed during the lead-in stage where key concepts clearly demonstrate what is going on (see page 60). We also need to know whether the students have understood the new language so that we can organise our teaching accordingly. Not only is the lead-in stage vital, therefore, but it will also be necessary for the teacher to check frequently that the students have understood. If they have not we will have to re-present the key concepts.

Checking meaning can be done in three ways, *information checking*, *immediate creativity* and *translation*.

(a) Information checking

The teacher will often need to find out if students have understood the information in the lead-in, or whether students understand what a model means. We can do this in a number of ways. We might, for example, ask a question. An example of this would be 'Does Carlos like spaghetti?' (see page 74). If the students answer 'Yes' they clearly haven't understood the way the chart on page 74 is organised, or they haven't understood the meaning of the new language. Another way of checking is to say sentences which are incorrect, e.g. 'Carlos likes spaghetti but he doesn't like fish'. The students will then, if they have understood, correct this error. The same effect can be created by reading students' models and asking them to say whether they are true or false (see 6.6.5(a)).

(b) Immediate creativity and different settings

The immediate creativity stage is a good indicator of whether or not students have understood the meaning and use of the new language (as well, of course, as its form). We may ask students to produce sentences of their own even before we get to this stage in order to check that they have understood the new language.

Another good check of meaning is to ask the students something using the new language which is not part of the context that is being used for the presentation. Thus, for example, if the teacher introduces 'can' and 'can't' with the kind of simulated story context we mentioned on page 57 he or she may ask (at any stage during the presentation) 'Juan, can you run?'. Unless Juan has broken his leg or is in some way disabled he should answer 'Yes' to this question. If he does the teacher is confident that he has understood the meaning of 'can' that is being introduced.

(c) Translation

Where the teacher is teaching a monolingual class, translation is obviously an excellent technique if the teacher is fluent in the students' language. The main advantages are that it is quick and efficient.

There are, however, two disadvantages to the use of translation: the first is that it is not really possible with groups of different nationalities, although where there are two or more speakers of a language one student can translate for the others, and secondly it is not always possible to translate exactly. Not all languages have words for exactly the same concepts, and it is often the case that in a given language there is not really a word which means the same as a word in another language.

6.4. Discovery techniques

In our model for introducing new language (see 6.3) we saw how the teacher creates a context (or uses one from some materials) and elicits language which is then given as models for the students to repeat. The whole procedure is basically teacher-led since it is the teacher's job to explain the language and conduct a cue-response drill before moving quickly to immediate creativity and pairwork (where the students start to take over control a bit).

Discovery techniques,[3] on the other hand, aim to give students a chance to take charge earlier. The idea is simple: give students a listening or reading text – or some examples of English sentences – and ask them to discover how the language works. We might give students a text which is a story, for example, and we could then ask them to look at it again to see how many ways they could find in it for referring to the past. They could listen to a tape and write down any sentences which had 'if' in them. Then they could see if there was any pattern to those sentences.

What is being suggested is that there is a range of techniques where the teacher gets the students to do most of the work. There are good pedagogical and methodological reasons for this since the students will be more involved and since this kind of activity invites them to use their reasoning processes.

The use of discovery activities does not mean that our model in 6.3 should be changed, however. In general we can still say that we should give students a lead-in to the topic, text or context. But the elicitation stage will be different. Instead of saying 'Can anyone tell me . . . Shiona . . . yesterday . . . New Zealand go . . .' to get the sentence 'Shiona went to New Zealand yesterday' we get students to look at the material and, working individually or in pairs, they find examples of the grammar we are interested in. When the teacher asks them what they have found and discusses the language with them we have reached an explanation stage, but because the teacher is talking with the students (rather than to them) the process appears to be more egalitarian, less dictatorial (see the discussion on the role of the teacher in 11.1).

Of course discovery techniques are not suitable for all students on all occasions. Frequently this problem-solving approach takes more time than a more controlled presentation. And although students may be very involved there is not the kind of dynamic tension that makes whole-class presentations such fun (when they go well). It is also true that designing material for discovery activities – or finding a text that will suit this approach – is far easier at intermediate and advanced levels than it is when teaching beginners.

Despite some of these apparent drawbacks, the use of discovery activities is a welcome alternative to other types of presentation: if it instils an interest in language and grammar in our students over and above their learning of English, so much the better!

In the examples of teaching contexts and procedures in 6.6 some of our examples will be of the 'discovery' type.

**6.5
The position of writing during presentation**

In this chapter we have been advocating a primarily oral approach in which the first thing students do with the language is to say it. At any stage, however, the teacher may ask the students to write the new language.

Often the teacher will use the writing as reinforcement for an oral presentation such as the type we have so far described. Thus either immediately before or after the immediate creativity stage the teacher asks students to write sentences using the new language. The sentences may be the original models the teacher used during the accurate reproduction stage, and the students might be asked to copy these sentences from the blackboard. They might see the same sentences, but the teacher might leave out certain words (this is commonly called a *fill-in* exercise).

The students might be shown model sentences and then be asked to write similar sentences of their own. This is a written version of the immediate creativity stage. The students might see a short piece of connected writing using the new language and then be asked to write a similar piece. This is often called *parallel writing*.

All of these techniques have their merits, although copying is often unchallenging and boring. The main object, though, is to relate the spoken and written forms of the new language, and to enable the students to write the new pattern as well as say it.

Sometimes, of course, we may want the students only to write the new language, not say it. In this case we might go through the explanation phase in the normal way, but then, after giving a clear written model we can ask students to write sentences using one of the techniques mentioned above.

Where students write in class as part of the introduction of new language it is often advantageous to 'correct' the written work in front of the whole class. One useful way of doing this is to ask the students to do the written work in their books. When we see that a student has finished (before the others) we ask him or her to write the first sentence on the blackboard. The second student writes the second sentence, and so on. When all the sentences are on the board we go through them one by one, asking the class if they are correct. If they are not we can ask another student to write the correct sentence or correct the sentence ourselves. This technique is particularly useful since it gives the students feedback, and allows the teacher and the whole class to focus on grammar points if such focus is necessary.

We will see a number of different ways of introducing writing during the presentation stage in 6.6.

6.6
Introducing new language: examples

In this section we will look at a number of examples of language presentation. We will consider procedures for introducing new language under five headings: *the student's world*, *stories*, *situations*, *language examples* and *formulated information*.

6.6.1
The students' world

In this section we will look at examples that need only a teacher, the students and the classroom.

(a) Physical surroundings: prepositions

In this example the teacher uses an approach much like Total Physical Response (see page 36) to teach imperatives and prepositions.

The teacher starts by producing some objects. They can be very ordinary, for example a stapler, a pen, a bag, a pencil, a pencil case, etc. The teacher elicits the words for these objects from the students and if they do not know them models the words and leads choral and/or individual repetition.

The teacher gives one of the objects (a book, for example) to one of the better students and then says something like 'Put the book on the table.' If the student does not understand the teacher helps by pointing and by gesture. When the student has put the book on the table the teacher says 'Well done' and then chooses another student who is told to 'Put the ruler in the box', etc. As the students gradually do what they are asked they are getting wonderful listening practice.

The teacher now asks the students if they can give instructions, thus eliciting the new language. When the students give their instructions the teacher will decide whether it is necessary to interrupt and model some or all of the new language or whether to move straight on to the immediate creativity stage where students are giving whatever instructions they want (within reason!).

As a written stage the teacher can write up some instructions on the board as models. Students can now be asked to write their own instructions which they give to their classmates who then have to do what is written there (see 8.2.1).

(b) Likes and dislikes

This presentation will consist of two stages. In the first students will learn to say 'Do you like ____?' and in the second they will be presented with 'He/she likes/doesn't like ____'.

The teacher starts the sequence by asking students 'Do you like coffee?'. With mime and expression he or she will soon convey the meaning of the question and a student will answer 'Yes' or 'No'. The teacher then gets choral and individual repetition of the answers ('Yes I do/No, I don't') if this is necessary. For a very brief period the teacher asks students questions and they give their answers. Then the teacher elicits the question (which the students have heard the teacher using). If necessary the question is explained and the teacher goes through the accurate reproduction stage, cueing students to ask and answer different questions. The students then work in pairs doing the same thing. This is a form of immediate creativity.

While the students are working in pairs the teacher puts the following on the blackboard:

NAME	FISH	CAVIAR	SPAGHETTI	LIVER	BANANAS

The teacher selects a student, for example, Carlos, and puts his name in the name column. The other students now ask him whether he likes the items on the chart and the teacher puts a tick (√) if he does and a cross (×) if he doesn't. The procedure is now repeated with other students until the chart looks like this:

NAME	FISH	CAVIAR	SPAGHETTI	LIVER	BANANAS
Carlos	√	√	×	√	×
Maria	√	×	√	×	√
Juan	×	×	√	√	√
Celia	√	√	√	√	√

The teacher then asks the students what they can say about Carlos and fish, hoping to elicit 'Carlos likes fish'. This new presentation (of the third person singular of the present simple with 'likes') now proceeds in the normal way using Carlos' likes and dislikes for the accurate reproduction stage and the others' preferences for immediate creativity, very like the flight timetable example on page 87. The teacher can later introduce the question 'Does Carlos like fish?', etc.

For the introduction of writing the teacher can use the fill-in idea (see (a) above) or the students can see the following model:

Carlos likes fish, caviar and liver, but he doesn't like spaghetti or bananas.

They can then be asked to write similar sentences about one of the other names on the list. This is a simple form of parallel writing.

This type of presentation seems enjoyable and motivating since it immediately involves the students in talking about themselves. The same type of procedure can be used when teaching such language as 'It looks/smells/tastes ____', 'Have you ever been to/visited/seen ____?',

'What do you do/Where do you live?', etc. We will see how questionnaires (which are similar) can be used in 7.1.5(c) and 8.4(a).

(c) Student lives: birthday chart/birthday line

This activity shows another way in which the students themselves can be used to help the presentation of new language including the accurate reproduction and immediate creativity stages.

The teacher wishes to present and teach numbers for use in dates (e.g. January the thirty-first, etc). The presentation can start with a figure on the board and the question 'When's her birthday?' To help students understand the teacher can draw a quick birthday cake like this:

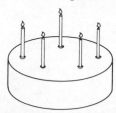

or (in a monolingual class) sing a snatch of the traditional birthday song. The teacher then says 'Her birthday's on April the thirtieth' (for example).

The teacher now teaches the numbers. He or she can hold up different numbers of objects and the students have to say 'first', 'second', 'third', etc. Then the teacher elicits the names of the months and gets choral and/or individual repetition so that the students' pronunciation can be worked on.

The teacher can write dates on the board (e.g. 24/5 for May the twenty-fourth) and conduct a cue-response drill by indicating the numbers and having the students say the dates correctly.

The teacher now elicits the question 'When's your birthday?' and gets students to repeat it.

Now the students' own lives get involved as the teacher tells them that they have to get in a line from January the first to December the thirty-first depending on their birthdays. In order to do this they have to ask 'When's your birthday?' and give the answer.

The ensuing activity is chaotic and often fairly noisy, especially in a big class, but it is also fun. The teacher goes around making sure that the students ask and answer in English and gradually a line is formed. Then the teacher checks that students have got it right by conducting a question and answer drill while students are still in the line.

This activity is an example of a way to use details about the students as the raw material for a lesson. It is a lot more involving than simply asking about other people's birthdays – though that too may have its uses.

**6.6.2
Stories**

In the following three examples we will see how different types of stories are used to promote the presentation and practice of certain structural patterns, though the third example is to a large extent a 'false' presentation.

(a) Sylvie[4]

In the following example on page 76, a story and some picture prompts provide the context for the practice of negative questions.

reading a book

overslept

television

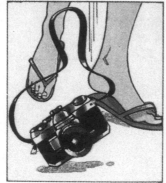

dropped her camera

sunburnt

cold water

1

Read this about Sylvie and look at the pictures.

Sylvie is on holiday. Yesterday she said, 'Tomorrow I'm going to get up early and go swimming. Before lunch I'm going to take some photographs. In the afternoon I'm going to lie in the sun and write postcards. In the evening I'm going to watch television.'

Now it is the afternoon. Sylvie isn't writing postcards and she can't lie in the sun. This evening she isn't going to watch television. In the morning Sylvie didn't get up early, she didn't go swimming and she didn't take any photographs.

2

Ask and answer, like this:

Why didn't Sylvie take photographs this morning?
- Because she dropped her camera.
Why can't Sylvie lie in the sun?
- Because she is sunburnt.

The teacher asks the students to read the text. The teacher can say 'get up early?' to prompt the question 'Did she get up early?', 'photographs' to prompt the question 'Did she take any photographs?' or 'television' to prompt the question 'Is she going to watch television?' The answers will obviously be 'no'.

The teacher will then want to try and elicit the negative question by saying 'Can anyone ask "why"' to see if any of the students can ask 'Why didn't she get up early?'. If students seem comfortable with this question the teacher can prompt the use of the other questions and answers. If they seem to be having trouble the teacher can model the question by saying 'Did Sylvie get up early? (No). Why? Why didn't she get up early?' etc.

If the students need practice the teacher can conduct a quick question and answer drill before putting the students in pairs to practise with the six models.

For an immediate creativity stage the teacher can encourage the students to ask each other 'Did you get up early? Did you do your homework last night? Are you going to watch TV this evening?' If the answer is 'no' they can go on to ask 'Why didn't you do your homework last night?' etc.

(b) Martha[5]

This material, from a book published many years ago, is perhaps the perfect example of how teachers can construct stories which will not only provide a good context for language presentation, but also provide the raw material for a large number of language models.

The teacher tells the class the following story:

"A Series of Coincidences"

Quite by chance Martha went into a coffee-bar one Saturday morning where she happened to meet an old friend of hers who was going to the races. His girl-friend was ill and he did not fancy going alone, so he asked Martha to come. She had never been before.

She decided to bet 10 shillings on a horse called "Dublin Boy" simply because she had once spent a very pleasant holiday in that city. However, when she got to the betting-window, all she had in her purse was a £10 note. She did not realise she could ask for change and hesitated. The man behind her shouted "Hurry up!", Martha became nervous and confused and bet the whole £10.

The odds on the horse were 100—1. At the last fence it was running second. The leading horse suddenly stumbled and fell, and "Dublin Boy" won. When Martha went to collect her £1,000, a television-reporter happened to hear what had happened before.

That evening she was interviewed on a news programme. The regular interviewer was ill and his place was taken by a young man who fell in love with Martha. They got married shortly afterwards and now have three children.

Comprehension questions are then asked to check that the students have understood the story, e.g. 'Did Martha plan to meet her old friend? Was her old friend's girlfriend at the coffee bar? Had Martha been to Dublin on holiday?' etc.

The teacher now asks the students if anyone can make a sentence with 'if', 'Martha', 'coffee bar' and 'old friend' to prompt the response 'If Martha hadn't gone to the coffee bar she wouldn't have met her old friend.' If students have difficulty with this sentence, the teacher can break it up into segments, e.g.

> *T*: Listen .... would not have met ... would not have met ... (*makes gesture for contraction*) wouldn't've met ... wouldn't've met ... everybody
>
> *SS*: Wouldn't've met   *etc.*

The teacher can give more prompts, e.g. 'holiday in Dublin ...' 'won a lot of money ... interviewed' etc. to prompt more sentences.

This story can provoke a lot of (not very serious) sentences, including the incredible 'If Martha hadn't gone to the coffee bar she wouldn't have had three children'!

This is the kind of teaching material that could be used for what one colleague describes as 'pressure teaching'. Faced with younger students who are most reluctant to talk and participate he plays games with them which force them to participate. In one example (which would be appropriate here) he makes them all stand up. They may only sit down when they have given a correct sentence. Even with big classes this can be great fun, provided that the teacher does it with humour, not cruelty!

(c) George's Marvellous Medicine[6]

There is no reason why teachers should limit themselves to stories from their textbook or stories which they invent. There are tapes and books all over the place which can provide a rich resource for more advanced classes.

In this example of a discovery activity (see 6.4) the teacher asks the students to decide on an adjective to describe grandmothers (they will frequently come up with words like 'nice' and 'wise'). They are now asked to read the following extract from a children's book called *George's Marvellous Medicine* by the well-known writer Roald Dahl. Their only task is to decide on an adjective which describes *this* grandmother.

'You know what's the matter with you?' the old woman said, staring at George over the rim of the teacup with those bright wicked little eyes. 'You're *growing* too fast. Boys who grow too fast become stupid and lazy.'

'But I can't help it if I'm growing fast, Grandma,' George said.

'Of course you can,' she snapped. 'Growing's a nasty childish habit.'

'But we *have* to grow, Grandma. If we didn't grow, we'd never be grown-ups.'

'Rubbish, boy, rubbish,' she said. 'Look at me. Am I growing? Certainly not.'

'But you did once, Grandma.'

'Only *very little*,' the old woman answered. 'I gave up growing when I was extremely small, along with all the other nasty childish habits like laziness and disobedience and greed and sloppiness and untidiness and stupidity. You haven't given up any of these things, have you?'

'I'm still only a little boy, Grandma.'

'You're eight years old,' she snorted. 'That's old enough to know better. If you don't stop growing soon, it'll be too late.'

'Too late for what, Grandma?'

'It's ridiculous,' she went on. 'You're nearly as tall as me already.'

George took a good look at Grandma. She certainly was a *very tiny* person. Her legs were so short she had to have a footstool to put her feet on, and her head only came half-way up the back of the armchair.

'Daddy says it's fine for a man to be tall,' George said.

'Don't listen to your daddy,' Grandma said. 'Listen to me.'

'But how do I stop myself growing?' George asked her.

'Eat less chocolate,' Grandma said.

'Does chocolate make you grow?'

'It makes you grow the *wrong way*,' she snapped. 'Up instead of down.'

Grandma sipped some tea but never took her eyes from the little boy who stood before her. 'Never grow up,' she said. 'Always down.'

'Yes, Grandma.'

'And stop eating chocolate. Eat cabbage instead.'

'Cabbage! Oh no, I don't like cabbage,' George said.

'It's not what you like or don't like,' Grandma snapped. 'It's what's good for you that counts. From now on, you must eat cabbage three times a day. Mountains of cabbage! And if it's got caterpillars in it, so much the better!'

When the students have decided in pairs and/or groups what adjective they wish to use the teacher discusses their choices with the whole class. The teacher now asks the students to find any sentences with 'if' in them and work out how they are different and what they mean.[7] They can work on this in pairs very much as a problem-solving activity.

The sentences they will find in the text are:

1 'But I can't help it if I'm growing fast, Grandma,' George said.
2 'If we didn't grow, we'd never be grown-ups.'
3 'If you don't stop growing soon, it'll be too late.'
4 'And if it's got caterpillars in it, so much the better!'

The teacher can then check up on the students' conclusions, making sure they identify the present and likely nature of sentence 1 which is represented by the use of present tenses; the hypothetical but generally present nature of sentence 2 which, in order to signal that hypotheticality uses past tenses; the future and likely nature of sentence 3, signified by present tenses and 'will'; and the use of the present to talk about a general condition in sentence 4 (and the verbless clause which goes with it).

If necessary the teacher can write grammar tables, etc. on the board before encouraging students to make sentences of their own expressing the same time and/or degree of hypotheticality as the examples. For example the teacher could say things like 'Why are you looking so glum?' and the student has to reply with 'I can't help it if . . .' in sentences like 'I can't help it if I'm feeling depressed'. The type 2 conditional (example 2) can be used to say what people would do if they won money, they were prime minister, they met the man or woman of their dreams, etc.

The point about this kind of activity is that it is in some ways a 'false' presentation: we know that students will be able to find the sentences and we expect that we can discuss grammar and meaning with them (as opposed to beginners who would find it more difficult). They will probably have seen all these grammatical patterns before, but we are focusing on them in a completely different way. Discovery activities like this frequently help to make language study at intermediate levels and above more involving than some of the techniques we use with beginners which are more appropriate to that level.

6.6.3
Situations

The examples in this section show language presented in situations. In the first two examples we deal with functional language whereas the second two use pictures and plans as contexts for language presentation and practice.

(a) Advice[8]

This example (from an American English course) is teaching students how to ask for and give advice. It employs a mixture of straight presentation and an element of discovery-like problem solving which is appropriate for this (lower intermediate) level.

Students look at the pictures. The teacher asks them where Ellery and Monica (two characters they recognise) are. They listen to the dialogue on tape. Now the teacher asks them where some of the dialogue utterances fit on a map of the conversation. (1 = agreeing, 2 = giving strong advice, 3 = asking for advice)

The teacher now asks the students to close their books (or cover the pictures) for a bit. The dialogue is elicited from the students line by line. Each time a new line is added the teacher models it (if this is thought to be necessary) so that the students gradually reassemble the whole dialogue, e.g.

T: OK. How does the dialogue go . . . Kim?
S1: How do you think I should go to Shreveport, Monica? By car or by plane?
T: Go on, Akiko.
S2: You'd better go by car.
T: Kim?
S1: Why?
T: Can anyone go on?   *etc.*

The teacher will model the correct intonation and stress, particularly with expressions like 'Well, I guess you're right'.

Students now practise the dialogue in pairs, with or without their books open. For a writing stage the teacher can write the dialogue on the board, omitting some words or phrases. Students come to the board and fill in the

How do you think I should go to Shreveport, Monica? By car or by plane?

You'd better go by car.

Why?

Well, for one thing it's more convenient, and there's only one plane a day.

Yeah, but it's more tiring by car.

I know, but you do want to get there early, don't you?

Sure. But ... well, I guess you're right. I'll drive.

OK. Do you want me to call ahead and say you're coming?

Interaction focus

1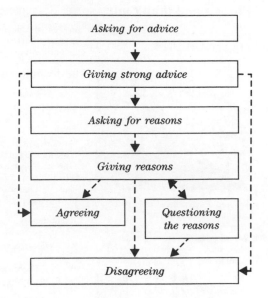

Look and listen. Where do these sentences go in the diagram?

1 I guess you're right. I'll drive.
2 You'd better go by car.
3 How do you think I should go to Shreveport, Monica? By car or by plane?

```
        Asking for advice
               │
               ▼
        Giving strong advice
               │
               ▼
        Asking for reasons
               │
               ▼
         Giving reasons
           ╱        ╲
          ▼          ▼
      Agreeing   Questioning
                 the reasons
               │
               ▼
          Disagreeing
```

2

Have similar conversations about one of the subjects below.

1 Going to the beach or going to the mountains for your vacation.
2 Buying a new coat or buying a new suit/dress.
3 Going by plane or going by bus.
4 Taking exercise classes or taking art classes.

J. Harmer and H. Surguine   Coast to Coast
Student's Book 3   Page 29

81

blanks. The teacher then elicits more dialogues, encouraging students to use the flow diagram to structure their conversations.

This example shows how language can be presented in a realistic situation and with a social context. The use of flow diagrams like this gives students insights into how conversations are structured.

(b) Please and thank you[9]

Please and thank you

PRESENTATION

Woman Excuse me. Could you open the door for me, please?
Man Yes, of course.
Woman Thank you very much.
Man Shall I take the bags for you?
Woman No, it's all right, thank you.

Man I'm dying of thirst. Would you make me a cup of tea?
Boy OK. I'll put the kettle on.
Man And could you bring some biscuits?
Boy Yes, I'll open the new packet.

● Grammar question

In the two dialogues, underline three *requests* like this: _____
Underline three offers like this:
_ _ _ _ _

PRACTICE

Speak
Work in pairs.
You are in a hotel.
One of you is the receptionist, the other a guest.
The guest has several requests, and phones reception from her/his room.

Example
There's no hot water.
A *Hello. Reception. Can I help you?*
B *Yes. There's no hot water in my room. Could you see to it, please?*
A *Certainly. I'll send someone straight away.*

– You'd like some tea in your room.
– You want the telephone number of the railway station.
– You're expecting a Mr Smith and want to know if he's in Reception yet.
– The television doesn't work.
– You want to change some travellers' cheques.
– You'd like to be woken at 7.00 in the morning and have breakfast in your room at 7.45.
– You want to leave a message for Mr Halliday in room 301.

This example for students at the same level as (a) above shows a slightly different discovery element.

The students read the two dialogues and the teacher can then check their understanding by saying 'What does the woman want? What does the man suggest?' etc. The students are then asked to identify the language used for requests and offers (see 'Grammar question').

The teacher can write up the language the students have found, e.g.

Requests	Offers
Could you _____.	Shall I _____ for you?
Would you _____.	I'll _____ .

The teacher now asks students to work in pairs to make dialogues (see 'Practice'). A decision will have to be taken as to whether the teacher should elicit some dialogues from the students first to make sure they can use this language before they do this work. The teacher may feel it necessary to conduct a short drill, giving prompts like 'open the window' for students to say 'Could you open the window?'.

When the students have had a chance to practise in pairs the teacher will want to listen to some of their efforts with the whole class so that attention can be drawn to any outstanding problems and mistakes, but also so that students may see how well they have completed the task.

(c) There's an attic[10]

This example, from a beginner-level book for young adolescents, provides grammar practice in the context of a house plan. Instead of a dialogue, students read a short text and then answer comprehension questions about it.

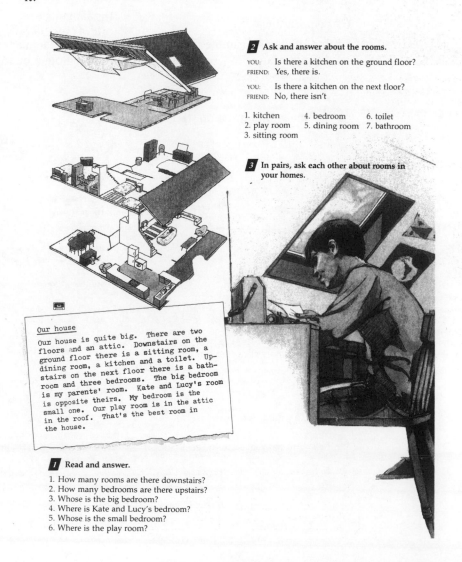

2 Ask and answer about the rooms.

YOU: Is there a kitchen on the ground floor?
FRIEND: Yes, there is.

YOU: Is there a kitchen on the next floor?
FRIEND: No, there isn't

1. kitchen   4. bedroom   6. toilet
2. play room   5. dining room 7. bathroom
3. sitting room

3 In pairs, ask each other about rooms in your homes.

Our house

Our house is quite big. There are two floors and an attic. Downstairs on the ground floor there is a sitting room, a dining room, a kitchen and a toilet. Upstairs on the next floor there is a bathroom and three bedrooms. The big bedroom is my parents' room. Kate and Lucy's room is opposite theirs. My bedroom is the small one. Our play room is in the attic in the roof. That's the best room in the house.

1 Read and answer.

1. How many rooms are there downstairs?
2. How many bedrooms are there upstairs?
3. Whose is the big bedroom?
4. Where is Kate and Lucy's bedroom?
5. Whose is the small bedroom?
6. Where is the play room?

When the students have completed the 'Read and answer' section of the material the teacher can then ask 'Is there a kitchen on the ground floor?' to elicit the answer 'Yes there is.' The teacher can continue asking questions whilst the students practise giving the answers (the teacher may have to model them, isolating 'isn't' if students are having trouble and getting choral repetition).

Now the teacher elicits the question (which the students have been listening to), and depending on whether the students can say it correctly or not may model it and get choral and individual repetition. The students can now take part in a SQ–SA session with the whole class and/or in pairs. For an immediate creativity stage the students can ask each other 'Is there a kitchen on the ground floor in your house?' etc.

For a first written stage the teacher can write sentences on the board with some words missing. The students can copy and complete the sentences in their own exercise books before the teacher invites individuals up to the front to complete the sentences on the board.

(d) Appearances[11]

In the following example for elementary students, language is taught in a more utilitarian way – without a surrounding dialogue or text.

A Sheila has got long dark hair

1 Put the right names with the pictures.

Sheila has got long dark hair and brown eyes.
Helen has got long red hair and green eyes.
Mary has got long fair hair and green eyes.
Lucy has got short grey hair and blue eyes.

2 Ask the teacher questions.

What's this?
It's your mouth.
What are these?
Ears.

3 Test other students. Do they know these words?

hair   eyes   nose   ears   mouth   face
arm   hand   foot   leg

TOUCH YOUR RIGHT EYE.
TOUCH YOUR LEFT EAR.

4 Talk about yourself and other people. Examples:

'I've got small hands. My mother has got pretty hair.'

5 Write three sentences with *and*, and three with *but*. Examples:

I've got blue eyes, and my mother has, too. I've got straight hair, but my brother's got curly hair.

The teacher first asks the students to match the sentences with the pictures (the original of this material is in colour, of course). They can do this in pairs (a discovery activity again) and the teacher can help if they are having difficulty with some of the words. This material is relying on the fact that at least some of the students will know some of the language and they can help each other to understand the sentences.

The students then ask the teacher questions, and the teacher's replies form the basis for modelling and choral repetition (if this is felt to be necessary).

The students use the words connected with the body, etc. in a kind of Total Physical Response session (see page 36), asking each other to touch parts of the body, before they move on to making statements using 'have got'. Here, once again, the teacher will decide if it is necessary to go through explanation and accurate reproduction stages before having students making their own sentences as part of an immediate creativity session. The writing exercise then consolidates the new language and allows students more time to make their own sentences.

6.6.4
Language
examples

In the following two examples students are simply shown examples of sentences or phrases and asked to identify grammatical differences (in the first example) and functional differences (in the second). Both examples use a 'discovery' or problem-solving approach, and follow the example of the first book which made a special point of this kind of activity, Rod Bolitho and Brian Tomlinson's *Discover English*.[12]

1 *Study the examples*

Why is it necessary to use *will be able to* rather than *can* in two of them?

1 My eyesight is very poor at the moment, but the doctors tell me after the operation I'll be able to see almost perfectly.
2 I'm very busy today but perhaps I can see you tomorrow.
3 This article says that some day soon we'll be able to cure almost all forms of cancer.
4 You're young and healthy and you can find a job if you really want to! You really can!

Which two are examples of:

a something that hasn't happened but which the speaker can already do?
b an ability purely in the future – something that needs something else to happen first, such as a new discovery or something else?

(a) *Can* or *will be able to*?[13]

In this example students have read a text in which the new language occurs and they have done comprehension work on the text. They now look at a grammar issue which arises in the text.

2 *See if you can decide*

In which of these sentences is it possible to use *can*? In which is it necessary to use *will be able to*? Why?

1 He lost a leg in the accident. But with a new artificial one, he ___ walk again.
2 After a few more lessons, I think you ___ ski very well.
3 I don't really feel like going to the cinema this evening but we ___ go tomorrow instead.
4 If we meet in town tomorrow, we ___ have lunch in that new restaurant.
5 Do you think that some day people ___ live and work on other planets?
6 I'm hard-of-hearing but if I get a deaf-aid I ___ hear everything people say.

Here the teacher will probably ask the students to work in pairs on exercise 1 before checking with the class. The focus is entirely on the meaning and grammar of the language. The teacher then asks the students for their conclusions, before letting them do exercise 2. If necessary the teacher can spend some time on an explanation stage (although the material makes the form of the language fairly clear) and even conduct an accurate reproduction stage using *can* and *will be able*.

(b) Making the right noises[14]

In this example students identify examples of reacting to good or bad news before using the language in their own dialogues. Once again the first part of the activity is a discovery exercise.

D3 Which of the following are answers to good news and which to bad news? Put a tick (✔) for good news and a cross (✘) for bad news. (Two of them could be good or bad.)

D4 Work in pairs. You are A or B. Cover up your partner's card. Your partner will tell you some news. Reply with one of the phrases in *D3*.

A Tell your partner that . . .
1 Your cat has just died.
2 You've passed your driving test.
3 You're worried about the exam tomorrow.
4 You've lost your passport and all your money.
5 You've won a free trip to Los Angeles.

B Tell your partner that . . .
1 You saw a UFO last night.
2 You've crashed your car.
3 You've just got engaged.
4 You've just got a new job.
5 You've scratched your partner's favourite record.

Once the students have identified which of the expressions are for good or bad news the teacher may wish to model the phrases, paying special attention to intonation so that the pitch and rise–fall of expressions like

'That's marvellous' is attention-catching and helps students to learn the expressions correctly.

The teacher now conducts a T–S drill by saying (e.g.) 'I've just crashed my car' and nominating a student who must use one of the 'bad' phrases. When the students have shown that they can handle these phrases to some extent they can work in pairs using the 'A' and 'B' cards.

6.6.5
Formulated
information

In this section we will look at two examples of contexts which provide 'formulated information' – that is, where the information used for presentation and practice is formulated as a chart, in a graph or as notes or some other tabular form.

The advantage of charts and tables, etc. is that there is potential for a much greater quantity of information than in a picture or a dialogue.

(a) Flight timetable[15]

We have already used the following flight timetable for examples in 6.3. The flight timetable has the advantage of introducing a perfectly natural use of the present simple tense (presented here for the first time) but suffers from not showing that language being used in the context of other language. Nevertheless it adequately conveys one meaning and use of the new verb tense.

The students look at the following flight timetable:

FLIGHT NUMBER	DESTINATION	VIA	DEPARTURE	ARRIVAL
714	New York	Dallas	08.15	11.45
603	Chicago	St. Louis	14.30	16.45
309	Paris	Miami	23.30	16.40
873	Montreal	Detroit	19.05	21.50
312	London	Bermuda	13.10	07.55

The teacher then ascertains that students understand what a flight timetable is, and what the words 'destination', 'via', 'departure' and 'arrival' mean.

The teacher now tells the students that they must listen to some sentences and circle the correct letter for each item. Here are the letters:

1 Listen, and put a circle round	1 D	2 D	3 D	4 D	5 D
the correct letter for each item	V	V	V	V	V
(D = destination; V = via;	6 Dp	7 Dp	8 Dp	9 Dp	10 Dp
Dp = departure; A = arrival).	A	A	A	A	A

Here are the sentences the teacher reads:

1 Flight 309 goes to Paris.	D
2 Flight 873 stops in Detroit.	V
3 Flight 714 arrives in New York at 11.45.	D
4 Flight 312 stops in Bermuda.	V
5 Flight 603 goes to St. Louis.	V

6 Flight 873 leaves at five past seven.	Dp
7 Flight 603 departs at 2.30.	Dp
8 Flight 312 arrives in London at 7.55.	A
9 Flight 873 gets to Montreal at ten to ten.	A
10 Flight 603 reaches Chicago at a quarter to five.	A

This procedure has a double advantage: it gives the students ample listening practice and it tells both the teacher and the students (during the feedback session) whether the students understand the new language (see 6.3.4).

The teacher now proceeds to teach the new language using four models about, for example, 'flight 309' ('Flight 309 goes to/stops at/leaves at/arrives at ...'). For the immediate creativity stage students can make more sentences of their own about the other flights.

The teacher can also introduce the two questions 'Where does flight 309 stop/go to?' and 'What time does flight 309 leave/arrive?'. Students can obviously work in pairs practising questions and answers.

For the written stage the students do the following exercise:

Read the following sentences and complete them appropriately, according to the departure board.

a Flight .... goes to Paris. It stops in ......
b Flight ..... at 14.30 and it ..... in Chicago ..... 16.45.
c What time .....? At 13.10.
d Does flight 309 ..... Miami? Yes, it does.
e Does flight 603 .....? No, it stops in St. Louis.

Once again the teacher can write the exercise on the blackboard and get students to fill in the blanks there after they have done·so on a piece of paper.

(b) Airmail zones[16]

In this example for elementary students (studying American English) a world map, divided into zones, forms the basis for language presentation and practice of 'How much does it cost to send a letter/postcard to _____?'. On the following page is the material the students see.

The teacher asks questions to find out the correct zones for the different countries (note that the original material is in colour): the students can then ask and answer 'Which zone is Venezuela?' etc. They can do the same with the price of stamps, e.g. 'How much are letters for zone A?' etc.

The teacher then asks the question 'How much does it cost to send a letter to France?' to try and elicit the answer '44 cents.' After a session of TQ–SA the question can be elicited and then students can practise in pairs.

For an immediate creativity stage students can imagine that they are in an American post office, asking about the price of stamps and buying the ones they need.

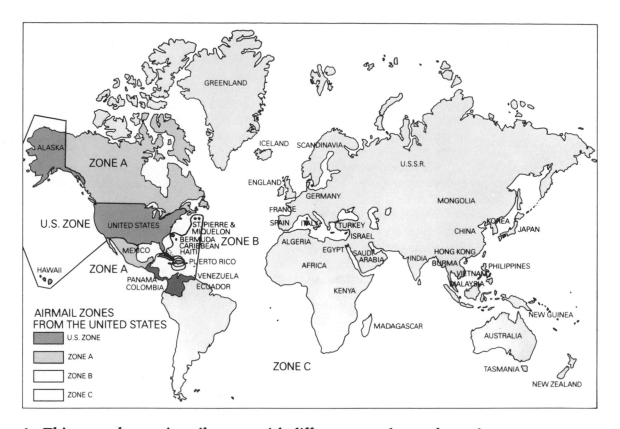

1. **This map shows airmail zones with different postal rates from the United States. Find the airmail zone for each of these countries, and write it on your paper.**

Australia	Colombia	England	Israel	Mexico	Saudi Arabia
Bermuda	Ecuador	Haiti	Italy	New Zealand	U.S.S.R.
Canada	France	India	Japan	Panama	Venezuela

2. **Look at the chart of rates for letters and postcards to each zone. Then ask and answer questions about these rates.**

AIRMAIL RATES

	Letters	Postcards
United States	22¢	14¢
Zone A	22¢	14¢
Zone B	39¢	33¢
Zone C	44¢	33¢

6.7
Conclusions

In this chapter we have discussed the introduction of new language. We have seen how we need to identify what we are going to teach and what patterns it occurs in.

We have seen how we can use a number of different contexts for language presentation and we have looked at a general model for the introduction of new language which places special stress on the importance of elicitation to see how much of the new language the students are already aware of.

We have discussed different ways of giving feedback and leading drills and we have looked at ways of showing students when they have made mistakes, thus giving them opportunities for self-correction.

We have discussed the place of discovery activities and seen how they allow students – through problem-solving – to become deeply involved in the language they are studying.

We have looked at a number of different activities for introducing new language which illustrate some of the many and varied contexts for language presentation.

Exercises

1 Which parts of the model *John's taller than Mary* would you isolate during an explanation stage? Why?
2 Design a context of your own for introducing the meaning and use of the past continuous (e.g. *Olivia was playing the guitar.*)
3 Take a dialogue from any textbook you know and write down exactly the procedure you would follow when using it to introduce some new language.
4 Design a context and presentation sequence which uses the students' world rather than material from a coursebook (for example).
5 You have used a map of an imaginary town to teach 'There's a cinema on South Street; there's a hospital on Green Street', etc. What could students do for an immediate creativity stage?

References

1 H Widdowson described the difference between meaning and use as the difference between signification and value (1972), concepts which he later developed into usage and use (1978).
2 For more on controlled drills see J Willis (1981) Unit 15, L G Alexander (1985), D Byrne (1986) Chapter 5 and D Byrne (1987) Chapters 3–6.
3 For more on discovery techniques see R Bolitho and B Tomlinson (1980) who constructed a series of materials on the basis of this kind of approach, and J Harmer (1987) Chapter 4.
4 From J Harmer (1988a).
5 From R O'Neill (1970).
6 From *George's Marvellous Medicine* by Roald Dahl (Puffin 1982).
7 An extremely interesting article about how conditionals work – often in ways which coursebook writers ignore – is D Maule (1988).
8 From J Harmer and H Surguine (1988).
9 From J Soars and L Soars (1986).

10 From B Abbs and I Freebairn (1986).
11 From M Swan and C Walter (1984).
12 See reference number 3.
13 From R O'Neill and P Mugglestone (1989a).
14 From V Black et al. (1986).
15 From R Rossner et al. (1979a).
16 From G Iantorno and M Papa (1986).

7 Practice

In this chapter we will consider techniques and materials designed to give students practice in specific items or areas of language (see 4.3 'Input and output'). The activities will all fall somewhere between the two extremes on the communication continuum (see 5.3). We will look at *oral practice* and *written practice*.

7.1 Oral practice

In this section we will look at ways of getting students to practise oral English. We will consider *oral drills*, *information gap activities*, *games*, *personalisation* and *localisation* and *oral activities*.

7.1.1 Oral drills

Drills are usually very controlled and therefore they have limited potential.[1] Because they are fairly repetitive and not very creative they should not be used for too long or too frequently. However, they do give students the opportunity for 'safe' practice; accuracy can be focused on as the students get a chance to rehearse language.

In the following examples the first three concentrate on practising question forms whilst the fourth looks at a way of making drills a bit more fun.

(a) (Four)-phase drills

(Four)-phase drills are so called because there are (four) phases or stages, e.g. Q–A–Q–A. The reason why 'four' is in brackets is, of course, because we can also have six- or eight- phase drills – or any number, for that matter, although four seems to be the most useable

The students are encouraged to ask a question and on the basis of the answer follow it up with another question, for example:

A: Is John English?
B: No, he isn't.
A: Where's he from, then?
B: He's Australian.

In this case the drill is designed for beginners to practise the question form 'Is X [nationality]?' and 'Where is she/he from?'

We can start the activity by showing flashcards of people with some indication of their nationality. We then conduct a cue-response drill (see 6.3.2 (c)) in which students ask questions such as 'Is John English?'. For example:

T: Question . . . . Maria . . . French? (*Nominates S1*)
S1: Is Maria French?
T: Answer . . . . Gloria
S2: No she isn't.   *etc.*

We can then move on to the next question, adding the word 'then' if the answer to the first question is negative, for example:

T: Question . . . Maria . . . French? (*Nominates S1*)
S1: Is Maria French?
T: Answer . . . anyone.
S3: No she isn't.
T: Good . . . ask somebody a question with 'where' . . .
S4: Where's she from?
T: Good . . . but you can say 'Where's she from, then?' so . . . ask again Jorge . . .
S4: Where's she from, then?
T: Answer, Gloria.
S2: She's from Mexico.   *etc.*

The teacher conducts this drill with the whole class for a short space of time and the students then practise the drill in pairs. The teacher can give them flashcards or they can think of famous people to ask about.

In our example the drill depended on a negative answer to the first question. But of course (four)-phase drills can be constructed with any question sequence, for example:

A: What's your favourite hobby?
B: Tennis.
A: How often do you play?
B: Once a week.

(Four)-phase drills are useful for practice and revision of specific question forms and can be successfully used for quick five-minute sessions after these questions have been introduced, perhaps in a previous class.

(b) Mixed question and answer drills

The difference between mixed question and answer drills and (four)-phase drills is that the former have more questions than the latter and they can be asked in any order.

In the following example the teacher works with the whole class who see the following wall picture:

The teacher then elicits the following questions:

– What's his/her name?
– Where's he/she from?
– What's his/her job?
– What does he/she do?
– How old is she/he?

This can be done by conducting a cue–response drill:

T: OK. Ask me about Pierre's age, Hans.
S1: How old is Pierre?
T: Answer . . . Heidi.
S2: He's twenty-three. *etc.*

Students are then put in pairs to work with similar pictures and they might use the answers to write short paragraphs, for example:

Jean-Paul's from France. He's a pilot and he's forty-six years old.

Mixed question and answer drills provide a good opportunity for quick revision of language the students have previously studied. Like (four)-phase drills they are suitable for short practice sessions.

(c) Talking about frequency of activities[2]

In this drill students work with a specially prepared set of flashcards. The cards show various activities taking place.

Students are put in groups of four and a set of flashcards is placed in front of them, face downwards. A student picks up a card and has to ask another student how often a relative of that student performs the activity shown on the card. The drill might go in the following way:

S1: (*Picks up a card showing a man brushing his teeth.*)
How often does your brother brush his teeth, Tomiko?
S2: Twice a day, I should think. (*Picks up a card showing someone playing tennis.*) How often does your mother play tennis, Monica?

S3: She doesn't play at all! (*Picks up a card showing a person getting on a bus.*) How often does your sister travel by bus, Tarek?
S4: Never ... she always gets me to drive her everywhere!

This is a simple cue–response drill, but the students are conducting the drill themselves rather than being controlled by the teacher. The random selection of the cards makes the drill enjoyable and quite challenging, and the use of groupwork means that many students get a chance to participate in a co-operative and friendly way.

Cards of this kind have a use in many kinds of drill activities where students can practise specific items of language without being inhibited by the teacher.

(d) Chain drills

Chain drills are ways of practising a particular structure over and over again in the context of either a game and/or a personal element.

With large classes students can sit in groups. Otherwise this is a whole-class activity. The teacher chooses the structure and then says (for example):
'My name's Katie and I'd like to travel round the world.'
The student next to the teacher then has to say:
'Her name's Katie and she'd like to travel round the world.
My name's Paul and I would like to write a novel.'
The third student then has to remember the first two speaker's ambitions and then give his or her own. There are many other structures that can be used for this kind of drill, for example *like DOING, I've always wanted to DO, I've never DONE, at seven thirty last night I was DOING* etc. Chain drills are an amusing way of getting quick and involving practice of a particular structure. If the memory element is added (as in our example here) they can be made into a game.

Drill work is very useful since it provides opportunities for students to practise a new bit of language in the most controlled way. Most drills can be adapted for pairwork and groupwork.

It is important to remember the limitations of drills, however, and to use them sparingly.

7.1.2
Information gap
activities

With information gap activities different students are given different bits of information. By sharing this information they can complete a task.

In 5.2 we saw that an information gap was an ingredient in much real life communication (the majority of the activities in Chapter 8 will have an information gap built into them). The three examples we are going to show here, however, use the information gap to provoke the practice of specific items of language. Information gap activities, in other words, are drills, but because they have a slightly communicative element built into them they are more involving and motivating than a lot of question and answer practice.

(a) The map[3]

This example (from an elementary American English course) shows the most straightforward kind of information gap. It is designed to practise the pattern 'Where's the ____?' to elicit the answer *next to*, *between*, *across from*.

Students are put in pairs. In each pair one student is A and the other student is B. This is the material that Student A looks at:

2 Share information (Unit 7)

Student A: You and Student B have different maps. Ask Student B where these places are:

the Art <u>Theater</u>   a <u>high</u> school   the Garden <u>Restaurant</u>   Mc<u>D</u>onald's
a <u>li</u>brary   a <u>church</u>   a <u>men's</u> store   Joe's Caf<u>é</u>

Don't look at Student B's map. When Student B gives you the information, write the name of the place in the right place on your map.

Student B: Your map is on page 74.

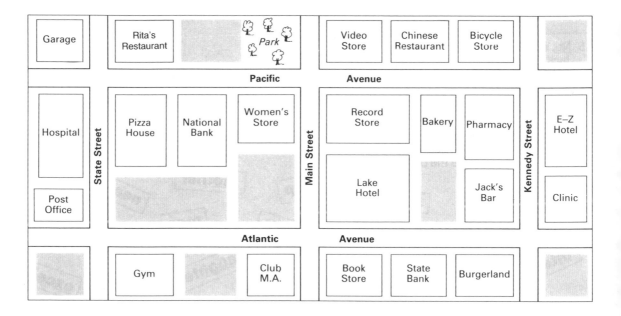

Notice that some of the squares on the map are blank. Student A is told to find out where the Art Theater is, for example. Student B has the answer of course since she or he looks at the following material:

2 Share information *(page 61)*

You and Student A have different maps. Ask Student A where these places are:

the E-Z Hotel   a <u>hos</u>pital   a Chinese <u>rest</u>aurant   a <u>rec</u>ord store
a <u>phar</u>macy   a <u>book</u>store   the National <u>Bank</u>   Burgerland

Don't look at Student A's map. When Student A gives you the information,
write the name of the place in the right place on your map.

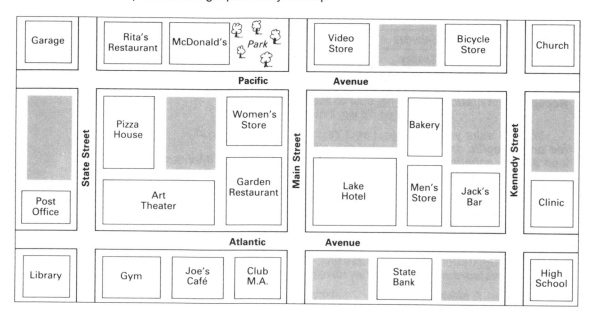

Student B has blanks, too, which only Student A can fill.
The point is that A and B will have to ask each other questions in order
to complete their maps, e.g.

A: Where's the Art Theater?

B: It's across from Joe's gym. (*A writes 'Art Theater' in the correct place
on his or her map*). Where's the National Bank? . . .

Remember that this activity only works if the students realise that they
are not supposed to look at each other's maps. The information gap is
created precisely because each student does not know the information that
the other student has.

(b) The Bailey Gold Cup[4]

There is no reason why information gap activities can only be used with
pairs, however. In this example for the intermediate level the students are
put into groups of three.

The activity is designed to practise the passive with questions like 'Who
is (name of horse) owned by?' 'Who is (name of horse) trained by?' 'Who is
(name of horse) going to be ridden by?'

When the teacher puts the students in groups Student A looks at the
following material:

Read this first

Which horse will win the Bailey Gold Cup? A lot depends on the owner, trainer and jockey. Here is a list of how many winners they have owned, trained or ridden so far this year.

Owners		Trainers		Jockeys	
Lady Melchett	3	Sally Flower	4	Leslie White	8
Sir John Prescott	2	Fred Dubbs	2	Mark Platt	5
Jim Green	0	George Makem	1	Pete Mayer	3

The Bailey Gold Cup

	1	2	3
Name of horse:	Trumpet Player	Lucky Lady	Dublin Boy
Owner:	Lady Melchett		
Trainer:		Fred Dubbs	
Jockey:			Pete Mayer

Student B get the same information about owners, trainers and jockeys, but the chart has different information in it.

Read this first

Which horse will win the Bailey Gold Cup? A lot depends on the owner, trainer and jockey. Here is a list of how many winners they have owned, trained or ridden so far this year:

Owners		Trainers		Jockeys	
Lady Melchett	3	Sally Flower	4	Leslie White	8
Sir John Prescott	2	Fred Dubbs	2	Mark Platt	5
Jim Green	0	George Makem	1	Pete Mayer	3

The Bailey Gold Cup

	1	2	3
Name of horse:	Trumpet Player	Lucky Lady	Dublin Boy
Owner:		Sir John Prescott	
Trainer:			Sally Flower
Jockey:	Mark Platt		

Student C's material is slightly different, too.

Read this first

Which horse will win the Bailey Gold Cup? A lot depends on the owner, trainer and jockey. Here is a list of how many winners they have owned, trained or ridden so far this year:

Owners		Trainers		Jockeys	
Lady Melchett	3	Sally Flower	4	Leslie White	8
Sir John Prescott	2	Fred Dubbs	2	Mark Platt	5
Jim Green	0	George Makem	1	Pete Mayer	3

The Bailey Gold Cup

	1	2	3
Name of horse	Trumpet Player	Lucky Lady	Dublin Boy
Owner:			Jim Green
Trainer:	George Makem		
Jockey:		Leslie White	

The students ask each other questions about the trainers, owners, etc. They fill in the blanks in their chart. When they have done this they can decide which horse they would put their money on, based, obviously, on the past record of the owners, trainers and jockeys. In other words, the filling in of the chart has had some purpose.

Once again it is vital that students do not look at each other's charts.

(c) Application[5]

This information gap activity is designed for intermediate students and shows how such an activity can be used not only for oral practice but also for reading and form-filling, etc.

Students are again divided into pairs with the usual restriction about not looking at each other's papers. They are told that they must each complete the paper in front of them.

This is what Student A receives:

By asking Student B questions, fill in the missing information in the letter of application below. (Student B will also ask you questions.)

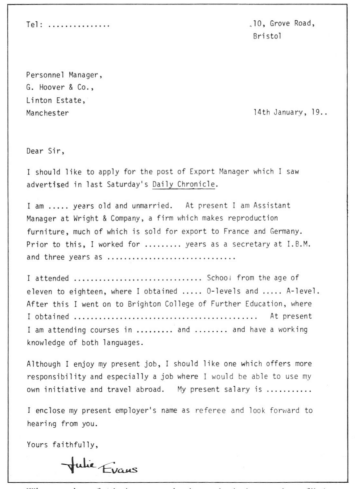

```
Tel: ..............                        .10, Grove Road,
                                           Bristol


Personnel Manager,
G. Hoover & Co.,
Linton Estate,
Manchester                                 14th January, 19..


Dear Sir,

I should like to apply for the post of Export Manager which I saw
advertised in last Saturday's Daily Chronicle.

I am ..... years old and unmarried.  At present I am Assistant
Manager at Wright & Company, a firm which makes reproduction
furniture, much of which is sold for export to France and Germany.
Prior to this, I worked for ........ years as a secretary at I.B.M.
and three years as .............................

I attended ........................... School from the age of
eleven to eighteen, where I obtained ..... O-levels and ..... A-level.
After this I went on to Brighton College of Further Education, where
I obtained ...........................................  At present
I am attending courses in ........ and ........ and have a working
knowledge of both languages.

Although I enjoy my present job, I should like one which offers more
responsibility and especially a job where I would be able to use my
own initiative and travel abroad.  My present salary is ..........

I enclose my present employer's name as referee and look forward to
hearing from you.

Yours faithfully,

Julie Evans
```

When you have finished, compare books to check that you have filled in the missing information correctly.

And this is what Student B receives:

By asking Student A questions, fill in the missing information in the application form below. (Student A will also ask you questions.)

APPLICATION FORM   Job applied for: ....

Name: ...... JULIE EVANS ....

Address: .... Tel: **327497**

Age: ...**30**....   single ☐ married ☐

Education: School: ...... HOVE COMPREHENSIVE ....

College/University: ....

Qualifications: School: .... 7 O-LEVELS, 1 A-LEVEL ....

College/University: ...... CERTIFICATE OF BUSINESS STUDIES

Present job: .... Salary: **£25,000**

Previous jobs (state number of years and start with most recent):

...... SALES MANAGER AT SUFFOLK CHEMICALS (   ) ..

.... (2 YEARS)

Foreign languages spoken:

French ☒   German ☒   Italian ☐   Spanish ☐   Others: ....

Reasons for leaving present job: ....

....

....

....

Date: ... JANUARY 14ᵗʰ 19...   Signature: ...... Julie Evans

When you have finished, compare books to check that you have filled in the missing information correctly.

The material makes students ask a large number of questions in order to complete their task. In order to ask these questions both students have to read their material and work out what questions to ask.

This is an impressive example of an information gap exercise which integrates skills.

Information gap tasks, then, provide students with a reason to communicate with each other, and can be designed to practise more or less specific language.

If students have not done an exercise of this type before the teacher would be well advised to demonstrate the technique before putting the students in pairs. Thus for the first example the teacher could write up a similar (but different) map on the blackboard with different information. A student then goes up to the front of the class. The student asks the teacher the questions; the teacher gives answers and the student has to complete the map on the blackboard.

When an activity of this type is over the teacher can conduct feedback by getting students to ask and answer the questions with the whole class listening. This serves to check not only the students' language production, but also whether they have got the information right.

7.1.3
Games[6]

Games are a vital part of a teacher's equipment, not only for the language practice they provide, but also for the therapeutic effect they have. They can be used at any stage of a class to provide an amusing and challenging respite from other classroom activity, and are especially useful at the end of a long day to send the students away feeling cheerful about their English class. We will look at four well-known examples.

(a) Ask the right question[7]

Students are divided into pairs in which there is A and B. Student A in each pair is given cards such as the following:

| a car | yesterday | Madonna | newspaper |

Student A then has to ask B questions so that B gives exactly the answer written on A's card. If B fails to give the exact answer A has to ask the question again until B gets it exactly right.

This game, suitable for all levels (although the teacher would choose more difficult answers for more advanced students) is great fun and quite difficult since A has to think of exactly the right question to get exactly the right answer.

(b) Twenty questions and other 'yes/no' games

Twenty questions is a team game which originated from a popular BBC radio programme.

Students are divided into teams. Each team must think of a number of objects. The game commences when one person from Team A asks someone from Team B a question which can only be answered with 'yes' or 'no'.

If Team B finds out what the object is after only a maximum of fifteen questions they get two points. If it takes them between sixteen and twenty questions they get one point. They get no points if they do not discover what the object is after asking twenty questions.

There are many varieties of this game, of course. Instead of objects the teams could be thinking of famous people and the questions could start with 'Is this person a man?' (notice that 'Is this person a man or a woman?' is not acceptable because it is not a 'yes/no' question).

A charade element can be added to the idea so that students can mime either actions ('Are you smoking a cigarette?') or occupations ('Do you work with other people?').

(c) Noughts and crosses/tic-tac-toe

This popular children's game can easily be adapted for the English classroom enabling the teacher to ensure practice of specific language items in an amusing context.

The class is divided into two teams; one represents noughts (0) and the other crosses (X). The teacher puts the following on the board:

this	never	running
their	can't	are
isn't	play	can

The team selects the square it wishes to play for, and a member of the team has to say a sentence using the word on that square. If the sentence is correct the square is filled with a nought or a cross, depending on the team the player comes from.

The game can be adapted to any language the teacher wishes to have practised. The squares could all contain question words, for example, or modal auxiliaries, frequency adverbs, etc. More fun can be added if the teacher brings in the game on a card and the squares are all covered. The students select a square which the teacher uncovers, and the team has to make a sentence with whatever is underneath.

(d) Quizzes

Quizzes can always be used to practise specific language items in an enjoyable and motivating way. In this example students will be practising the use of the 'was/were' past.

The students are divided into two teams. Each team is given time to write a number of general knowledge questions using the 'was/were' past. Their questions might be like the following:

Who was the first man on the moon?
What was the name of the last American president?
Where was the 1990 World Cup?
When were the Seoul Olympics?   *etc.*

In the game a member of Team A asks a question to a member of Team B. If the question is said correctly Team A gets one point. If the member of Team B gets the answer immediately the team gets two points. If he or she has to confer with the rest of the team to get the answer the team gets one point.

Games like these have been widely used for many years. They are great fun and provide practice in an amusing context.

**7.1.4
Personalisation
and localisation**

Personalisation and localisation refer to those stages of practice where students use language they have recently learnt to talk about themselves and their lives. Such stages can obviously be very controlled or very free, but here we are concerned with personalisation and localisation which have been designed to practise specific items of language – rather than with general discussion sessions.

When students are involved in immediate creativity (see 6.3) we ask them to produce sentences of their own using the new language. But we tend to stop there. In other words, students often produce language one sentence at a time. In personalisation and localisation for practice purposes, however, we will want to be a bit more realistic about the way in which language is used.

Language teaching materials in general sometimes give students a highly grammatical (and not very real) idea of how questions are asked and answered. Students practise questions such as 'Do you smoke?' and are expected to answer 'Yes I do/No I don't'. Even more exaggerated are textbook drills such as the following, 'Where's John?', 'John's in the kitchen'.

Research[8] has suggested, however, that answers to questions in real life are seldom grammatically parallel to the questions. The answer to a question such as 'Are you happy?' is seldom 'Yes I am/No I'm not'. Much more likely are responses such as 'More or less', 'Can't complain' or even 'Why do you ask?'

Teachers should encourage this type of response and a way of doing so is to insist on an additional remark being made. This means that where a student gives a yes/no type answer he or she must then add a comment to it. The following example shows such a remark being prompted:

S2: Do you like swimming?
S1: Yes.
 T: Yes ... and?
S1: Yes ... I go every Sunday.

Another feature of conversation is that people rarely ask a question, get an answer, and then finish the conversation (although many textbook drills are like this). The following exchange therefore is unlikely:

JOHN: Hello, Mary. Have you been to the movies recently?
MARY: Yes I have.
     (*John walks away*)

The conversation would be more likely to run in one of the following ways:

JOHN: Have you been to the movies recently?

MARY: Yes, actually.   *or*   No ... no I haven't.

JOHN: What did you see?   Really. Don't you like films?

MARY: Oh ... I saw *Born on the*   Yes, but I don't have the
    4th of July.   time to go to the cinema.

JOHN: Hadn't you seen it   Why?
    before?
    It's ancient!

        etc.   *etc.*

In other words, John's original question starts a conversation which he continues by asking questions which follow up the answer to the original conversation starter.

Particularly during personalisation and localisation stages the teacher can prompt the use of additional remarks and follow-up questions in order to encourage realistic communication.

We can now look at three examples of personalisation and localisation stages, bearing in mind the need for the teacher to prompt the use of additional remarks and follow-up questions, etc.

(a) Personalisation plans

In this case students have recently been learning the use of the present continuous to express future plans (e.g. 'He's going to Rome tomorrow').

The teacher then asks students what they are doing at the weekend and they give sentences using the present continuous, for example:

T: What are you doing this weekend, Gunter?
S1: I'm visiting Scotland.
T: Oh really ... When are you leaving?
S1: Early on Saturday morning. *etc.*

The teacher then gets students to ask each other questions of the same type (making sure they use follow-up questions in the same way). They can work in pairs or groups to do this.

This type of personalisation may form an immediate creativity stage (see 6.3) or it may be used at some stage after students have learnt the new item of language.

(b) Localisation: Guadalajara

Students are learning English in Guadalajara, Mexico. They have recently learnt how to talk about the location of places (e.g. 'There's a cinema in South Street', etc.).

The teacher then gets students to ask and answer questions about Guadalajara in a similar way:

T: OK ... well ... is there an airport in Guadalajara?
S1: Yes ...
T: Where is it exactly?
S1: It's on the road to Chapala ... about 11 kilometres from here. *etc.*

Students are then encouraged to ask and answer questions of the same type, and they will be put in pairs to do so. Once again this activity could be used as an immediate creativity stage, but it would also be suitable for language practice some time after the new language has been originally introduced.

(c) The hot seat

In this activity a student is put in the 'hot seat' and subjected to a barrage of questions. Obviously the technique has to be used sensitively by the teacher, but in the right atmosphere and carried out in the right spirit the activity provides enormous opportunity for practice.

A student is selected to be the focus of attention. The idea is to get students to ask him or her as many questions as they know, for example:

T: OK Juan ... ask Maria about yesterday evening.
S1: What did you do yesterday evening, Maria?
S2: I went to the supermarket.
    (Pause)
T: Well Juan ...
S1: Oh ... why?
S2: Because I needed some things.
S3: What did you buy?
S2: Eggs ... meat ... that kind of thing.   *etc.*

Supermarkets may not be very exciting as a topic for social conversation of this type, but of course the topic will depend on the students. In this example the teacher was controlling the proceedings, even to the extent of encouraging Juan to use a follow-up question. But the advantage of this kind of whole-class conversation is that the teacher may, if necessary, help out with prompting and gentle correction (see page 237) at the same time as getting a good idea of how the students are progressing with language that has recently been used for conscious learning.

Any subject of current interest can be used for such a session and it will be suitable for the beginning of classes particularly, where it will serve to 'warm the class up'.

Personalisation and localisation, then, are techniques for getting students to practise language in a way that ensures appropriate language use. Students have to be able to make the connection between the grammar that they have learnt and the way to apply it to things that have real meaning for them. Personalisation and localisation are useful for various stages of practice as well as the immediate creativity stage that we looked at in Chapter 6.

7.1.5
Oral interactions

We will look at three activities designed to encourage practice of specific language in an enjoyable and active way.

(a) Find someone who[9]

This activity is designed to get the students asking a number of different questions in an active way.

Each student is given the following card:

```
┌─────────────────────────────────────────────┐
│  FIND SOMEONE WHO                             │
│                                               │
│  1  likes chocolate_____                 │
│                                               │
│  2  often goes to the cinema_____        │
│                                               │
│  3  has three brothers_____              │
│                                               │
│  4  went to bed late last night_____     │
│                                               │
│  5  plays the guitar_____                │
│                                               │
│                                  (etc.)       │
└─────────────────────────────────────────────┘
```

All the students then stand up and circulate, asking each other questions such as 'Do you like chocolate?'. If they get the answer 'yes' they write that person's name in the space provided. They can only ask someone a question once. The activity ends when a student has got names for each question.

The activity is obviously noisy but it is great fun. Teachers can ensure practice of whatever questions they like by altering the items on the card. The activity is particularly suitable for a group that has only recently met since it helps students to get to know about each other.

It is a good idea to check that the 'winning' student has written down the names correctly.

(b) Likes and dislikes

This activity starts as a way of practising like/dislike language and the language of agreement and disagreement. If it is successful it may well develop into a free conversation.

The teacher and the students decide on a topic. The teacher then asks the students to write down two reasons why they like or dislike the topic, using the following formula:

I like/don't like (*the topic*) because _____ .

Before the activity starts the teacher will introduce agreement and disagreement language. In a fairly elementary class the following language might be introduced:

Agree   I agree, and + additional remark *Disagree* I'm afraid I don't agree. (I think) + opinion

The teacher now asks a student to read a sentence and asks another student to agree or disagree with it. The opinion or additional remark consists of what the second student had originally written down for that topic.

Suppose the topic were bullfighting, the session might start like this:

T: Read one of your sentences Juan.
S1: I like bull fighting because it's very exciting.
T: Agree or disagree, Maria.
S2: I'm afraid I don't agree ...
T: I think ...
S2: I think it's cruel because the bull always dies.
T: (*Nominates S3*)
S3: I'm afraid I don't agree. The bull sometimes wins.
S2: But he doesn't receive the ears of the matador!

The teacher starts the activity by cueing students and treating it like a drill. Thus he or she has to prompt *S2* to add an opinion to her disagreement. *S2*'s final contribution shows how the conversation is 'taking off'. If this happens (and it will probably not happen as quickly as in our example) the teacher will stop treating it as a drill, and cease prompting or correcting, perhaps joining the discussion as a participant (see 11.1.5).

This activity is equally suitable for groupwork. Once the students understand the procedure they can be put into groups to continue the activity.

(c) Questionnaires

Questionnaires are a useful way of encouraging practice of specific language items in an interesting and motivating way. In this example students will ask each other about films they have (or have not) seen and what their opinions of the film were.

The teacher and the students discuss some of the most recent films that have been shown. The students are then given the following form:

NAME OF FILM	Tick if seen	Tick if		
		good	satisfactory	bad

Students then question each other asking questions such as 'Have you seen *Parenthood*?', 'What did you think of it?/Did you like it?', etc. As the form suggests they put ticks (√) where indicated.

When they have filled in their questionnaires they will then write a short paragraph such as the following:

More people have seen *Family Business* than any other film, but most of them did not like it very much. The film that everybody thought was good was *Parenthood.*   *etc.*

The activity thus provides practice of the present perfect and past simple tenses and shows how oral and written skills can be integrated. The writing also encourages the use of comparatives.

The questionnaire, then, is a useful practice technique. We have already seen its use in presentation (see 6.6.1(b)) and we will see how the idea can be considerably extended in 8.4(a).

(d) Changing sex

The following activity[10] is designed to practise second and third conditional sentences, but instead of creating a story situation it asks students to make statements about themselves. What would life be like if they were the other sex?

♀ or ♂

Level   Intermediate and above

Time   30-40 min.

Grammar structures   'Second' and 'third' conditional

Preparation

Copy the completion sentences below enough times for each person to have one copy.

In class

1   Ask each student to imagine what life would be like were they a member of the other sex, and to individually complete the sentences you give out.

2   Ask the students to get out of their seats and to mill. When they are all up, ask each person to find a partner, if possible of the other sex, and explain their sentence completions to them. Get the students to re-pair 2 or 3 times.

Completion sentences

- If I was...
- If I belonged to the other sex...
- Had I been born (a)...
- Supposing I were (a)...
- My parents would've...
- If I wasn't the sex I am...
- Were I (a)...

ADD 10 more sentences of your own about what it would be like to belong to the other sex.

This exercise can be as light-hearted or as serious as the students and teacher want to make it. The point is that the students are practising specific language whilst at the same time talking about themselves.

**7.2
Written
practice[11]**

In this section we will consider ways of encouraging written practice. We will look at *sentence writing*, *parallel writing*, *cohesion*, *oral compositions* and *dictation*.

7.2.1
Sentence writing

We will look at three examples of sentence writing which aim to give students practice in specific written language.

(a) The fill-in

One way of providing controlled written practice is to get students to fill in blanks in sentences. This is extremely restricted, of course, though it is often useful during presentation stages and as controlled homework practice. In the following example[12] the authors use a postcard with multiple fill-ins for both practice and humour.

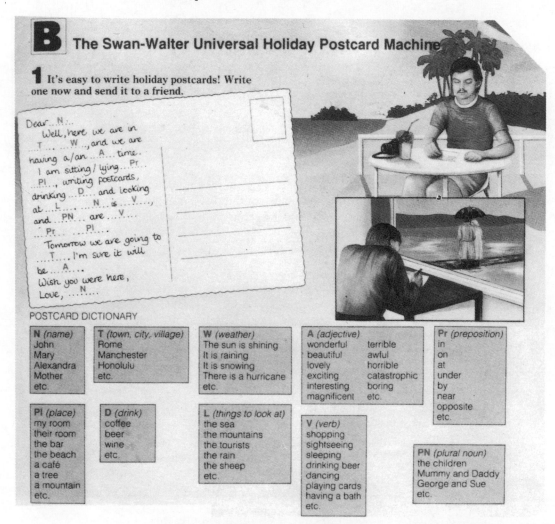

B The Swan-Walter Universal Holiday Postcard Machine

1 It's easy to write holiday postcards! Write one now and send it to a friend.

Dear ...N...,
Well, here we are in ...T... ...W..., and we are having a/an ...A... time. I am sitting / lying ...Pr... ...Pl..., writing postcards, drinking ...D... and looking at ...L..., ...N... is ...V..., and ...PN... are ...V... ...Pr... ...Pl...
Tomorrow we are going to ...T... I'm sure it will be ...A...
Wish you were here,
Love, ...N...

POSTCARD DICTIONARY

N *(name)*	**T** *(town, city, village)*	**W** *(weather)*	**A** *(adjective)*		**Pr** *(preposition)*
John	Rome	The sun is shining	wonderful	terrible	in
Mary	Manchester	It is raining	beautiful	awful	on
Alexandra	Honolulu	It is snowing	lovely	horrible	at
Mother	etc.	There is a hurricane	exciting	catastrophic	under
etc.		etc.	interesting	boring	by
			magnificent	etc.	near
					opposite
					etc.

Pl *(place)*	**D** *(drink)*	**L** *(things to look at)*	**V** *(verb)*	**PN** *(plural noun)*
my room	coffee	the sea	shopping	the children
their room	beer	the mountains	sightseeing	Mummy and Daddy
the bar	wine	the tourists	sleeping	George and Sue
the beach	etc.	the rain	drinking beer	etc.
a café		the sheep	dancing	
a tree		etc.	playing cards	
a mountain			having a bath	
etc.			etc.	

The students get a lot of good sentence-writing practice, and the task is made more involving and challenging by having them choose between all the alternatives in the various boxes.

(b) What are they doing?

In this example students are asked to look at a picture and write four sentences about what the people in the picture are doing. This is the picture:

This exercise has the advantage of getting the students to use specific language (in this case the present continuous) to make their own sentences. It is thus slightly more challenging than the first example.

(c) Christmas

In this example students use personalisation (see 7.1.4) to write sentences using time clauses.

    The students have recently learnt how to make time clauses using words such as 'before', 'after', 'when', 'while', etc. To start this sentence-writing activity the teacher might proceed in the following way:

T: What happens on December 25th?
S1: Christmas.
T: Right . . . do you do the same thing every Christmas?
S1: Yes . . . more or less.
T: OK . . . do you go to church Juan?
S1: Yes.
T: OK . . . and what happens after you've been to church?
S1: After we've been to church we open the presents.
T: Good . . . now I want you to write me four sentences using 'after', 'when', 'before' and 'while' about what you will do this Christmas.

Clearly this topic will only be suitable in Christian countries, and is probably appropriate for use near December the 25th. But other national holidays, both sacred and secular will work (e.g. Divali, Hannuka, New Year, Thanksgiving, etc.).

This exercise has all the advantages of oral personalisation since it is asking students to use specific language in what is, for them, a meaningful way. Topics such as this can serve as the basis for composition work, of course.

The three examples we have considered have all been concerned with the production of accurate written sentences. Connected written discourse is also necessary, however, and in the next three sections we will look at ways of encouraging students to write in this way.

7.2.2
Parallel writing

The concept of parallel writing is central to the teaching of connected discourse since it suggests that students should have a model from which to work. In other words, students will first see a piece of writing and then use it as a basis for their own work. The original piece that they look at will show them how English is written and guide them towards their own ability to express themselves in written English.

We have already discussed parallel writing during the presentation stage (see 6.5) We can now look at three practice examples using the same technique.

(a) Hotels

With this stimulating material students have to write descriptions of hotels based on a guide book after first seeing how the symbols are used in a written model. On the following page is the material the students see.[13]

The teacher starts by getting the students to look at the 'Key to symbols' either singly or in pairs. He or she then finds out if there is any vocabulary the students do not understand. When it is clear that the students understand all the symbols they study the entry for the Hotel Concorde. They are then asked comprehension questions to check they have understood the text. If necessary the teacher can then elicit similar sentences about, for example, the Castille Hotel as a further check that they can apply the symbols to the model. Students are then asked to write (either singly, or in pairs, or in groups) a similar paragraph about one of the other hotels. They might write something like the following:

> The Windmill Hotel in Mykonos is a simple hotel. It has no telephone. It is in the countryside.

The kind of writing which the students have to do here is very controlled; the activity is very like an oral substitution drill. Nevertheless the fact that students have to interpret symbols and relate them both to the original text and to the one they wish to write makes the activity extremely involving for them.

This is a page from a hotel GUIDE BOOK.

(1) Read the symbols and their meanings:

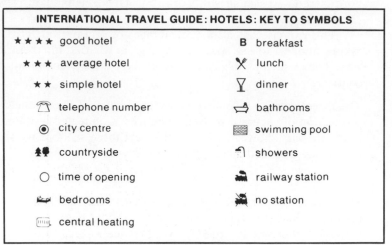

INTERNATIONAL TRAVEL GUIDE: HOTELS: KEY TO SYMBOLS	
★★★★ good hotel	B breakfast
★★★ average hotel	lunch
★★ simple hotel	dinner
telephone number	bathrooms
city centre	swimming pool
countryside	showers
time of opening	railway station
bedrooms	no station
central heating	

(2) Here is the entry for the Hotel Concorde, Paris.

HOTEL CONCORDE: PARIS, FRANCE

★★★★ 📞 88-66-21 ◉ ○ all year
40 🛏 central-heating. B 7-9 🍴 11-3 🍷 8-11
25 🛁 15 🚿 ▨ in hotel 🚂 2km

It means:

The Hotel Concorde in Paris is a good hotel. The telephone number is 88-66-21. It is in the city centre.

The hotel is open all year and there are forty bedrooms. There is central heating in the hotel.

Breakfast is from seven to nine, lunch is from eleven to three, and dinner is from eight until eleven. There are twenty-five bathrooms and fifteen showers. There is also a swimming pool in the hotel. The nearest railway station is two kilometres away.

Now read these symbols, and describe the hotels in the same way:

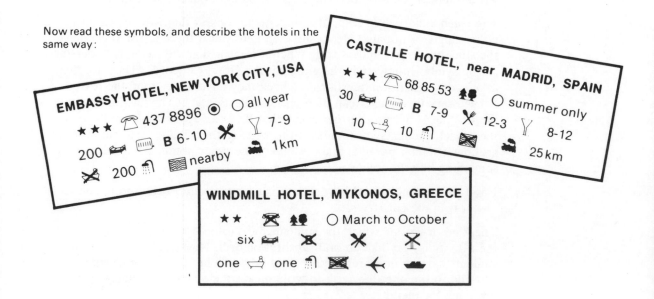

EMBASSY HOTEL, NEW YORK CITY, USA

★★★ 📞 437 8896 ◉ ○ all year
200 🛏 central-heating B 6-10 🍴 🍷 7-9 🚂 1km
🍴 200 🚿 ▨ nearby

CASTILLE HOTEL, near MADRID, SPAIN

★★★ 📞 68 85 53 🌳 ○ summer only
30 🛏 central-heating B 7-9 🍴 12-3 🍷 8-12
10 🛁 10 🚿 ▨ 🚂 25 km

WINDMILL HOTEL, MYKONOS, GREECE

★★ 📞 🌳 ○ March to October
six 🛏 🍴 🍴 🍷
one 🛁 one 🚿 ▨ ✈ ⛴

(b) Hetty Green[14]

Of course parallel writing does not always need to be as controlled as in the hotels example. In this example for upper intermediate classes, the students are drawn into the activity by a sentence-ordering task.

Writing skills

1 Here is an account of the life of Hetty Green. Fit the sentences a–e into the text.

a His leg was eventually amputated.

b Hetty Green, one of the richest and meanest women who ever lived, was born in New Bedford.

c When Hetty Green died at the age of 82, she left more than 100 million dollars.

d By the age of six she was reading the stock market reports for pleasure.

e When her son Ned had an infected leg, she dragged him around free clinics rather than pay for proper treatment.

2 Write an account of the life of somebody you know about – alive or dead!

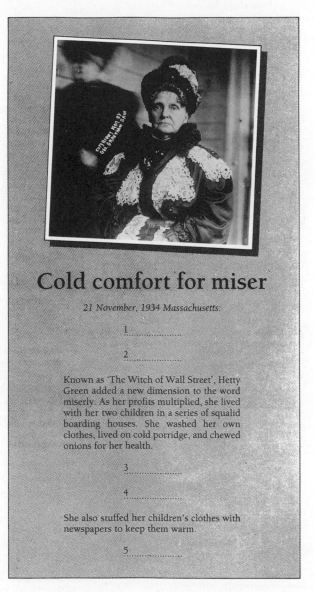

Cold comfort for miser

21 November, 1934 Massachusetts:

1 ....

2 ....

Known as 'The Witch of Wall Street', Hetty Green added a new dimension to the word miserly. As her profits multiplied, she lived with her two children in a series of squalid boarding houses. She washed her own clothes, lived on cold porridge, and chewed onions for her health.

3 ....

4 ....

She also stuffed her children's clothes with newspapers to keep them warm.

5 ....

102

113

When the teacher has checked that the students have got the sentences in the right place, they then study the organisation of the text (see 7.2.3 (c)). Now they are in a position to use the text as a model for their own description of a famous person.

These two examples show parallel writing at the controlled and free ends of the spectrum. It is probably the case that students at lower levels will respond best to more controlled examples while the freer activities may suit intermediate students better. However parallel writing is only one technique, and we will look at many more ways of encouraging freer writing in 8.2.

7.2.3
Cohesion

In 5.6 we discussed some of the differences between speaking and writing and in particular we saw the need for coherent organisation and logical thought. We saw how this was in some ways more difficult in writing than in speaking, particularly since readers are often not in a position to clarify points they do not understand with the writer in the same way that participants in a conversation can stop the speaker and ask for repetition and re-explanation. In this section we will look at a number of exercises designed to help students to organise their writing clearly and coherently. This involves not only the ordering of sentences, but also the use of cohesive devices (i.e. language that is used to join sentences together). We will look at three examples of exercises designed to teach students about coherence and cohesion.

(a) Co-ordinators: Sunshine

In this example we will look at a simple exercise for elementary students designed to teach them how to join sentences with 'and' and 'but'.

The students are given the following exercise:

Join the following pairs of sentences using 'and' or 'but'.

1 Sunshine makes people happy. Sunshine can be bad for you.
2 Sunbathing feels good. People with light skins can get skin cancer from sunbathing.
3 People are more cheerful in the sunshine. People are more friendly to each other when the sun is out.

The students will not only have to select 'and' or 'but'; they will also have to change 'sunshine' and 'sunbathing' to 'it'. The use of words like 'it', 'they', 'she', etc. to refer back to subjects mentioned earlier will be discussed in detail in (c) below.

(b) Concession: The photocopier

The aim of this exercise for advanced students is to train them in the use of concession language such as 'in spite of' and 'although', etc. It also reminds students how spoken language can be formalised for written style.

This is the spoken text which the students either read or listen to on tape.

You want to hear a story? I'll tell you. Four weeks ago I finally got round to buying myself a brand new photocopier – I've been needing one for some time. Anyway so I finally got it, and quick as a flash it started to go wrong. First of all it copied everything completely black. Now the copies are so faint you can hardly see a thing. I phoned the company of course, but nobody came. After a week I was pretty mad so I wrote a rather angry letter. Nobody came. In the end I turned up at the shop and, well, they sent a man round after that, I can tell you. He said he'd fixed it but it still isn't working properly. I just don't know what to do. Oh, and to make matters worse they sent me a bill. A bill! I ask you. The thing's under guarantee . . . .

Re-tell the basic facts of the story in written style using *'in spite of (the fact that)'*, *'despite (the fact that)'* and *'although.'*

Example: *Although the photocopier was completely new it started to go wrong immediately.*

This exercise is fairly advanced, but the same principle can easily be used at lower levels.

(c) Princes, grandmothers and bears[15]

In this example we will look at a lesson sequence designed to train students how to write more coherently by using pronouns as cohesive devices (see (a) above). A four-stage sequence exposes students to the issue and gets them to practise using the pronouns.

The teacher writes the following on the blackboard:

a It will give her more time to wash all the dishes so she's very happy now.
b John and Mary have six children.
c It takes Mary three hours to clean it.
d They live in a large flat.
e Luckily she was given a vacuum cleaner for her birthday this morning.

The students are asked to re-order the sentences by putting the letter of the sentence against the following numbers.

1 ___ 2 ___ 3 ___ 4 ___ 5 ___

When they have done this individually the teacher asks them what order they have chosen and asks them why. With luck they will have realised that sentence *b* has to be the topic sentence because it introduces the subject matter of the paragraph. Sentence *d* follows, and the clue to this is the use of *they* which refers to 'John', 'Mary' and the 'six children'. The sentence ends with the information about the flat which is then picked up by the second '*it*' in sentence *c*. And so on. The teacher helps the students to be aware of elements of cohesion and how they are used in paragraph organisation.

Of course this domestic tale of typical housewifery may not be to everyone's taste. Stories of princes rescuing princesses tend to portray women as subservient victims, too. That's why a children's story called *The Bear* may therefore be something of a relief.

The students are told that Kitty Redcape's grandmother lives in the woods and Kitty frequently goes to have tea with her. The students are then given the following cards and told to re-order them to finish the story, paying particular attention to clues such as the use of he and she. (The first one is done for them.)

1 | One day, on her way to visit her grandmother, Kitty Redcape saw a handsome prince.

So he rode away, sadder, but alas, no wiser.

'Oh, shut up, you silly old woman,' he retorted.

The bear, who by this time was fed up with being ignored, followed the prince into the forest and ate him.

At that moment the prince rode by and charged into the garden.

'I'm sure you were,' said the prince. 'Come on, let's get away from that silly old lady and go to my castle for lunch.'

'I have come to save you, young maiden,' he cried, knocking the grandmother down in his haste to be by her side.

Her heart skipped a beat or two, but the prince hardly noticed her as he rode by.

'Hey! Watch what you're doing!' said Kitty Redcape's grandmother.

'Thank you for coming to our rescue,' Kitty Redcape said to the prince, 'though I have a gun and was quite capable of looking after myself.'

'That silly old lady is my grandmother, actually,' said Kitty, 'and I didn't like the way you spoke to her. And now that I can see you close to, I can't imagine why I thought you were good-looking. Why don't you rejoin your hunt?'

By the time she got to her grandmother's house, Kitty had forgotten about the prince, but she was horrified to see the old lady being attacked by a bear.

After pairs and/or groups of students have completed the task the teacher checks to make sure they all have the correct order.

The teacher could then ask students to imagine what happened after the end of the story using personal pronouns to start their sentences, e.g.

He _____

She _____

The students are now putting into effect what they have learnt from the previous sentence-ordering tasks.

Another exercise that could be used is the following:

Where you think it is necessary replace the words 'Kitty Redcape', 'the prince' and 'the bear' by 'she', 'her', 'he', 'him' and 'it'.

The Bear tells the story of Kitty Redcape, her grandmother, a bear and a prince.
Kitty Redcape often goes to visit Kitty Redcape's grandmother in the woods. One day, on Kitty Redcape's way to Kitty Redcape's grandmother's house, Kitty Redcape sees the prince and Kitty Redcape thinks the prince is very attractive. The prince does not notice Kitty Redcape.

When Kitty Redcape arrives at the cottage Kitty Redcape sees Kitty Redcape's grandmother being attacked by a bear. Just then the prince rides into the garden to save Kitty Redcape and the prince is rude to Kitty Redcape's grandmother.

The prince asks Kitty Redcape back to his castle for lunch but Kitty Redcape says no because Kitty Redcape doesn't like the prince's treatment of Kitty Redcape's grandmother and Kitty Redcape doesn't fancy the prince. Kitty Redcape suggests that the prince should go back to the prince's hunt and leave them alone. And that's what the Prince does.
The bear follows the prince into the forest and eats the prince.

This lesson sequence clearly shows students how and why paragraphs are organised in the way they are (clearly children's stories – however witty – will not be suitable for some classes). The variety of exercises in the sequence gives students practice not only in working out the logic of such organisation but also in putting their newly acquired understanding into practice.

7.2.4
Oral compositions

Oral compositions have been popular in language teaching for a long time. The idea is that the teacher and the class together build up a narrative before the students are then asked to write it. This process allows the teacher and the students to focus in on a variety of language items from verb tenses to cohesive devices, etc.

Oral compositions can be handled with visual[16] or aural[17] stimuli. In other words, the teacher can show the students a series of pictures, mime a story, or play them a tape with a series of sounds. The example we are going to look at uses pictures.

Saved by the rats![18]

The teacher is going to work from the following set of pictures:

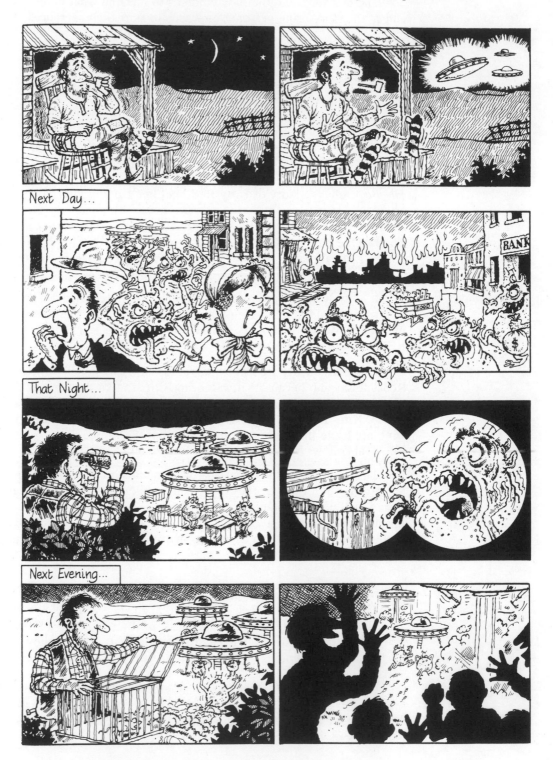

The teacher starts by getting students to look at the first picture in the sequence. The students are encouraged to say what the man is doing, e.g.

T: So ... what can you say abut the man ...
S1: The man sitting?
T: OK .. but when .?
S2: Last night?
T: Hmm ... a bit before that.
S3: Last Monday ...
T: OK. So can someone give me a sentence.
S1: Last Monday evening a man was sitting on his porch. He was smoking a pipe.   *etc.*

Of course it probably won't go that smoothly!

The teacher then produces the next picture and elicits the same kind of language until the first four pictures have been dealt with. Students could then be given the last four pictures as homework.

Clearly oral compositions work better if students do not see all the pictures at the same time.

Oral compositions are useful for the teaching of narrative style and the use of various past tenses. However, they take a long time and should, therefore, be used sparingly.

7.2.5 Dictation

Like many teaching techniques that go completely out of fashion for a time, dictation is making a comeback. This is largely due to the work of Paul Davis and Mario Rinvolucri[19] who have looked at the subject and changed it out of all recognition by asking the question, who should dictate what and to whom? In other words, they have found dynamic alternatives to the dictation of large chunks of uninteresting prose by a stern teacher – the situation that many students used to have to suffer. Two examples show how dictation can be a useful way of getting into a topic.

(a) Beautiful things

Teachers frequently complain that their students 'have nothing to say'. Partly that is because they tend to spring discussions on them without any warning. If you ask a class 'What is beauty?' you probably won't get an answer!

Little dictations can get the process moving, however, as in the following example.

Tell the students to get out a pen and paper and then dictate the following:

One of the most beautiful things I have ever seen is .....

Now tell them they have to complete the sentence for themselves. They may do it seriously or superficially. It doesn't matter. The point is that you now have something to work with and all the students, because they have had a chance to write something down, will have something to say.

(b) Poetry dictation[20]

In this activity students dictate to each other in an involving and exciting way.

The teacher brings one copy of a poem into the classroom and either keeps it on the desk or pins it to a board. The students are put into groups. Each group sends a member up to the poem where they read only the first line. They take this line back to their group and dictate it. Now a second member of the group goes to the poem and reads the second line so that it can be dictated to the group. A third student goes up for the third line and so on.

The technique works beautifully because the students are kept guessing about what the next line(s) will be. They are far more involved in the meaning of the poem than they would be if they were just reading it, and they are getting writing practice.

A lot of modern poetry – which is often short and clear – is useful for this kind of activity. But you can also use dialogues and prose passages, too, provided that they are not too long.

7.3
Conclusions

In this chapter we have looked at ways of getting students to practise specific items of language both in speech and in writing. We have seen that the object of practice is to allow students to focus on the accuracy of what they are saying and writing. But we have shown that this does not mean that such activities have to be dull and manipulative: on the contrary, many practice activities are great fun and provide the students with a satisfactory blend of confidence and enjoyment.

Exercises

1 Select a language item or items that you are going to teach and then design an information gap activity to practise that language.
2 Take a unit from a textbook you are using (or are familiar with) and design the following supplementary practice material:
   a) a noughts and crosses game
   b) a personalisation/localisation stage
   c) a 'find someone who' activity.
3 Look at your textbook (or one that you are familiar with) and say what kinds of written practice the book contains.
4 Take an English written text from any source and identify cohesive devices that are used in that text.

References

1 Alexander discusses the relative merits of drills in an article called 'To Drill or not to Drill' (LG Alexander 1985).
2 This idea originally comes from J Kerr (1979) Teacher's Book page 74. Kerr's cue cards are still very useful for this kind of activity, but teachers can, of course, produce their own picture or word cards. Another source of both cards and ideas is De Bono's set (De Bono (1982)). (See also reference 7.)
3 From R Maple (1988).
4 From J Harmer and S Elsworth (1988).

5 Taken from P Watcyn-Jones (1981), one of the first sets of materials devoted exclusively to information gaps. Others include A Matthews and C Read (1981). Watcyn-Jones' material was in two separate books, one for Student A, one for Student B. Others put the material for different students on different pages of a book.

6 For more on games see D Byrne (1986) Chapter 9, A Wright et al. (1984) and W Lee (1980). C Frank and M Rinvolucri (1983) and M Rinvolucri (1985) contain a wealth of interesting game-like activities. P Ur (1988) is a rich source of grammar activities.

7 A slightly different version of this game can be found in J Willis (1981) page 122.

8 See J Richards (1977). An excellent comparison of textbook 'short answers' and real life exchanges was made by W Plumb (1979).

9 This activity comes originally from G Moskowitz (1978). A nice adaptation can be found in S Deller (1990) page 25.

10 From C Frank and M Rinvolucri (1983).

11 For more on controlled writing see D Byrne (1988), especially Chapter 4, and J Willis (1981) Unit 20.

12 Taken from M Swan and C Walter (1984).

13 From E Davies and N Whitney (1979).

14 From R O'Neill and P Mugglestone (1989b).

15 This class sequence was planned by Anita Harmer.

16 See for example L Markstein and D Grunbaum (1981).

17 See for example A Maley and A Duff (1977).

18 The pictures are from A Doff et al. (1983).

19 See P Davis and M Rinvolucri (1989).

20 This idea is based on activities in Davis and Rinvolucri (see above).

8

Communicative activities

In this chapter we will consider activities which comply as far as possible with the characteristics we said were necessary for communicative activities (see Figure 8 on page 50). In the first half of the chapter we will look at activities with a largely oral focus (although we should not forget the points about skill integration in 5.5); in the second part we will consider written communication. Many teachers worry about the management of such activities and the students' use of their mother tongue. These issues are dealt with in 11.1 and 11.2.4.

8.1 Oral communicative activities

The following activities are all designed to provoke spoken communication between students and/or between the teacher and the students. We will divide the activities into seven categories: *reaching a consensus*, *discussion*, *relaying instructions*, *communication games*, *problem solving*, *talking about yourself*, *simulation and role play*. (Where the organisation of the activities seems complicated, teaching stages have been included.)

8.1.1 Reaching a consensus

In these examples students have to agree with each other after a certain amount of discussion. The task is not complete until they do.

Consensus activities have been very successful in promoting free and spontaneous language use and we can now look at three examples.

(a) Going to New York[1]

In this activity students are told that they are going on holiday and have to decide what ten objects to take with them. They will have to reach a consensus on these objects.

Stage 1 All the students are asked to write down the ten items they would choose to have in their luggage if they were going to stay in New York for two weeks.

Stage 2 When all the students have completed their lists they are put into pairs. Each pair has to negotiate a new list of ten items. This will involve each member of the pair changing their original list to some extent.

Stage 3 When the pairs have completed their lists two pairs are joined together to negotiate a new list that all four students can agree to.

Stage 4 Groups can now be joined together and the lists re-negotiated.

Stage 5 When the teacher thinks the activity has gone on for long enough a feedback session is conducted with the whole class in which each group explains and justifies its choices.

This activity, which can be used from the elementary level upwards, is great fun and produces a lot of English. Of course there is no particular reason for selecting New York as the destination. Other places can be used.

(b) Moral dilemmas

Students are given a situation and alternative suggestions for acting in such a situation are given. The following is an example:

Stage 1 Students are told that they are invigilating an important school/ university exam. They see a student cheating with notes he or she has illegally brought into the exam room. They have four possible courses of action:
– Ignore the incident.
– Warn the student that if she or he cheats again she or he will be reported to the authorities.
– Ask the student to leave the exam, tear up his or her exam and mark him or her as absent.
– Report the student to the authorities, in which case he or she will have to leave the school/university.

Stage 2 Students are put in small groups to reach a consensus on this issue.

Stage 3 Pairs of groups are combined and have to reach a consensus on which alternative to adopt.

Stage 4 The procedure can be repeated with groups joining each other. Alternatively after Stage 3 the teacher can conduct a feedback session in front of the whole class in which groups justify their choices.

(c) Learning decisions

There are many other occasions when we will ask students in groups to come to a consensus about things they are learning. Reading tasks might involve this kind of agreement (students decide which is the correct answer together); some vocabulary study involves reaching a consensus about which meanings are correct (see 9.5.2 (g)) or which words to select for comprehension work (see 9.6.1 (d)).

8.1.2
Discussion[2]

Many teachers can be heard complaining that their students 'have nothing to say': they complain, for example, that they have no opinions and are not prepared to discuss anything.

Part of the problem here is the way in which some teachers approach discussion as an activity. If students are asked to express themselves fluently on a difficult topic in front of their peers in a foreign language (often with no warning) they may find themselves reluctant to do so!

Of course some discussions develop spontaneously during the course of a lesson. A student reacts to something that is said, another student joins in, and soon the whole class is bubbling with life. Such discussions are often the most successful sessions that the teacher and the class ever have together, but they can't be planned.

Between these two extremes (the students with nothing to say and the spontaneous outbreak of conversation) there are techniques that can be used to get students talking. Before looking at three examples, however, we can give some hints about organising discussions:

1 **Put students in groups first**. Before asking students to discuss as a whole class, put them in groups to try out the topic. This will allow them to give opinions in a less threatening environment than in front of the whole class. It will also give the teacher a chance to see if the topic is interesting for the students. If it is not and the teacher decides to end the discussion, this can be done without the 'loss of face' that accompanies the cancellation of a discussion session in front of a whole class.

2 **Give students a chance to prepare**. Where a more formal discussion is due to take place students need a chance to prepare their opinions. If they are to discuss the role of the family or the relative merits of radio and television they need time to marshall their thoughts and come up with arguments to support their case. This is especially true for debates (see (c) below).

3 **Give students a task**. One way of promoting discussion is to give students a task as part of the discussion process. They can be given a list of controversial statements about a topic and asked to score them from 0 (= very negative) to 5 (= very positive). They can do this in pairs and groups; once again this will be excellent preparation for any full-class session.

We can now look at three types of discussion activity:

(a) The buzz group

One way of encouraging short sharp bursts of discussion is through the use of 'buzz groups'. This is where students are put into loose groups of three or four (the number is unimportant) and asked to think of the topic. Frequently the teacher may ask them to think of 'as many .... as possible'. Examples might be: the students are going to read a text about addiction. First the teacher puts them into groups for a two-minute session. They should think of as many forms of addiction as they can. The class pools the information. Perhaps the students are doing some work about seaside holidays (in an elementary group this might be for tense practice, e.g. 'What's Jenny doing?' 'She's swimming', etc.). They could be put into buzz groups to think of as many seaside activities as possible.

Buzz groups can form the prelude to a larger discussion session (see 1 above).

(b) Controversial topics

In (2) above we said that controversial statements were good discussion provokers. Here is an example. The students are given the following statements about smoking and told that they have to circle the number which best reflects their agreement or disagreement with the statement (0 = totally disagree, 5 = totally agree).

1 Smoking should be banned in all public places.	0	1	2	3	4	5
2 Smokers should be forced to give up the habit.	0	1	2	3	4	5
3 People who smoke in no-smoking areas should be put in prison.	0	1	2	3	4	5
4 There should be separate areas for smokers in all restaurants, bars and cafés.	0	1	2	3	4	5

When they have done this they proceed as if for a consensus activity (they compare their answers in pairs and then groups and they have to agree a score).

This technique is a good example of using a small task to provoke discussion.

(c) The debate

There is still room for the more formal debate – where two sides argue a case which is then put to the vote. The activity is suitable for more advanced classes.

Students are given a controversial proposition such as *People who buy fur coats should pay a 100% tax*. They are then put into two groups which have to prepare arguments *either* in favour of the proposition *or* against the proposition. When the arguments are ready the teams elect a proposer and a seconder who make formal speeches to argue their case. All the other students can then take part with short interventions. At the end of the discussion the teacher can organise a free vote to see whether the proposition wins or not.

A variation on the formal debate is the 'Balloon' debate. Students must each choose a character. They are then told that all the characters are in the basket of a hot-air balloon. The balloon is losing air and so people must jump from the basket to save the lives of others. Who should be chosen as the sole survivor? The 'characters' must make convincing arguments in favour of their own survival. A final vote decides which characters should jump and which should remain.

Discussion activities are an important part of many lessons. The main thing to remember is that proper organisation can ensure their success. Lack of it can provoke their failure.

8.1.3 Relaying instructions

In this type of activity students have to give each other instructions. The success of the activity depends on whether the students to whom instructions are being given perform the tasks successfully – in other words, were the instructions the right ones, and were they understood?

(a) Exercises

Stage 1 The teacher writes down the names of a number of common exercises (e.g. press-ups, sit-ups squat jumps, etc.) – or better still has drawings of them. These are given to individual students (without the others seeing).

Stage 2 Students have to get their colleagues to do the exercises using only words (no gestures, etc.).

This activity can be very amusing, and certainly involves real communication. Apart from physical exercises, students can instruct each other in a dance, in certain mimes, etc.

(b) Making models

Stage 1 A small group of students is given material to make models with (e.g. building bricks, *Lego*, etc.) They are told to make a model.

Stage 2 The original group now has to instruct another group or groups so that they can duplicate the original model. It is, of course, necessary for the original model to be hidden from the second group or other groups at this stage.

(c) Describe and draw

One of the most popular instruction games is 'describe and draw' in which one student is given a picture which the other student cannot see. The second student has to draw an identical picture (in content, not style) by listening to the first student's instructions.

The students must be put in pairs and they must be told not to look at each other's pictures until they have finished the activity. It is because Student B cannot see Student A's picture that the communication takes place.

8.1.4
Communication
games

Communication games are based on the principle of the information gap (see 5.2). Students are put into a situation in which they have to use all or any of the language they possess to complete a game-like task.

(a) Find the differences (or similarities)[3]

Students are put into pairs. In each pair Student A is given a picture and Student B is given a picture which is similar, but different in some vital respects. They are told that they must not look at each other's material but that they must find out a certain number of differences between the two pictures through discussion only. In the following example[4] Student A looks at this picture:

And Student B gets this picture:

(Note that the originals are in colour so that differences in shirts, etc. can be used.)

(b) Describe and arrange

Students are told they are going to work in pairs. In each pair Student A is given the following pictures and told not to show them to Student B:

Student B, on the other hand, is given the same pictures, but cut up so they are not in any order, e.g.

It is now Student B's job to arrange the pictures in the same order as Student A's.

(c) Story reconstruction: The hospital case[5]

Students are given different parts of a picture story. They have to reconstruct the whole narrative even though individually they have seen only a small part of it. This is done because each member of the group has seen a different picture; by talking about their pictures together the narrative emerges.

Here is a procedure for the technique:

Stage 1 The class is divided into four large groups, A, B, C and D.
Stage 2 Each group is given one of the following pictures and told to study it.

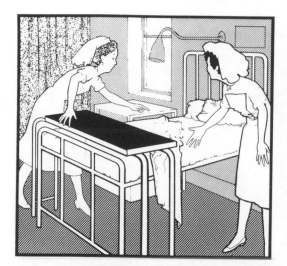

Stage 3 After a couple of minutes the teacher takes the pictures back from the groups.

Stage 4 The teacher makes new groups with one student from each of the original groups (i.e. one from A, one from B, one from C, one from D).

Stage 5 The students in the new groups have to try and reconstruct the story by discussing what they saw on each of their pictures.

Stage 6 The teacher then gets the different groups to tell their stories. Often with picture sequences there will be more than one version of the story. The teacher then shows the students all the pictures.

(d) Poem reconstruction

The same principle (of reconstruction) can be applied to simple poems. Students have to reassemble lines which they are given. The activity mixes reading, listening and discussion.

Stage 1 The students are put into groups.

Stage 2 In each group each of the students is given one of the following cards and instructed not to show it to anyone else:

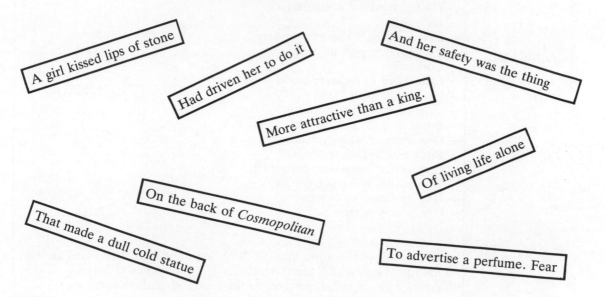

Stage 3 The groups are told that they must reassemble the poem – it is a one stanza poem. Students can read the lines aloud, but they may not show them to anyone else.

Stage 4 The groups are told that they must decide on a title for the poem.

8.1.5 Problem solving

Problem-solving activities encourage students to talk together to find a solution to (a set of) problems or tasks. We will look at two examples:

(a) Desert dilemma[6]

Students are given a complex situation and told to work out a means of survival.

All the students are told to read the following:

THE SITUATION

It is about ten o'clock in the morning in July, and you have just crashed in a small aeroplane in the Sonora desert in Northern Mexico. The pilot and co-pilot are dead and the aeroplane is a burnt-out shell. One of the passengers is injured.

The aeroplane had no radio, and the survivors think that they were about 100 kilometres off course when they crashed. Just before the crash the pilot told the passengers that they were 120 kilometres south of a small mining camp.

From experience you know that daytime temperatures can reach 43° centigrade (110° Fahrenheit) and night-time temperatures reach freezing. All the passengers are dressed in light clothes. The area is flat and arid as far as the eye can see.

Instructions

The following is a list of items that came out of the crash in good order:
— Flashlight with four batteries
— Jack knife
— Detailed pilot's chart of the area
— Large plastic poncho
— Compass
— Instrument to measure blood pressure
— Loaded .45 pistol
— One red and white parachute
— Bottle of 1000 salt tablets
— One quart of water per person
— Book *Edible Desert Animals*
— One pair of sunglasses per person
— Two bottles of vodka
— One overcoat per person
— One pocket mirror

Now do the following:
(a) Individually write down a list of the seven most important items on this list to ensure survival and/or rescue.
(b) Agree with the other members of the group what these items are.

They are then put in groups. Each group must follow the instructions and work out how to survive this desert situation. The teacher can then check to see how ingenious (or otherwise) the solutions are. (One proposed solution is as follows: the seven important items are the mirror, the flashlight, one quart of water per person, the plastic poncho, sunglasses, overcoats and a parachute. Walking is inadvisable owing to the heat, so a signalling mirror (by day) and flashlight (by night) will be useful. The parachute can be used for shelter and as a sign for searching planes. Sunglasses can prevent blindness and overcoats keep people warm in the cold desert nights. The water is clearly important, and the plastic poncho can be used to create more water, e.g.

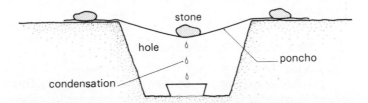

This reading/discussion exercise is suitable for intermediate students. Apart from organising the groups and conducting feedback, the teacher can leave the students very much on their own.

(b) Fast food[7]

A welcome development in language teaching has been the introduction of computers into the classroom. Despite the scepticism of some teachers they provide a valuable aid for language learning.[8]

Fast Food is one of a series of computer games where the user has to take decisions which will affect the outcome of the game. In this program students run a fast food stall and they have to decide how many rolls, sausages, drinks, etc. to order for their stall and what price to charge for them. They are given information about the weather, etc. If they make the right decisions they prosper, if they make the wrong decisions they start to lose money.

After the game has been explained, the teacher puts students into small groups. Each group is assigned to a computer and told to run their stall. The discussion that takes place is frequently fast and furious with students anxious to ensure the success of the venture (see also 'Co-operative writing' in 8.2.3).

Where a school only has one or two mini-computers activities like *Fast Food* can be reserved for students who finish other groupwork early; teachers can set up small English computer clubs so that students who are keen can work after class.

8.1.6
Talking about yourself[9]

The students themselves are often an underused resource[10]: in particular we can use their lives and feelings for any number of interpersonal exchanges. Such activities fall into the 'Humanistic' category (see 4.1.5) and are often useful at the beginning of classes to warm things up ('warmers') or to create a good and positive atmosphere in new groups which are a bit 'icy' ('ice breakers').

We will look at three simple activities that are quick and easy to organise:

(a) Your name[11]

The teacher puts the students in pairs and asks them to tell each other:
• how they feel about their first name (do they like it, etc.)
• what name they would choose for themselves if they had to choose one that was different from the one they have (and why)

Clearly this activity is very simple, but it demonstrates the advantages of 'talking about yourself'. Many people have strong opinions about their names and from such simple questions an interesting personal discussion can develop.

(b) What we have in common[12]

This is an ideal ice breaker. Students are put in pairs at random and told to discover five things which they have in common. This encourages them to cover a number of areas and topics including musical tastes, sports, families ('Do you have any brothers or sisters?'), etc. It is also a positive activity since it investigates what joins people together, not what breaks them apart!

(c) Musical associations

In this activity the teacher encourages the students to use the title of a song to provoke discussion of feelings and memories, etc.

Stage 1 The teacher asks the students to write down the name of a song which they like. It can be a pop song, a folk song, a song from the opera, anything. They should not show this title to anybody else for the moment.

Stage 2 The teacher then tells the students that they are going to discuss this song with a partner. They should tell their partner the title of their song and the following:
  • how the song makes them feel
  • what the song makes them think of
  • what the song makes them feel like doing
  • where they would most like to hear the song

Stage 3 When the students have had enough time to tell each other about their songs the teacher can ask if anyone heard anything particularly interesting that they would like to share with the group.

Most students seem to enjoy this activity since, like (a) and (b) above, it is positive in tone and allows them to talk about themselves.

Any activities which invite students to share themselves with others – even though they are fairly light like the ones here – should be done in a calm and supportive atmosphere. Teachers must decide whether students want to do activities like this and how far they should be encouraged to reveal their feelings.

8.1.7 Simulation and role play[13]

The idea of a simulation is to create the pretence of a real-life situation in the classroom: students 'simulate' the real world. Thus we might ask them to pretend that they are at an airport, or we might organise them to get together to plan an imaginary reunion. What we are trying to do – artificially of course – is to give students practice in real-world English.

For a simulation to work it needs certain characteristics. Jones (1982) says that there needs to be a *'reality of function'* (students must accept the function; they must not think of themselves as language students but as the people in the simulation), a *simulated environment* (we do not take the students to a real airport – that would no longer be a simulation, it would be the real thing!) and *structure* (there must be some structure to the simulation and essential facts must be provided).

Within these guidelines we can add another variable: sometimes the students take part as themselves (if we ask them to organise a party, for example, we are not asking them to pretend to be someone else) and sometimes we ask them to *play a role*, pretending to be someone that they are not (we may ask them to be a distraught policeman or a bad-tempered child). In the latter case we are talking about *role plays*. All role plays are simulations, in other words, but not all simulations are role plays. However, even where the students are not asked to play a role they must still accept Jones' 'reality of function': they must still be themselves at an airport (even though it is simulated) rather than students in a classroom. And this acceptance means that students will have to be prepared to enter into the activity with enthusiasm and conviction.

There is some controversy about the usefulness of simulations, particularly where students are asked to play roles, but many teachers feel that they have certain advantages because students do not have to take responsibility for their own actions and words – in other words, it's the character they are playing who speaks, not themselves. It has certainly been noticed that some shy students are more talkative when playing roles.

During a simulation teachers may act as participants (see 11.1.5), that is to say as one of the people involved. The advantage of this is that they can help the simulation along if it gets into difficulty.

Where simulations get off to a shaky start – and where the teacher is not a participant – he or she may want to act as a prompter (see 11.1.4), making suggestions about what the students could say and do next. But this must be done as unobtrusively as possible and only when absolutely necessary for the success of the activity. Otherwise the simulation becomes teacher-dominated and this restricts the students from communicating amongst themselves.

After the simulation has finished the teacher will want to conduct feedback with the students. The object here is to discuss with them whether the activity was successful, why certain decisions were reached, etc. If the teacher has been recording the proceedings (either by writing down good and bad points, or by using a tape recorder or a video) this will be a good opportunity to show where students performed particularly well (they may have used a convincing argument or a particularly effective piece of English) and to point out where poor English, for example, made communication less effective.

It is important for the teacher to conduct feedback about the content of an activity such as simulation as well as discussing the use of English. If only the latter is focused on the students will perceive the object of the exercise as being concerned only with linguistic accuracy rather than the ability to communicate efficiently – which is the main motive for this kind of activity.

We will now look at four examples of simulations.

(a) The travel agent

In this example students are divided into pairs in which they play the roles of a travel agent and a customer. The latter wants to book a holiday in a hotel, but insists that the hotel should have a number of qualities (such as the right price, good food, etc.). The travel agent has all the information about the hotels.

Stage 1 Students are told that they are going to work in pairs.

Stage 2 Students in each pair are given the letters *A* and *B*.

Stage 3 Students are told that *A* is a travel agent and *B* is a customer who wants to book a holiday in Miami.

Stage 4 The teacher tells the students not to show each other the information they are going to get, and then gives the following piece of paper to *B*.

B.   CUSTOMER

You want: (a) to go to a hotel in Miami for a week and
you can spend up to $1400 on a hotel

(b) to be as near as possible to the town centre

(c) to go to a hotel with a good discotheque

(d) there to be a children's swimming pool for your small son

(e) there to be someone to look after your son at the hotel

(f) the hotel to serve good food

(g) a comfortable room (with a good view)

Get all the information from the travel agent and then write down the hotel of your choice.

A gets the following hotel list:

A.   TRAVEL AGENT

Study the following information carefully so that you can answer B (the customer)

	SUN INN	REGENCY PARK	PARADISO	OASIS
COST (double) per night	$180	$175	$210	$130
DISTANCE FROM CENTRE	10 kms.	12 kms.	20 kms.	3 kms.
DISCO	*	**	***	—
RESTAURANT	**	***	***	**
VIEW	***	*	**	*
SWIMMING POOL Adults	***	*	**	*
Children	*	**	***	—
CHILDCARE FACILITIES	—	**	*	—

Note: Various features (e.g. view, discos, restaurants, etc.) have been given stars to indicate quality. *** = very good, ** = good, * = fair. As an example we can say that you get a better view if you're staying at the Paradiso than if you're staying at the Regency Park.

The students are told to study their information for a short period.

Stage 5 B is told to select a hotel based as far as possible on the six qualities he or she is looking for. The activity commences.

Stage 6 When all the pairs have completed the activity (or when the majority have finished) the students and the teacher will discuss what choices have been made. Clearly, in this simulation, the Regency Park is the logical choice since it has most of the qualities that *B* is looking for.

(b) Arranging to meet

In this simulation groups of students are going to arrange a reunion to celebrate some event (a birthday, anniversary, etc.). They have to agree when and where the reunion will take place.

Stage 1 The teacher tells the class that they are going to work in groups of five, and that they are going to arrange to meet in honour of . . . (here the teacher can invent a reason based on the members of the class).

Stage 2 The teacher explains that each group must decide where they should meet and when, based on the information that they will be given.

Stage 3 The teacher tells the students that they are going to get some pieces of paper, and that they should not show them to each other. The teacher then distributes the following:

```
STUDENT A: You want to have lunch in a restaurant.
           You should think of reasons why this is
           the best choice.
```

```
STUDENT B: You want to have dinner at your home.
           You should think of reasons why this
           is the best choice.
```

```
STUDENT C: You want to have lunch at your home.
           You should think of reasons why this
           is the best choice.
```

```
STUDENT D: You want to have dinner at a restaurant.
           You should think of reasons why this is
           the best choice.
```

```
STUDENT E: You are undecided. You should listen to
           the others' ideas and then agree with
           the suggestion you like best.
```

Stage 4 The teacher tells the students to think about their instructions for a short time. Then they are told to start the activity.

This activity is very successful and produces a great deal of spoken English. The teacher will need to keep an eye on each group and perhaps act as a prompter to make sure that they realise there are two variables – where they are going to meet and when.

(c) The Loch Ness monster[14]

The monster, who is supposed to inhabit Loch Ness in Scotland, has long been the object of interest and speculation. In this simulation, which forms part of a unit about 'Nessie', four people have seen the monster and describe it to a police inspector who has to build up an 'identikit' picture.

Stage 1 The class discusses the Loch Ness monster and the teacher tells them they are going to take part in an activity about it. Students are told that the monster has been seen by a number of people who are going to describe it to the local police in Scotland.

Stage 2 Students are told they are going to work in groups of five. One student in each group will be the police inspector who should question the other students (witnesses) about what they saw and then fill in the following identikit form and draw a picture of the monster in the space provided.

Form PK IR4	IDENTIKIT PICTURE
Age :	
Sex :	
Height :	
Weight :	
Distinguishing features :	

Stage 3 The students in each group are given the following role cards:

1ST WITNESS

You were having a stroll along the shore and you distinctly saw a small, flat thing moving on the surface of the water. You believe it was the head of the monster. It had a large mouth, two bulging red eyes and two small horns.

2ND WITNESS

You were having a nap in the grass when you were woken up by loud tramping noises. When you got up you had just enough time to see a very large greenish animal diving into the water.

3RD WITNESS

As you were fishing early one morning, you saw the monster splashing on the surface of the water. You estimated its overall length to be perhaps between 20 and 30 feet and it had a very small head in comparison with the size of its body.

4TH WITNESS

You were surveying the loch from the top of the hill with a pair of binoculars. You saw a large animal with a stout body, two humps on its back, four legs and a long neck, grazing on the shore of the loch.

INSPECTOR CAMERON

Ask each witness how and when he saw the monster. Draw up an identikit picture by putting together the various accounts you get.

The activity can start after each 'witness' has had a chance to study the role card.

Stage 4 The different groups study the final identikit picture of the monster to compare their versions.

This simulation is highly amusing, and although designed for intermediate groups could also be suitable for elementary students since it mixes the best elements of simulation with the describe and draw technique we discussed in 8.1.3(c).

(d) Knife in the school

In the following simulation all the participants have definite roles to play – they are asked to assume personalities and realities that are not their own.

The situation revolves around a troublesome boy at a secondary school. After a report that the boy has been seen at school with a knife, the head teacher decides to call the parents and the boy in to discuss the incident.

Stage 1 The teacher puts students into buzz groups (see 8.1.2 (a)) and asks them to list various 'crimes' for which school children are punished.

Stage 2 The teacher gets feedback from the groups and then asks the students what they would expect a head teacher to do if a student was found at school with a flick knife.

Stage 3 The teacher then tells the students that they are going to role play an interview between a boy who reportedly brought a knife to school, his parents and the head teacher of the school.

Stage 4 The students are put into groups of four. They are given the roles of head teacher, mother, father, Brian (the boy). They are given the following role cards and told not to show them to anyone else:

Head teacher

You have been told that Brian was seen in the school with a knife. The problem is that no teacher actually saw it; they were told about it by the other pupils. You must not let this fact slip out.

If the situation becomes impossible you may consider suspension from the school. Otherwise a severe warning about Brian's behaviour will do.

> **Father**
>
> You are aware that Brian is a persistent troublemaker and your own patience with him has worn a bit thin. You suspect, though, that he is always led on by Sam Richards, and you will try to use the interview to establish this fact.

> **Mother**
>
> You think Brian is a much nicer boy than people give him credit for. You think the school is unfairly prejudiced against him and will do everything in the interview to support him.

> **Brian**
>
> It is true that you had a knife: it belonged to Sam Richards and you don't want anyone to know about this because Sam is your friend – and you are afraid of what he will do if you give him away. You will either pretend that it is your knife or that the whole story is a lie – after all, did any teacher actually talk to you about it? The one thing you are really frightened of is suspension from the school. You will do anything to avoid it.

Stage 5 When the role play is over the teacher will lead a feedback session discussing what happened in each group and whether the boy, the parents and the head teacher behaved appropriately. The issues raised by the situation will be discussed and only then will the teacher discuss any language errors that he or she collected while listening to the groups.

Simulations are a valuable part of the teacher's armoury. The examples shown here are on a fairly small scale. Of course they can be considerably bigger and last for longer than the ones here, but whatever the size and design of the activity they give students a chance to step out of the role of language students and to use their language in realistic (but safe) contexts.

8.2.
Written
communicative
activities

It is often easier to provide opportunities for spoken communication in the classroom than it is for the written medium. Frequently writing is relegated to the status of homework. This is a pity since writing, especially communicative writing, can play a valuable part in the class.

   We will look at *Relaying instructions*, *Writing reports and advertisements*, *Co-operative writing*, *Exchanging letters* and *Writing journals*.

8.2.1
Relaying
instructions

Just as in 8.1.3, one group of students has information for the performance of a task, and they have to get another group to perform the same task by giving them written instructions. We will look at three examples.

(a) Making models

This is the same as the activity in 8.1.3(b) except that instead of passing on oral instructions the original group of students have to write directions.

Stage 1 A small group of students is given material to make a model with (e.g. building bricks, *Lego*, etc.) and they are told to make a model.

Stage 2 The group now writes instructions which will enable other people to duplicate the model.

Stage 3 Other students are given the instructions and told to build the model by reading the instructions.

There is, of course, immediate feedback. The original group can see how well they have written instructions by watching the efforts of the other students to duplicate their model.

(b) Giving directions

In this activity students write directions which other students have to follow.

Stage 1 Students are told to write directions from the place where they are studying to some other place in the same town or city. They are told not to mention the destination by name.

Stage 2 Students give their directions to a partner who has to guess what the destination is by following the directions.

The same effect can be created by letting the students work from a street plan of a town with clearly marked buildings, etc.

(c) Writing commands[15]

Students write each other messages which contain commands.

Stage 1 The teacher tells students to write a command for one of their classmates on a piece of paper. The student might write something like this:

> Maria:
> Take off your left shoe!

Stage 2 The written messages are then passed to the students who have to obey the commands.

This activity is especially appropriate for beginner students and is most enjoyable.

8.2.2
Writing
reports and
advertisements

We will look at three activities in which students write news reports or advertisements.

(a) The news broadcast[16]

Students write items for a news broadcast which they then organise for 'transmission'.

Stage 1 The teacher asks all the students in the class to write two news items on a piece of paper.

Stage 2 The teacher then collects all the pieces of paper and forms the class into small groups.

Stage 3 The teacher then distributes the pieces of paper equally between the groups in no special order. The students are asked to combine the items (making changes where necessary) to make up a complete news broadcast.

Stage 4 Each group then reads its broadcast to the rest of the class. Ideally, of course, each group could record their broadcast to make it more realistic.

This activity is attractive because it involves all the skills, as well as the ability to order and organise ideas. It also involves current events and is thus interesting and motivating.

(b) The tourist brochure

In much the same way as the news broadcast, students can be asked to join together to write a brochure about the place they live in or are studying in.

Stage 1 The students are all told to write two sentences (or more) about the attractions of the place they live or study in.

Stage 2 The class is then divided into small groups.

Stage 3 In each group the students pool their sentences and use them to devise a short brochure about the place they live or study in for a tourist magazine.

Stage 4 Students from each group may read out their final version. A better alternative, however, is to put the texts in a folder which can be passed round the class or to stick them to a notice board in the classroom.

(c) The advertisement

After discussing what successful advertisements contain, students can write and design their own.

Stage 1 The class discusses (together and/or in pairs/groups) what makes a successful advertisement.

Stage 2 The class is divided into groups. They are told that their task is to select a product and write an advertisement for it which will appear in a magazine.

Stage 3 When they have completed their advertisements they can pass them round the class. Alternatively they can be given a period of time (e.g. a weekend) to design the artwork for their text. The advertisements can then be pinned to the class notice board.

8.2.3
Co-operative
writing

In this section we will look at more activities where students actually write things together; where the process of co-operation is as important as the actual fact of the writing itself. In the first two of these activities there is a definite game-like quality present.

(a) The fairy story

In this activity students are put into groups and told that they are going to write joint stories. This example shows a fairy story being used for this process.

Stage 1 Students are put into groups. Where possible, they should be of equal numbers.

Stage 2 Students are told to tear a page from their exercise books and write the following sentence on it:
Once upon a time there was a beautiful princess who lived in a large castle at the edge of a forest.

Stage 3 The students are then instructed to continue the story by writing the next sentence.

Stage 4 The students are then told to give their piece of paper to the student on their left. They should now continue the (new) story they have in front of them by writing the next sentence. The procedure is repeated until the papers have gone round the whole group but one. The teacher then tells the students to write the penultimate sentence.

Stage 5 The stories are now returned to their originators (by passing the papers to the student on the left). They must write the concluding sentence. Students can read the resulting tales to the rest of the class.

This activity can be immensely enjoyable, and often produces wildly differing stories. Of course there is no reason why the activity should concern a fairy story. Another alternative is not to supply the original sentence.

(b) Story reconstruction

This activity follows a similar procedure to that for oral story construction (see 8.1.4 (c)). In other words, students are put into four groups (A, B, C, D) each of which is shown a picture from a story sequence. Instead of talking about the pictures, however, the activity continues as follows:

Stage 1 The students individually write two sentences (in the past) about the pictures they have seen.

Stage 2 The teacher forms new groups of four (i.e. one student from the original group A, one from the original group B and so on).

Stage 3 The students show each other their sentences and they then use them to construct a narrative.

The finished stories can be circulated round the class, put on the board or used for student–student correction (see 8.3).

(c) The word processor[17]

One of the best uses for the computer in language teaching is as a word processor. When students have been asked to complete a written task – the writing of a story, a letter, a report, etc. – they can, of course do it on their own in their books or on their own with a word processor.

However, we have already seen the benefits to be gained from students writing in groups in the two examples above. There seem to be distinct advantages when such co-operation takes place in front of a screen.

Groups working on a piece of writing with a word processor seem to focus much more clearly on the language. Editing decisions can be taken far more quickly, and changes can be effected simply and clearly. The end result looks neat and tidy, not a mess of crossing out. And the piece of work can be stored so that it can be continued over a series of classes.

8.2.4
Exchanging
letters

In this section we will consider ways of getting students to exchange letters with each other. Particularly with the more realistic tasks students have a good chance to practise real written communication.

(a) Writing messages

The most basic form of letter writing is the message. This can be used at beginner levels to generate written questions and answers, as in this example:

Stage 1 Students are told to write a message to another member of the group which demands an answer.
Stage 2 The completed messages are then given to the student who has been written to.
Stage 3 The student who has received the message then writes a reply which is passed back to the original writer.

The original message might be something like this:

> To Maria
> What kind of house do you live in?
> from José

and the reply might be:

> To José
> My house has three bedrooms,
> and a small garden at the front.
> from Maria

143

(b) The agony column

This activity has long been a favourite with both teachers and students. It involves students writing letters to 'agony columns' – those parts of newspapers and magazines where supposed experts give advice on everything from marital problems to trouble with the neighbours. In this activity students invent some problem and then have it answered by other members of the class.

Stage 1 The class and the teacher discuss 'agony columns', getting examples from the students' knowledge of their own countries. Where students say there is no such thing in their newspapers and magazines the teacher will show them examples from English or American agony columns.

Stage 2 The teacher arranges the class into small groups and asks each group to think of a problem and then write a letter.

Stage 3 The letters from each group are then given to another group who have to consider the best answer and then write a reply.

Stage 4 The replies are then given to the original groups to consider. The teacher can put them into a folder which can be passed round the class. If there is a notice board the best and/or most amusing letters can be pinned up for all to see.

This activity is particularly suitable, of course, after the students have been working on the language of advice. It can be used at a fairly elementary level, but is even more successful with intermediate and advanced students.

(c) The complaining customer

In this activity students write complaining letters about goods they have bought after seeing an advertisement. The students representing the company who make the goods then have to reply to these letters.

Stage 1 Students are divided into small groups. Each group is given an advertisement. It would be ideal if they could be given advertisements prepared by their classmates.

Stage 2 The groups are told to imagine they have bought the item that is advertised but are not satisfied with it for some reason. They should write a letter of complaint to the company.

Stage 3 The letters are then given to different groups. The new group has to study the letter of complaint and decide what to do about it. When the decision has been reached they can write a reply to the original letter.

Stage 4 The letters are then returned to the original groups who read them and discuss what they have been sent.

This is an enjoyable and useful activity involving a number of different skills. It is particularly suitable for intermediate and advanced classes.

(d) The job application

This activity involves applying for a job. The application will then be judged and a decision taken about whether it should be successful. There is no reason why students should not be given role cards. In this example, however, we will ask them to create their own roles.

Stage 1 Students are shown the following advertisement:

GREAT FUTURE: GREAT PAY

Work in Public Relations for A Major Airline.

Experience in transport not necessary, but good personality and bright ideas are essential.

Applications in writing are requested, giving any information about yourself you think might be relevant.

Write to: The Manager, Box 247.

Stage 2 Students are asked to apply for the job in writing, making their applications as attractive as possible.

Stage 3 The teacher divides the class into small groups. The groups are then given some of the letters (which must not be the work of anyone in the group).

Stage 4 Each member of the group must read each letter, giving the applicant a score of 0 (= very poor) to 5 (= excellent) depending on suitability for the job.

Stage 5 The scores are added together and the winning applicant chosen.

Stage 6 The group writes two letters. One is to the successful applicant asking him or her to come to a meeting. The other is the letter they will send the applicants who were not successful.

Stage 7 The letters of the winning applicants can be read to the whole class and comments made on them.

This is a good exercise for skill integration and forces the students to write for a purpose. It is particularly suitable for intermediate and advanced classes.

8.2.5
Writing journals

One area of writing that we have not touched on so far is the written communication between students and teachers. In an important article Mario Rinvolucri described how he had become involved in letter writing with his students.[18] At the beginning of the course he wrote to them telling them something about himself and inviting them to write letters to him which he would reply to personally (they all got the same letter). Some of them took up his offer, and over the period of the course he engaged in a lengthy correspondence about language learning, the students' experiences, how he and they felt about the classes, etc.

The advantage of this activity is that students get a chance to use writing for genuinely communicative purposes and they get an extraordinary level of individual attention from the teacher. The disadvantages of this procedure, as Rinvolucri readily admits,[19] are firstly that some students get 'too close' to the teacher and secondly that it takes a lot of time. His group was small, but imagine doing it with a group of thirty or forty students!

Reading and writing that number of letters every week on top of preparation and other kinds of homework marking would be quite impossible.

There is a way of using this communication which is not so impractical, however, and that is the use of student journals. In these diaries students can write what they want about anything that interests them. They can comment on the classes they are experiencing, they can write about their personal lives, they can talk about politics (not an easy subject in the classroom) or they can write stories. On more than one occasion teachers have been surprised and delighted by the level of English displayed in journals and by the interest and creativity which they have found there.[20]

Two issues have to be considered if students are to be asked to keep diaries, however. When should they write them and what should the teacher do with them if and when he or she reads them?

Lonon Blanton (1987) got her students to write their journals for five minutes at the end of every class, but others feel that students should write their journals when they themselves want to, not when they are told to.

There are advantages in the regular journal-writing spot: it ensures frequent writing practice and it means that all students have a chance to use English to reflect their own thoughts and feelings. On the other hand it is a bit arbitrary in the sense that students may not have much to say in those particular five minutes.

When students have written the journals teachers have to decide whether they should read them or not. If the answer is yes – and the teacher collects the journals every week or fortnight, for example – they must then decide how to react to them. What is important is that teachers should not treat these diaries as they do other pieces of written work. They are not there primarily to be corrected, but rather to be reacted to. Content feedback is clearly more important than form feedback here. Teachers can write short reactions to what they read. These do not have to be lengthy, but they should respond to the spirit of the journal. Areas of language difficulty can be pointed out, of course, but this should be done more in a written conversational way than in a 'marking' way.

Students respond well to teachers who are interested in their journals: teachers have the advantage of interacting with their students as individuals.

8.3 Correcting written work[21]

The correction of written work can be organised on much the same basis as the correction of oral work (see 6.3.3 and 11.1.2). In other words there may well be times when the teacher is concerned with accuracy and other times when the main concern is the content of the writing. Certainly the tendency is for teachers to be over-preoccupied with accuracy. This means that the student's work is often covered with red ink and no comment is made about whether the work was interesting or succeeded in its purposes.

Correction of written work can be done by both teacher and student. If you are correcting written work always remember to react to the content of the work, showing the student where the work was effective and where it was not.

Where teachers wish to correct the English in the written work, they may wish to use a variety of symbols. They can underline the mistake in the written work and put a mark in the margin to show what kind of mistake it was. The following example shows how the teacher can indicate that the student has made an error in word order:

WO   I like very much tennis.

The teacher will need symbols for spelling, wrong tense usage, concord (the agreements between subject and verb), wrong word order, inappropriate language, punctuation, a word missing and unclear meaning, among others. Whatever the symbols are the students should understand clearly what they mean.

When teachers first use the system of symbols they may underline the word in the text and put the symbol in the margin. Later it will only be necessary to put the symbol in the margin for the students to identify the error. When students correct each other's work (see below) no symbols will be necessary.

When teachers hand back written work with comments on content and the correction symbols in the margin, they should allow the students time, during the class, to identify their mistakes and correct them. In this activity the teacher is acting as a resource, and can help where students do not know what is wrong. If this kind of stage is not gone through, however, students may not be able to take advantage of the system of correction symbols.

Ideally written work can form the basis for student–student correction, which in itself can be classed as a communicative activity. Students work in pairs, exchanging their work. They then look for mistakes in each other's writing and attempt to correct them.

Where a piece of student writing contains a number of common errors, the teacher may want to photocopy the work (erasing the writer's name) and show it to the whole class, asking them to identify problems. In this way the attention of the class can be drawn to common mistakes and the photocopied document can form the basis for remedial work.

Another variation which will help students to concentrate on particular aspects of language is to tell them that you are going to correct a piece of work for only one thing. It could be tense usage, it could be spelling, it could be punctuation. By doing this you ensure that the students' work will not be covered by red marks, and you also encourage them to concentrate on particular aspects of written language use.

8.4
Projects[22]

One way of ensuring genuinely communicative uses of spoken and written English is through the use of projects – longer pieces of work which involve investigation and reporting. The end-product is the most important thing here, and all the language use that takes place is directed towards the final version. Although students studying in target language communities (Britain, the USA, etc.) obviously have much greater access to English speakers, TV stations, radio and written material, etc., there are a whole range of project types that do not require this kind of contact. We will look at only two kinds of project here.

(a) The smoking report

In this project students devise a questionnaire and then use it to get results which are interpreted and written up as a report. The project can easily be used in non-target language situations since students can interview each other – or students in other classes – to get the results they want.
The project is organised in the following way:

Stage 1 Students are told they are going to work in groups to write a report on attitudes to smoking based on a questionnaire that they will design.

Stage 2 The teacher discusses with the class what kind of information they might want to obtain and the kind of questions they could use to get it. For example the following areas might be selected:

Smokers:
• their smoking habits
• their reasons for smoking
• their feelings about smoking in public places and on public transport
• their attitude to smokers who complain

Non-smokers:
• their reasons for not smoking
• their reasons for having given up (in some cases)
• their attitude to smoking in public places and on public transport
• their suggestions for change

Stage 3 The groups write their different questionnaires. The teacher can act as a resource (see 11.1.6) or as a prompter (11.1.4).

Stage 4 The groups then administer their questionnaires. In an English-speaking community they can question members of the public. In other countries they can question fellow classes and fellow students (see above).

Stage 5 The groups study the information they have collected and write a report in which they reach conclusions about the results of their investigations. The reports can then be compared. Groups can read other groups' work and discuss the similarities and differences with their own.

Clearly this project requires commitment and dedication from the students. It could well occupy two weeks of an intermediate class's time. Smaller versions could be done, however, simply focusing on how many people smoke and how many cigarettes they smoke a day. The same kind of thing could be done with other topics like hobbies, travel to and from work/study, eating habits, etc.

(b) Wheelchairs

One of the best-known projects for advanced students has been the 'Wheelchair User's Guide to Bath' reported in the *ELT Journal* by Diane Fried-Booth (Fried-Booth (1982)).

Students at the Bell School in Bath, England, surveyed Bath to see how easy it was for people in wheelchairs to gain access to public buildings, shops, etc. This involved making a number of visits, using wheelchairs, interviewing wheelchair users and theatre managers, etc.

The final result of all these investigations was a guide for wheelchair users telling them which sites and buildings were appropriate/inappropriate for them in terms of access. The guide was a genuinely useful piece of work which achieved a real communicative purpose and which, along the way, involved students in a wide range of interactions both written and spoken.

This particular project, like many others of the same scope and size, was possible because it was done in an English-speaking environment. Similar large-scale projects are possible in non-English environments, however, and students can use tape-recorders and video cameras to record interviews with any native-speakers they can find, or they can consult libraries, the British Council, etc. for source material.

8.5
Learner training

In recent years emphasis has been placed on training students to take charge of their own learning (see 4.1.6 and the references quoted there). The three main areas that are involved in this are *Personal assessment*, *Learning strategies* and *Language awareness*.

(a) Personal assessment

Try the following quiz. Tick (✓) your answers to the questions.

	Usually	Sometimes	(Almost) never	Don't know
1. Did/do you get good results in grammar tests?				
2. Do you have a good memory for new words?				
3. Do you hate making mistakes?				
4. In class, do you get irritated if mistakes are not corrected?				
5. Is your pronunciation better when you read aloud than when you have a conversation?				
6. Do you wish you had more time to think before speaking?				
7. Did/do you enjoy being in a class?				
8. Do you find it difficult to pick up more than two or three words of a new language when you are on holiday abroad?				
9. Do you like to learn new grammar rules, words, etc. by heart?				

One of the aims of learner training is to make students think about what kind of learners they are and about what they can do to help themselves. A vital stage in this process is getting students to think about their own learning behaviour, as in this example:[23]

The students are now given a score for usually/never, etc. and based on their total score have their answers evaluated, e.g. 'Your score does not mean that you are not a good language learner. Perhaps this is the first time that you have thought about the way you learn .....' (Ellis and Sinclair 1989:8)

In the same book, students are encouraged to keep a personal motivation graph, talk about the best way of tackling reading or extending vocabulary knowledge, etc.

The point of all these activities is to let students think hard about their learning and to use the insights they gain to help them to become more effective as learners.

(b) Learning strategies

If the teacher's job is to help students learn in a better way (see above) then he or she will have to encourage students to develop learning strategies. This will involve the students in personal assessment (see above) but it will also involve actually training students to behave in certain ways. This will include:

1 **training students to use textbooks**. Teachers can spend some time taking students through a new textbook, showing them how to make the best use of it.
2 **training students to use communicative activities properly**. This involves the issue of mother tongue use. Most of the activities in this chapter will be rather ineffective if the students use their own language. This point is discussed in more detail in 11.2.4.
3 **training students to read for gist** (see 10.4.4). We must give students the ability to cope with texts outside the classroom and if we can help them to approach such texts confidently – and not to get hung up on every word they do not understand – then we will have done them a service.
4 **training students to deal with unfamiliar vocabulary**. How should students cope with new words? An example is given in 9.5.2 (g).
5 **training students to use dictionaries** (see 9.6.1).

(c) Language awareness

Teachers can design material that makes students more aware of the way in which language is used. Many of the discovery activities in Chapters 6 and 9 of this book use that kind of awareness activity (see 6.4 and 9.5.2).

One way of doing this is to make students do an exercise about language just as they do exercises about other topics like hobbies, films, adventure, etc. Frequently such activities can be done by the students studying on their own. The pay-off is that as students complete the exercise they are being made more aware of how language works.

A small example will show the idea. Here students are involved in studying the way in which phrasal verbs operate.[24] This is the exercise they have to do:

Complete the following with '*before*' and '*after*':

> Sometimes the particle (on, up, down, away, etc.) comes _____ the object. Sometimes it comes _____ the object. It always comes _____ an object which is a pronoun (it, him, her). If the object is a noun, it can come _____ or _____ the object.

Learner training is vital if students are to achieve their full potential as learners. In its different forms it encourages them to think about their experiences, discuss them with the teacher and take action to make the whole process more effective.

8.6
Conclusions

In this chapter we have looked at activities designed to have the characteristics we said were desirable for communicative activities (see 5.3). We have looked at both spoken and written activities, and we have seen how journals and project writing can contribute to the students' ability to communicate in English. We have also seen how learner training contributes to the students' success.

The feedback that a teacher gives in such activities is seen as vitally important. It cannot be stressed enough that we have a responsibility to react to content and not just to the language that we hear from our students. Communicative activities mean getting students to actually do things with language, and it is the 'doing' that should form the main focus of such sessions.

Exercises

1 Design your own oral communicative activity for a beginners' class based on the ideas in this chapter.
2 Design your own written communicative activity for an elementary class based on the ideas in this chapter.
3 Take any simulation activity from a coursebook that you are familiar with and write out a procedure for using that activity using the 'stages' type of procedure which we have used in this chapter. Then give your plan with its stages to colleagues and ask them to try the activity following your stages.
4 Design your own symbols for the correction of written work.

References

1 I first saw this activity demonstrated by Peter Taylor.
2 On discussions see the excellent P Ur (1981).
3 This type of activity (and the one that follows it) were described in M Geddes and J McAlpin (1978). Communication games like this are still widely in use.
4 From J Richards, J Hull and S Proctor (1990).
5 I first saw this technique demonstrated by Alan Maley. The picture sequence is from D Byrne and S Holden (1978).
6 I have never been able to trace the source of this activity which was used by teachers at the Instituto Anglo Mexicano de Cultura in Guadalajara.

7 Developed by the British Council and published by Cambridge University Press.

8 See C Jones and S Fortescue (1987). In Chapter 9 they discuss activities similar to (and including) Fast Food although they describe them as role plays. I would dispute this categorisation (see 8.1.7).

9 See P Davis and M Rinvolucri (1990) for a series of activities which centre on having students talk about themselves in order to become more confident.

10 See S Deller (1990) who shows how students can be encouraged to generate their own language activities.

11 I was first told about this activity by Gillie Cunningham.

12 From C Frank and M Rinvolucri (1983).

13 For more on simulation see especially K Jones (1982). See also G Sturtridge (1981) who discusses the difference in meaning between simulation and role play.

14 Taken from D Hicks et al. (1979).

15 See D Byrne (1988) pages 40–2.

16 For this and other ideas in 8.2.2 see D Byrne (1988) Chapter 5, although I have often adapted his ideas.

17 For more on the use of the word processor in groupwork see the excellent article by Alison Piper (Piper 1982). For a variety of word processing activities see C Jones and S Fortescue (1987).

18 See M Rinvolucri (1983).

19 Personal communication.

20 A slightly different example can be found in T Lowe (1987) who records an experiment where teachers of English kept journals while they were taught a foreign language.

21 For more on correcting written work see J Willis (1981) pages 172–4, R White (1980) pages 106–9 and D Byrne (1988) Chapter 10.

22 For more on project work see especially D Fried-Booth (1986). G Carter and H Thomas (1986) and L Munro and S Parker (1985). T Hutchinson (1985) based a course for secondary students around a series of small projects.

23 From G Ellis and B Sinclair (1989).

24 From J Harmer and R Rossner (1991).

9 Teaching vocabulary

In this chapter[1] we will look at issues which are raised by the teaching and learning of vocabulary and we will study examples of vocabulary teaching. We will discuss the importance of dictionary use and we will look at exercises designed to train students in the use of (monolingual) dictionaries.

9.1 Language structure and vocabulary

If language structures make up the skeleton of language, then it is vocabulary that provides the vital organs and the flesh. An ability to manipulate grammatical structure does not have any potential for expressing meaning unless words are used. We talk about the importance of 'choosing your words carefully' in certain situations, but we are less concerned about choosing structures carefully – unless of course we are in a language classroom. Then structural accuracy seems to be the dominant focus. In real life, however, it is even possible that where vocabulary is used correctly it can cancel out structural inaccuracy. For example the student who says 'Yesterday ... I have seen him yesterday' is committing one of the most notorious tense mistakes in English but he or she will still be understood as having seen him yesterday because of the word 'yesterday'.

The need to teach language structure is obvious as we have seen in Chapters 2 and 3. Grammatical knowledge allows us to generate sentences (see 2.2). At the same time, though, we must have something to say; we must have meanings that we wish to express, and we need to have a store of words that we can select from when we wish to express these meanings. If you want to describe how you feel at this very moment you have to be able to find a word which reflects the complexity of your feeling. The words you choose to use when you want to invite someone out – especially if you think they may be reluctant – can make all the difference between acceptance and refusal.

153

For many years vocabulary was seen as incidental to the main purpose of language teaching – namely the acquisition of grammatical knowledge about the language. Vocabulary was necessary to give students something to hang on to when learning structures, but was frequently not a main focus for learning itself.

Recently, however, methodologists and linguists have increasingly been turning their attention to vocabulary,[2] stressing its importance in language teaching and reassessing some of the ways in which it is taught and learnt. It is now clear, for example, that the acquisition of vocabulary is just as important as the acquisition of grammar – though the two are obviously interdependent – and teachers should have the same kind of expertise in the teaching of vocabulary as they do in the teaching of structure.[3]

9.2 Selecting vocabulary

Part of the problem in teaching vocabulary lies in the fact that whilst there is a consensus about what grammatical structures should be taught at what levels the same is hardly true of vocabulary. It is true, of course, that syllabuses include word lists, but there is no guarantee that the list for one beginners' syllabus will be similar to the list for a different set of beginners. Whilst it is possible to say that students should learn the verb '*to be*' before they learn its use as an auxiliary in the present continuous tense (for example) there is no such consensus about which words slot into which future meanings.

One of the problems of vocabulary teaching is how to select what words to teach. Dictionaries for upper intermediate students frequently have 55,000 words or more – and there may be many meanings for a word – and they represent a small fraction of all the possible words in a language. Somehow we have to make sense of this huge list and reduce it to manageable proportions for our learners.

A general principle in the past has been to teach more concrete words at lower levels and gradually become more abstract. Words like 'table', 'chair', 'chalk', etc. have figured in beginners' syllabuses because the things which the words represent are there in front of the students and thus easily explained. Words like 'charity', however, are not physically represented in the classroom and are far more difficult to explain.

Other criteria which are rather more scientific have been used, amongst which two of the more important are *frequency* and *coverage*.

9.2.1 Frequency, coverage and choice

A general principle of vocabulary selection has been that of frequency. We can decide which words we should teach on the basis of how frequently they are used by speakers of the language. The words which are most commonly used are the ones we should teach first.

Another principle that has been used in the selection of vocabulary is that of coverage. A word is more useful if it covers more things than if it only has one very specific meaning – so the argument goes.

These two principles would suggest that a word like 'book' would be an early vocabulary item. It is frequently used by native speakers and has greater coverage than 'notebook', 'exercise book', 'textbook', etc.

In order to know which are the most frequent words we can read or listen to a lot of English and list the words that are used, showing which ones are used most often and which are used least often. This was done notably by Michael West (1953) who scanned newspapers and books to list his frequency tables. More recently Hindmarsh produced a list which is still used by exam and material designers to show what words should be 'known' at what level.[4]

Perhaps the greatest revolution in vocabulary investigation and design, however, has been the harnessing of the computer to the tasks of finding out which words are used and how they are used. The massive Cobuild computer-based corpus at Birmingham University has been used not only for the design of a learner's dictionary[5] but also as a resource for a vocabulary-driven coursebook.[6] Many other universities and research projects have computer-based corpuses too and now it is even possible for teachers and students to buy relatively small computer programmes which will scan texts and tell the users which words are used most often and how they are used.[7] That is the beauty of a computer, of course; you can key in a word and it will immediately give you examples showing you the sentences and/or phrases the word occurs in and the frequency with which it is used.

It should be possible, then, to design vocabulary syllabuses on the basis of computerised information. If we feed in enough text – from newspapers, magazines, books, letters, conversations, etc. – we will be able to make accurate statements about what words to teach.

There is no doubt at all that the use of computers has given us insights into the use of words, and teachers and materials designers have gained enormously from the information they have been able to access. But even with such scientific power at our fingertips the problem of selection has not been completely solved.

The fact remains that the frequency count will still be heavily influenced by the type of text that is fed into the computer. If you key in scientific textbooks you will get a different frequency count from the results you would get if you keyed in 10,000 Superman comics. If you keyed in the newspapers of twenty years ago you might well get a different frequency order from what would happen if you used today's newspapers. In other words, whilst computer-generated text study is considerably quicker, larger and more reliable than the word lists of an earlier age it does not necessarily give us the only information we need when selecting vocabulary. If you find that the word 'way' (for example) is the fifth commonest word in the English language according to one computer-based corpus does that necessarily mean that you will teach it fifth?

The point is that other factors come into play. Do the students need to know 'way' yet? How useful is it for them? And how well does it fit into the topics, functions, structures and situations that we want to teach?

Recently I walked into a group of upper intermediate students whom I had not taught before. I asked them to tell me what new words they had learnt and remembered recently. They all chose the word 'cuddle'. It turned out that this was because they had come across it in an amusing text which had formed part of a class which they had really enjoyed – because they thought the teacher was so good. There were other equally important reasons, too. The students liked the meaning of the word (it's a nice thing to do!) and they liked its sound. Perhaps the word 'cuddle' would have been a suitable word for beginner students if it could provoke such enthusiasm. But this would never be possible (even if it was desirable) if frequency (and coverage) were taken as the only information to be used when selecting vocabulary.

The decision about what vocabulary to teach and learn will be heavily influenced, then, by information we can get about frequency and use. But this information will be assessed in the light of other considerations such as topic, function, structure, teachability, needs and wants (see 3.6).

9.3
What do students need to know?

In Chapter 2 we looked at what native speakers need to know about language and in Chapter 3 we used this to discuss the linguistic understanding that we should expect of our students. We can now develop the comments we made there about vocabulary (see 2.3 and 3.3) and look at words in more detail since it is clear that there is far more to a vocabulary item than just one meaning. For a start we must look at what 'meaning' really is.

9.3.1
Meaning

The first thing to realise about vocabulary items is that they frequently have more than one meaning. The word 'book', for example, obviously refers to something you use to read from – '(a written work in the form of) a set of printed pages fastened together inside a cover, as a thing to be read', according to one learner's dictionary.[8] But the same dictionary then goes on to list eight more meanings of 'book' as a noun, two meanings of 'book' as a verb and three meanings where 'book' + *preposition* makes phrasal verbs. So we will have to say that the word 'book' sometimes means the kind of thing you read from, but it can also mean a number of other things.

When we come across a word, then, and try to decipher its meaning we will have to look at the context in which it is used. If we see a woman in a theatre arguing at the ticket office saying 'But I booked my tickets three weeks ago' we will obviously understand a meaning of the verb 'book' which is different from a policeman (accompanied by an unhappy-looking man at a police station) saying to his colleague 'We booked him for speeding.' In other words, students need to understand the importance of *meaning in context*.

There are other facts about meaning too. Sometimes words have meanings in relation to other words. Thus students need to know the meaning of 'vegetable' as a word to describe any one of a number of other things – e.g. carrots, cabbages, potatoes, etc. 'Vegetable' has a general meaning whereas 'carrot' is more specific. We understand the meaning of a word like 'good' in the context of a word like 'bad'. Words have opposites (*antonyms*) and they also have other words with similar meanings (*synonyms*) – e.g. 'bad' and 'evil'. Even in that example, however, one thing is clear: words seldom have absolute synonyms, although context may make them synonymous on particular occasions. As far as meaning goes, then, students need to know about *meaning in context* and they need to know about *sense relations*.

9.3.2
Word use

What a word means can be changed, stretched or limited by how it is used and this is something students need to know about.

Word meaning is frequently stretched through the use of *metaphor* and *idiom*. We know that the word 'hiss', for example, describes the noise that snakes make. But we stretch its meaning to describe the way people talk to each other ('"Don't move or you're dead," she hissed.'). That is metaphorical use. At the same time we can talk about treacherous people as snakes ('He's a real snake in the grass.'). 'Snake in the grass' is a fixed phrase that has become an idiom like countless other phrases such as 'raining cats and dogs', 'putting the cat among the pigeons', 'straight from the horse's mouth', etc.

Word meaning is also governed by *collocation* – that is which words go with each other. In order to know how to use the word 'sprained' we need to know that whereas we can say 'sprained ankle', 'sprained wrist', we cannot say *'sprained thigh' or *'sprained rib'. We can have a headache, stomachache or earache, but we cannot have a *'throatache' or a *'legache'.

We often use words only in certain social and topical contexts. What we say is governed by the *style* and *register* we are in. If you want to tell someone you are angry you will choose carefully between the neutral expression of this fact ('I'm angry') and the informal version ('I'm really pissed off'). The latter would certainly seem rude to listeners in certain contexts. At a different level we recognise that two doctors talking about an illness will talk in a different register than one of them who then talks to the patient in question – who has never studied medicine.

Students need to recognise metaphorical language use and they need to know how words collocate. They also need to understand what stylistic and topical contexts words and expressions occur in.

9.3.3 Word formation

Words can change their shape and their grammatical value, too. Students need to know facts about word formation and how to twist words to fit different grammatical contexts. Thus the verb 'run' has the participles 'running' and 'ran'. The present participle 'running' can be used as an adjective and 'run' can also be a noun. There is a clear relationship between the words 'death', 'dead', 'dying' and 'die'.

Students also need to know how suffixes and prefixes work. How can we make the words potent and expensive opposite in meaning? Why do we preface one with *im-* and the other with *in-*?

Students need to know how words are spelt and how they sound. Indeed the way words are stressed (and the way that stress can change when their grammatical function is different – as with nouns and verbs, for example) is vital if students are to be able to understand and use words in speech. Part of learning a word is learning its written and spoken form.

Word formation, then, means knowing how words are written and spoken and knowing how they can change their form.

9.3.4 Word grammar

Just as words change according to their grammatical meaning, so the use of certain words can trigger the use of certain grammatical patterns. Some examples will show what this means.

We make a distinction between *countable* and *uncountable* nouns. The former can be both singular and plural. We can say 'one chair' or 'two chairs'. The latter can only be singular; we cannot say 'two furnitures'. This difference, then, has certain grammatical implications. 'Chair' can collocate with plural verbs (provided that it is pluralised) whereas 'furniture' never can (unless it is the name of a pop group, for example). There are also nouns that are neither countable nor uncountable but which have a fixed form and thefore collocate only with singular or plural verbs, e.g. 'people', 'the news', 'mathematics', etc.

Verbs trigger certain grammar too. 'Tell' is followed by an object + to + infinitive, for example ('He told her to wake him up at six') and so is 'ask'. But 'say' does not work in the same way. Knowing modal verbs like 'can', 'must', etc. means also knowing that these verbs are followed by a bare infinitive without 'to'. When students don't have this kind of knowledge they come up with erroneous sentences which all teachers instantly recognise, e.g. *'He said me to come', *'I must to go', etc.

There are many other areas of grammatical behaviour that students need to know about: what are phrasal verbs and how do they behave? How are adjectives ordered? What position can adverbs be used in? Without this knowledge can we really say that students know vocabulary items such as 'look up' (as in a dictionary), 'tired' and 'worn', or 'greedily'?

What we have been saying in this section is that knowing a word means far more than just understanding (onc of) its mcaning(s). Somchow our teaching must help students to understand what this knowledge implies both in general and for certain words in particular. By being aware students will be more receptive to the contextual behaviour of words when they first see them in texts, etc. and they will be better able to manipulate both the meanings and forms of the word.

We can summarise 'Knowing a word' in the following way:

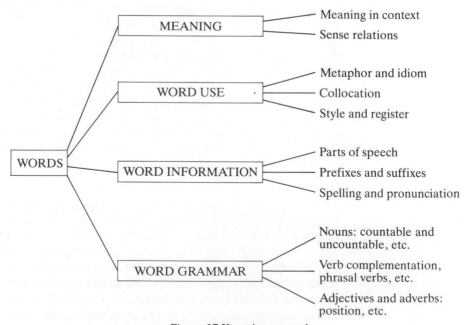

Figure 17 Knowing a word

**9.4
Teaching
vocabulary**

Teaching vocabulary is clearly more than just presenting new words. This may, of course, have its place (see 9.5.1) but there are other issues, too. For example, students see a lot of words in the course of a week. Some of them are used straight away, others are not. Should we teach some words (which we need for structure practice, for example) and not teach others (which occur incidentally in reading texts, for example)? Is there any way in which we can encourage students to really learn a word? We will look at *'Active' and 'passive'*, *Interaction with words*, and *Discovery techniques*

**9.4.1
Active and passive**

A distinction is frequently made between 'active' and 'passive' vocabulary. The former refers to vocabulary that students have been taught or learnt – and which they are expected to be able to use – whilst the latter refers to words which the students will recognise when they meet them but which they will probably not be able to produce.

This distinction becomes a bit blurred, however, when we consider what 'knowing a word' means and when we consider the way students seem to acquire their store of words.

It is true that students 'know' some words better than others, but it has not been demonstrated that these are necessarily the words which teachers have taught them, especially at higher levels. They might be words that are often used in the classroom or words that have appeared in the reading texts which students have been exposed to. If we have any belief in language acquisition theories (see 4.1.3) it is clear that many words which students know do come through that route rather than through learning (see page 33). Other words may be those that students have looked up because they wanted to use them. Or they may be words that students have met and somehow 'liked' (see 9.4.2.)

At beginner and elementary levels it certainly seems a good idea to provide sets of vocabulary which students can learn. Most of these early words will be constantly practised and so can, presumably, be considered as 'active'. But at intermediate levels and above the situation is rather more complicated. We can assume that students have a store of words but it would be difficult to say which are active and which are passive. A word that has been 'active' through constant use may slip back into the passive store if it is not used. A word that students have in their passive store may suddenly become active if the situation or the context provokes its use. In other words, the status of a vocabulary item does not seem to be a permanent state of affairs.

**9.4.2
Interaction with
words**

The students who remembered the word 'cuddle' (see 9.2.1) because they liked the experience of learning it and because they liked the word seem to provide another example of how students learn and retain words. We could predict that 'cuddle' is a word they are going to remember for a long time – though it may eventually fade through lack of use. This word touched them in some way. They had some kind of a relationship with it. It was not just a word they had repeated because it referred to a picture they had been shown, e.g. 'It's an apple'. It was a word that had personal meaning for them.

Not all vocabulary items have the warmth of a word like 'cuddle', however. But it would be nice if we could provoke the same kind of relationship with the words we teach as those students seemed to have had with their word.

Experiments on vocabulary seem to suggest that students remember best when they have actually done something with the words they are learning.[9] There is a definite advantage in getting students to do more than just repeat them. Tasks such as changing them to mean their opposites, making a noun an adjective, putting words together, etc. help to fix the words in the learners' minds.

Somehow or other, then, it seems that we should get students to interact with words. We should get them to 'adopt' words that they like and that they want to use. We should get them to do things with words so that they become properly acquainted with them. Vocabulary learning needs the 'deep experience' we mentioned on page 34.

9.4.3 Discovery techniques

Especially at intermediate levels and above, discovery techniques (where students have to work out rules and meanings for themselves rather than being given everything by the teacher – see 6.4) are an appropriate alternative to standard presentation techniques. This is certainly true of vocabulary learning where students will often be asked to 'discover for themselves' what a word means and how and why it is being used.

At intermediate levels we can assume that students already have a considerable store of vocabulary. Rather than teach them new words we can show them examples of words in action (in texts, etc.) and ask them to use their previous knowledge to work out what words can go with others, when they should be used and what connotations they have.

Even at beginner levels, however, we may want to ask students to try to work out what words mean, rather than just handing them the meanings: when students have 'had a go' with the words we can lead feedback sessions to see if they have understood the words correctly.

Discovery techniques used with vocabulary materials allow students to activate their previous knowledge and to share what they know (if they are working with others). They also provoke the kind of interaction with words which we have said is desirable (see 9.4.2). We will look at a number of discovery activities in 9.5.2.

The conclusions we can draw from this discussion about active and passive vocabulary and about interacting (and about discovery techniques) are best summed up by a quote from Adrian Underhill:

' ... engaging the learner ... is essential to any activity that is to have a high learning yield.' (Underhill 1985: 107)

We know that learners will select the words they want to learn. We know that the words they have acquired seem to move between active and passive status, and we know that involvement with words is likely to help students to learn and remember them. In other words, if we provide the right kind of exposure to words for the students and if we provide opportunities for students to practise these words then there is a good chance that students will learn and remember some or all of them. As Richard Rossner writes:

> The factors that are crucial, surely, are those least easily controlled, such as the relevance of a word to an individual's immediate wants, needs and interests, the impact on his or her 'affect' on the first few encounters, and the number of opportunities to bring it into active use.
> (Rossner 1987: 302)

9.5 Examples of vocabulary teaching

We have said that vocabulary teaching is as important as the teaching of structure, and in the following examples we will look at a range of activities which are designed to teach and practise words and their various uses. We will look at *Presentation, Discovery techniques* and *Practice*.

9.5.1 Presentation

Not all vocabulary can be learnt through interaction and discovery techniques. Even if such techniques are possible, however, they are not always the most cost effective. There are many occasions when some form of presentation and/or explanation is the best way to bring new words into the classroom. We will look at some examples:

(a) Realia

One way of presenting words is to bring the things they represent into the classroom – by bringing 'realia' into the room. Words like 'postcard', 'ruler', 'pen', 'ball', etc. can obviously be presented in this way. The teacher holds up the object (or points to it), says the word and then gets students to repeat it.

(b) Pictures

Bringing a pen into the classroom is not a problem. Bringing in a car, however, is. One solution is the use of pictures.

Pictures can be board drawings, wall pictures and charts, flashcards, magazine pictures and any other non-technical visual representation. Pictures can be used to explain the meaning of vocabulary items: teachers can draw things on the board or bring in pictures. They can illustrate concepts such as *above* and *opposite* just as easily as hats, coats, walking sticks, cars, smiles, frowns, etc.

(c) Mime, action and gesture

It is often impossible to explain the meaning of words and grammar either through the use of realia or in pictures. Actions, in particular, are probably better explained by mime. Concepts like *running* or *smoking* are easy to present in this way; so are ways of walking, expressions, prepositions ('to', 'towards', etc.) and times (a hand jerked back over the shoulder to represent the past, for example).

(d) Contrast

We saw how words exist because of their sense relations (see 9.3.1) and this can be used to teach meaning. We can present the meaning of 'empty' by contrasting it with 'full', 'cold' by contrasting it with 'hot', 'big' by

161

contrasting it with 'small'. We may present these concepts with pictures or mime, and by drawing attention to the contrasts in meaning we ensure our students' understanding.

(e) Enumeration

Another sense relation we looked at in 9.3.1 was that of *general* and *specific* words. We can use this to present meaning. We can say 'clothes' and explain this by enumerating or listing various items. The same is true of 'vegetable' or 'furniture', for example.

(f) Explanation

Explaining the meaning of vocabulary items can be very difficult, especially at beginner and elementary levels. But with more intermediate students such a technique can be used. It is worth remembering that explaining the meaning of a word must include explaining any facts of word use (see 9.3.2) which are relevant. If we are explaining the meaning of 'mate' (= friend) we have to point out that it is a colloquial word used in informal contexts and that it is more often used for males than for females.

(g) Translation

Translation is a quick and easy way to present the meaning of words but it is not without problems. In the first place it is not always easy to translate words, and in the second place, even where translation is possible, it may make it a bit too easy for students by discouraging them from interacting with the words.

Where translation can quickly solve a presentation problem it may be a good idea, but we should bear in mind that a consistent policy towards the use of the mother tongue is helpful for both teacher and students (see 11.2.4 for a discussion of this point).

All of these presentation techniques either singly or in combination are useful ways of introducing new words. What must be remembered with vocabulary presentation, too, is that pronunciation is just as important here as it is for structural material.[10] We should not introduce words without making sure that students know how they are said. Not only will this mean that they can use the words in speech, it will also help them to remember the words.

There are a number of ways of presenting the sounds of words:

1 **Through modelling.** Just as with structures (see 6.3.1) the teacher can model the word and then get both choral and individual repetition. When the teacher is modelling the word he or she can use gesture, etc. to indicate the main stress in a word.
2 **Through visual representation.** When teachers write up new words on the board they should always indicate where the stress in the word is. They can do this by underlining, e.g.

photograph

They can use a stress square, e.g.

photographer

They can use a stress mark before the stressed syllable, e.g.

photo'graphic

They can write the stress pattern of the words next to it, e.g.

photography □ □ □ □

3 **Through phonetic symbols.** Some teachers get their students to learn the phonetic symbols, at least for recognition purposes. Certainly for more advanced students a basic knowledge of the symbols will help them to access pronunciation information from their dictionaries (see 9.6).

9.5.2
Discovery

We will look at a number of discovery techniques from simple matching tasks to more complex understandings of connotation and context.

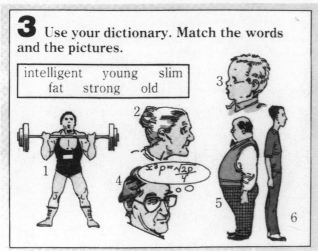

3 Use your dictionary. Match the words and the pictures.

| intelligent | young | slim |
| fat | strong | old |

(a) Adjectives[11]

This example from a book for elementary students shows the simplest form of matching discovery activity:

Students will be using their bilingual dictionaries (see 9.6), though some of them may know these words already.

Teachers can easily prepare their own versions of this activity. For example, students can be given numbered pictures and the teacher can then write words on the board which they have to match with the pictures.

The use of simple matching activities like these as a prelude to repetition and practice allows the students more involvement than a presentation led by the teacher. However the same procedure repeated for the introduction of all new words would become boring.

(b) Parts of the body[12]

This activity for intermediate students broadens the matching of words to pictures by not actually giving the students the words. They have to find them from their own memories or from their peers.

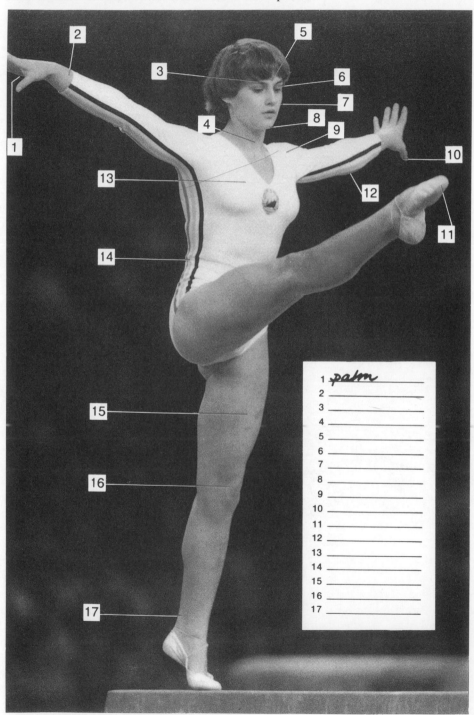

Notice how students are encouraged to come up with any more words they know to extend the list of vocabulary.

It is often a good idea to have students working in pairs or groups for this activity. Frequently a word that is unknown to one student will be known by another.

(c) Around the house[13]

In 9.3.1 we talked about sense relations and about general and specific words. The following activity expands the concept to include word fields – i.e. areas where a number of words group together.

The activity uses the 'mind map' technique to help students to put a list of words into different groups.

─── 1 ───────────────────

a Here is a 'vocabulary network'. Can you complete it with words from the box? (Then add *one more* object for each room.)

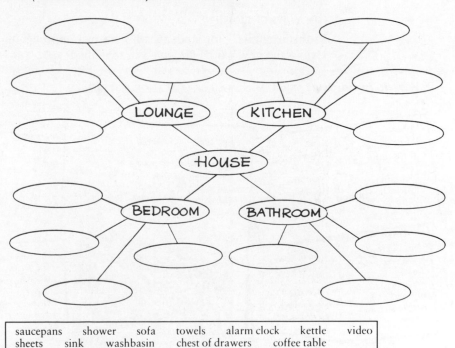

saucepans	shower	sofa	towels	alarm clock	kettle	video
sheets	sink	washbasin	chest of drawers	coffee table		

b In which room do you normally:

listen to music?   waste time?
daydream?   think about your problems?
have arguments?   feel most relaxed?

Now compare your answers with a partner.

c Why do you have certain things in certain rooms? For example, why not put the television in the bathroom? Why not put the sofa in the kitchen?
Think of some more examples and ask your partner to explain them.

Once again, because this activity is for intermediate students, we can assume that some of the students know some of the words. By sharing their knowledge they can complete the map – and add the extra bits of vocabulary. Notice how the follow-up activities in this material encourage practice of the words.

Using mind maps to create vocabulary fields is something that teachers can incorporate into their regular vocabulary teaching. Indeed such activities can form a useful prelude to work on specific topics. Thus if students are going to read a text about movement, the class might start with the basis for a mind map like this:

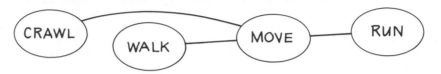

It would then be up to the students (in pairs or groups) to expand the map as far as possible.

(d) Ways of moving[14]

In this example – for students who are just approaching the intermediate level – the new words are given in texts first:

Words in context *Read the following passages and do the exercises.*

Robert couldn't get to sleep. He didn't know why. At two o'clock in the morning he decided to go downstairs and get some food from the fridge. Everyone in the house was asleep so he **tiptoed** down the stairs, making as little noise as possible. (Now answer question 1, Exercise 1.)

From the hotel window, you could see the green hills covered with tall trees, and in the distance was a little lake.
'Let's put on some strong shoes, take some sandwiches and spend the day **hiking** *in the mountains,' their father said. (Now answer question 4.)*

It was a dark day and it looked as if it might rain. From the hotel window, you could see the beach. No one was there.
'Let's **wander** round the town and get to know this place a little better,' their father suggested. (Now answer question 6.)

Jim and Sandy had met on holiday and were very much in love. This was their last day together. Now, as the sun went down over the sea, they **strolled** *hand in hand along the beach, looking into each other's eyes, saying nothing. (Now answer question 2.)*

The boxer took a hard punch on the chin. He stood still for a second and then his legs became weak. Almost falling, he started to **stagger** *like a drunken man. One more punch and he was down . . . seven, eight, nine, ten. It was a knock-out. (Now answer question 7.)*

'Oh no,' shouted Mike, 'my contact lens has fallen out.' Soon everyone was on their hands and knees, **crawling** around looking for it.
'You can all stand up now,' someone said. 'I've found it.' (Now answer question 3.)

The boys were sixteen years old and they were in the army. Every day they had to practise **marching** as the sergeant called out, 'Left, right. Left, right. Left.' (Now answer question 5.)

In the village, most people were happily getting ready to go skiing. There were only a few people who looked unhappy. They could not go skiing. They had each injured a leg, a knee or an ankle, and were now **limping** *around the village with nothing to do. (Now answer question 8.)*

When they have read the texts they are in a position to guess the meaning of the words, and the following chart helps them to do it:

Match each of these verbs with its meaning. Put a cross (X) in the right box, as in the example.

	stroll	wander	march	limp	hike	tiptoe	stagger	crawl
with each step equal			X					
quietly, on your toes								
pressing more on one foot than the other								
in a slow, relaxed way								
in an unsteady way								
in the countryside								
on your hands and knees								
in no particular direction								

This discovery activity is made usable because students had a chance to see the words in context. At their post-elementary level they would probably not know the words already so the text provides the information on which they can base their deductions – and, therefore, fill in the chart correctly.

This kind of activity can be used by teachers when working with any text. If there are a number of words that group into a vocabulary field (see (b) above) it will be easy to design a similar chart – which is a matching-word-and-definition activity.

(e) Suffixes and prefixes[15]

We said in 9.3.3 that students need to know about word formation. This exercise is designed to make them aware of how suffixes and prefixes work.

After the students are reminded of how suffixes and prefixes work they are asked to look at a list of words and see what they mean:

1 **Suffixes** and **prefixes**

In *Unit 1* (page 4) we saw how *prefixes* and *suffixes* are used to form different parts of speech.
fashionable = adjective
happiness = noun
electrician = person
They can also add a new meaning.

Example
bi = two
bilingual
biplane
If you understand the meaning of the suffix or prefix, you can often guess the meaning of a new word.

2 What meaning do the following *suffixes* and *prefixes* add?
a. **non**-fiction
b. **dis**honest
c. **mis**understand
d. **over**sleep
e. **under**cook
f. **re**decorate
g. an **ex**-president
h. a manager**ess**
i. help**less**
j. use**ful**
k. **anti**-social
l. **auto**graph
m. **pro**-American
n. **de**frost
o. **micro**scope
p. **post**-graduate
q. **pre**dict

167

Once again the point here is that students are being asked to interact with the words and work things out for themselves. Because this is an activity for upper intermediate students they can probably do so.

(f) Fear[16]

Understanding how words relate to each other also involves understanding which words are weaker or stronger than others. In this activity at the upper intermediate level students are being prepared to read a short story by Janet Frame called *You are Now Entering the Human Heart*. The materials designer takes the opportunity to do a quick discovery activity on words associated with 'fear' – a major theme of the story:

Ⓚ **Exercise 2** **Everybody experiences fear at some time or other, for example when you are woken by a strange noise at night, before you go to the dentist, or when you are on top of a high building. The following words describe different kinds of fear. Using a dictionary if necessary, put the words in the appropriate place on the lines. You may want to put more than one word on a line.**

afraid   nervous   terrified   petrified   scared   frightened

A little fear

————————————
————————————
————————————
————————————
————————————

A lot of fear

Notice the letter 'K' in the circle which indicates that users can find the answers to this exercise in the answer key. It is worth reminding ourselves that either the teacher or a self-study key must be on hand to help give students feedback on the discoveries they have made.

(g) Gibraltar[17]

The following example could only be used with very advanced students, but the principle (using a modified fill-in passage) can be adapted to almost all levels.

Students are going to read an account of the inquest into shootings which took place in in Gibraltar some years ago. This extract relates to the death of one of the victims, called Savage.

The students are told that in the passage a number of words have been blocked out by the symbol xxxxxx (this seems less disruptive to the reading eye than the more normal blank). Individually they have to think of as many words as possible to replace these symbols with, and they then have to compare their possibilities in pairs and groups until they have decided which words should be replace the xxxxxs (this consensus activity is similar to that in 9.6.1 (d)).

This is the text:[18]

Kenneth Asquez, a twenty-year-old bank clerk, alleged last April that he saw a man with his foot on Savage's chest, firing xxxxxx him at point-blank xxxxxx two or three times. Asquez made the claim in two statements, one hand-written and another made before a lawyer, which he refused to sign, because, he said he wanted to protect his xxxxxx. Thames Television used seventy-two words from his statements. But at the inquest Asquez - a surprise xxxxxx given his previous anonymity - said he had invented his account under 'xxxxxx' and 'offers of money', the first unspecified and the second unquantified (he received none, in any case). Sir Joshua Hassan, the colony's most distinguished lawyer and former chief minister, represented him in court. The coroner said that, retracted or not, his first account should still be xxxxxx by the jury.

Then there is Robin Arthur Mordue. He was a British holidaymaker, walking towards Savage in Landport Lane when the shooting started, and he was pushed to the ground by a woman on a bicycle (herself pushed by a third xxxxxx). He saw Savage fall at the same time. The shots stopped for a time, and then resumed as Mordue struggled to his xxxxxx; as he ran for xxxxxx behind a car, he looked back to see a man standing over Savage and pointing down with a gun. Mordue was a confused (and perhaps frightened) witness; coroner and counsel examined him ten times before he was released xxxxxx his oath. He may also have been a confused and frightened witness before he arrived in Gibraltar: in the weeks before the inquest, he received a number of xxxxxx phone calls ('Bastard...stay away'). His telephone number is ex-directory.

This activity reinforces the point about meaning in context (see 9.3.1), and gains a lot through the discussion that takes place between students about what the words should be. Interestingly enough some of the words are easy for a native speaker to guess because they form part of clichéd or fixed phrases (at point-blank *range*, he ran for *cover*, struggled to his *feet*), whilst others are more interesting and show the writer stretching words and meanings to his particular purpose (firing *into* him) and some respond to the legal register of the piece (a third *party*, released *from* his oath).

Clearly this extract is difficult because of the complexity of the information, the register and the general level of the language. But the same procedure can be used by teachers with texts at virtually any level.

The examples in this section have all encouraged students to work out meanings, etc. for themselves. By provoking this involvement with words, we make it likely that students will remember them at least for a short time (see 9.4.2). Clearly, though, we will want to encourage students to practise using the words so that they become more familiar. That is what we will look at in the next section.

9.5.3
Practice

In this section we will look at activities designed to encourage students to use words in an involving way.

(a) Actions and gestures[19]

In this example students have studied words connected with body language and movement (e.g. shrug, shake, cross + shoulders, fist, arm). They have done an exercise on the way verbs and nouns collocate (you can't shrug your fists, for example). Now they complete the following questionnaire:

What actions or gestures do you use to do the following?

INTERVIEWEE NUMBER	1	2	3	4
say hello				
say goodbye				
express anger				
express surprise				
express indifference				
express agreement				
express disagreement				

Do people from different cultures do any of these things differently?

(b) Bring, take and get[20]

In this example students at elementary level have studied the different uses of get, bring and take, verbs that are frequently confused. After doing a fill-in exercise they then take part in the following practice activity.

PRACTICE

2 Susanna Davies is an office manager. She keeps her staff very busy. It's Monday morning, and there are various jobs they will have to do before midday.

Look at the illustration and information, and give Susanna's orders. The first one has been done for you.
Example: *Bob, would you take the office car to the garage, get some petrol and bring it back here?*

1 Tracy . . .
2 Eric . . .
3 Phil . . .
4 Is that Miss Jones at Speed-o-Bike? . . .

3 In pairs, give each other instructions to move objects about.
Examples: *Hans, take this book to Marie, and give it to her.*
Sam, go and get Kate's pen, and bring it here.

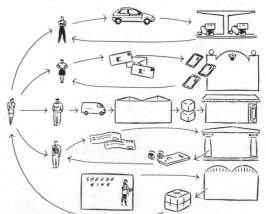

This is a very straightforward practice activity which will help students to fix the meanings and uses of these difficult verbs in their minds.

(c) Traits of character[21]

In this example for advanced students, students are led through three exercises which practise the use of 'character' vocabulary.

1 Ladies and gentlemen, which of these traits of character do you most dislike in a partner? Place them in order.

vanity	hypocrisy	pomposity	stubbornness
obstinacy	selfishness	dishonesty	pettiness
arrogance	snobbishness	timidity	possessiveness
shyness	meanness	rashness	aggressiveness

Ladies and gentlemen, which of these qualities is most important for you in a partner? Place them in order of importance.

compassion	vivacity	frankness	self-assurance
tolerance	patience	generosity	ambition
sincerity	imagination	passion	humility
modesty	sensitivity	courage	creativity

2 Discuss or write down the personal characteristics (good and bad) that you would expect to find in these people.

1 a nurse
2 the chairman of a multinational company
3 an actor
4 a politician
5 a teacher

We must assume that the students have a knowledge of a majority of the words. That being so, the genuine discussion in exercise 2 about the characteristics we would wish to see for various professions will provoke the use of a number of these words.

The same kind of activity can be done with emotional reactions, for example. How would students expect to feel if they went to see a horror movie, a love story, a Shakespeare play?

This activity demonstrates the desirability of making the words and what they stand for the centre of a practice session.

(d) Innismullen[21]

In 9.3.2 we discussed the importance of the metaphorical use of language. The following discovery–practice activity shows how students can be made aware of metaphorical use, and in a controlled practice session, how they can be encouraged to use some of the idioms.

Students at the upper intermediate level are shown the following text from an imaginary novel called *The Keeper of Innismullen*:

> Their ill-fated marriage started badly on the first night, for when they arrived at the hotel and had unpacked their things Charles found that he was unable to hide his unhappiness. Despite his apologies, and his claims that he had not meant to hurt her feelings, Matilda's pride was deeply wounded and since she was unable to guess at the cause of his distress she jumped to all sorts of conclusions.
>
> Charles was, by this time, ill at ease but had no way of explaining the true situation to his new bride. Sick at heart he continued to give unconvincing apologies or merely to murmur in monosyllables.
>
> Finally, after three hours, during which Matilda's injured pride pained her more with every passing second, she exploded. 'I am sick and tired of this ill-mannered behaviour,' she exclaimed. 'I consider our marriage to be already at an end.' She spoke in anger; how could she know that it would be five long years before her wish finally came true?

After being asked to speculate on the reasons for the situation the students see the following question:

How are the words 'sick', 'ill', 'injured', 'wounded' and 'hurt' used in the extract from *The Keeper of Innismullen*? What other meanings can you find for these words in the dictionary?

When the teacher and students have discussed the answers to the question they are given this practice activity:

Read this summary of a story called *Runaway Heart*.

> Sylvia and Gregorio are terribly in love and hope to get married. However, at a dinner party (which was the first time that Gregorio had met Sylvia's family) Sylvia's lover and her father had a terrible argument and Gregorio was thrown out of the house and told never to return. What are Gregorio and Sylvia to do now?

Tell the story in your own words, trying to use as many expressions with 'sick', 'ill', 'injured', 'wounded' or 'hurt' from the text as possible.

This activity shows how the metaphorical use of language can be approached. Notice that the practice activity has elements of parallel writing (see 7.2.2).

(e) Restaurants[22]

Once again for this activity at the intermediate level practice is preceded by a discovery activity.

a Working with your partner, put the following events into the correct order. The first one has been done for you.

look at the menu ....
give the waiter a tip ....
have dessert ....
pay the bill ....
book a table ....
decide to go out for a meal ...**1**...
leave the restaurant ....
have the starter ....
go to the restaurant ....
have the main course ....
sit down ....
order the meal ....
ask for the bill ....

Here the vocabulary is dealt with in phrases rather than single words since in the context of restaurants there would not be any point in listing the words without the vocabulary they collocate with. Students listen to an account of a meal where the sequence of events was different from the one given here and they are then given this practice activity:

Events do not always follow this sequence. What happens in:

• a hamburger (fast food) restaurant?
• a pub?
• a restaurant or bar in your country?

As the students discuss these situations they are recycling the phrases they have just been (re-)learning.

Using sequences of events in certain well-defined situations (shopping, travelling by air, getting up, going to bed, etc.) teachers can provide practice for a lot of the language that concerns those situations. The material shown here provides a clear example of how practice can lead on naturally from a discovery activity in such circumstances.

(f) Headlines

Headlines (both real and imagined) are a very good way of providing practice, particularly if they refer to certain well-defined topic areas. Suppose that students have been studying words related to age and ageing (infant, child, middle age, etc.) they could be asked to write an article to accompany the headline:

OLD LANGUAGE LEARNERS ARE BEST SAYS PENSIONER GRANDMA

If students have been studying vocabulary related to families and weddings they could be asked to expand a headline like this:

BIGAMY DOUBTS CAUSE WAR AT WEDDING

Students who have been studying vocabulary related to death and dying might write a story to accompany this headline:

CEMETERY FACES M–WAY THREAT

Of course, there is no reason why teachers should only use newspaper headlines. They could equally well use radio news items; they could describe the situation in a 'gossip' session with a 'neighbour' or they could tell the story in a letter.

The point is that headlines, etc. provide a powerful stimulus for freer work. They are easy to construct, too.

In this section we have looked at a number of practice activities designed to provoke the use of certain (areas of) vocabulary. For free practice, of course, the ideas in Chapter 8 are just as valid for vocabulary as they are for structures. At that stage it is not the particular type of language being used that is the main focus: it is the spontaneous use of language, both structural, functional and lexical.

9.6
The importance of dictionaries[23]

We have already said (see 9.2) that selecting words for teaching purposes is very difficult. We based this on the enormous number of words that any language contains. For the same reason we can be sure that students will want to know the meaning of many more words than we, their teachers, can teach them. Where can they get this information?

Obviously the dictionary provides one of the best resources for students who wish to increase the number of words they understand – or at least for students who wish to understand what a word means when they come across it in a text or in a conversation. Most students in such circumstances consult a bilingual dictionary to find an equivalent in their own language.

There is nothing wrong with bilingual dictionaries except that they do not usually provide sufficient information for the students to be able to use. We frequently find that one word in the L2 (English) has five or six equivalents listed in the L1. But the student cannot tell which one of these meanings is referred to. There is often no information either about the level of formality of the word, its grammatical behaviour, or its appearance in idioms, etc. Such a lack of information could lead to serious errors of translation: one trainer used an Italian–English dictionary to produce a completely inaccurate (and fanciful) letter which started 'Expensive Mary'![24]

One response to the limited nature of information available in many bilingual dictionaries is to say that they should not be used. This will not be sensible, however, since most students who are at all interested in learning a language will use a bilingual dictionary whether their teachers want them to or not. Our job is not to try to prevent their use, therefore, but to turn it to our advantage by incorporating them into good dictionary practice using monolingual dictionaries.

Perhaps the greatest resource we can give our students is a good monolingual dictionary. In it there are many more words than students will ever see in class. There is more grammatical information about the words than students get (usually) in class. There is information about pronunciation, spelling, word formation, metaphorical and idiomatic use – a whole profile of a particular word. There should also be examples of words in sentences and phrases. Of course not all dictionaries do this equally well, and teachers (and students) have their preferences; but we can and should expect this kind of information from a good dictionary.

The problem is that students at beginner and elementary levels simply cannot access this information. Even where the language used in the dictionary definitions has been restricted to make those definitions easier to understand, it is just too difficult for students at lower levels. Such students do not have any alternative to using bilingual dictionaries. But as their English starts to improve we can begin to introduce the monolingual dictionary to complement their bilingual one. We can encourage them to look up a word in their bilingual dictionaries and then check what they have found against the information in the monolingual dictionary. We can allow them to check information from their monolingual dictionaries against translations that they find in their bilingual dictionaries.

It is when students get to the intermediate levels and above that we can seek to change completely to monolingual dictionary use, and to prise the students away from their bilingual dependence. As their vocabulary improves so they can understand the definitions and appreciate the information that they can find. Advanced students can (and should) use their monolingual dictionaries as their chief source of information about meaning, pronunciation and grammar. There is no better resource for the learner.

A note of caution should be added here, however. Whilst we wish to encourage sensible dictionary use, we do not want this to interfere with other methodological concerns. We do not want students to be checking every word of a reading text in their dictionaries when they should be reading for general understanding (see 10.4.4). We do not want the students' ability to be spontaneous to be limited by constant reference to dictionaries. We will see one example of good dictionary use in reading classes below (see 9.6.1 (d)).

9.6.1
Examples of dictionary training material[25]

The fact that some students do not use monolingual dictionaries very much is not just because of language difficulty, however. Dictionaries are very daunting precisely because they contain so much technical information. Unless we train students in how to understand the information and use the

175

dictionaries, the money they spend in buying them will be largely wasted since they will never open them.

In training our students in dictionary use we will want to achieve three things: in the first place we will want to remove the fear that they may have when faced with the mass of information a dictionary contains. Secondly we will want to train students to understand that information, and thirdly we will want to make the dictionary a normal and comfortable part of language study and practice. We will look at four examples of activities which seek to achieve some or all of these aims.

(a) Authority[26]

In this activity for intermediate learners, the students are first asked to read texts about government in Britain and the United States without a dictionary. This is one of them:

HOW BRITAIN IS GOVERNED

Britain consists of four countries: England, Scotland, Wales and Northern Ireland. London, the capital, is the centre of government for the whole of Britain, but local authorities are partly responsible for education, health care, roads, the police and some other things.
Laws are made by Parliament. There are two 'houses': the House of Commons and the House of Lords (which has little power). Members of the House of Commons are called MPs (Members of Parliament); an MP is elected by the people from a particular area.

The material then asks the students:

2 **Read this entry from a dictionary. It gives several meanings for the word *authority*. Which of the meanings is the one used in the first paragraph of the text in Exercise 1?**

respected store of knowledge or information: *We want a dictionary that will be an authoritative record of modern English* —compare DEFINITIVE — ~ly *adv*
au·thor·i·ty /ɔːˈθɒrɪ̩ti, ə-‖əˈθɑ-, əˈθɔ-/ *n* **1** [U] the ability, power, or right, to control and command: *Who is in authority here?*|*A teacher must show his authority* **2** [C *often pl.*] a person or group with this power or right, esp. in public affairs: *The government is the highest authority in the country.*|*The authorities at the town hall are slow to deal with complaints* **3** [U] power to influence: *I have some authority with the young boy* **4** [U9] right or official power, esp. for some stated purpose: *What authority have you for entering this house?* **5** [C *usu. sing.*] a paper giving this right: *Here is my authority* **6** [C] a person, book, etc., whose knowledge or information is dependable, good, and respected: *He is an authority on plant diseases* **7** [C] a person, book, etc., mentioned as the place where one found certain information
au·thor·i·za·tion, -isation /ˌɔːθəraɪˈzeɪʃən‖ˌɔːθərə-/ *n* **1** [U] right or official power to do something: *I have the owner's authorization to use his house* **2** [C] a paper giving this right

This simple activity helps to train students to be able to pick out different meanings and to stop them from being daunted by long entries for one word. It is not a difficult activity for teachers to introduce when using reading texts.

(b) Ferry[27]

This activity, again for intermediate students, involves learners in actively discovering what the information in the dictionary actually means.

1 using the dictionary

Here are two definitions of the word *'ferry'*. Fill in the boxes using the words below.

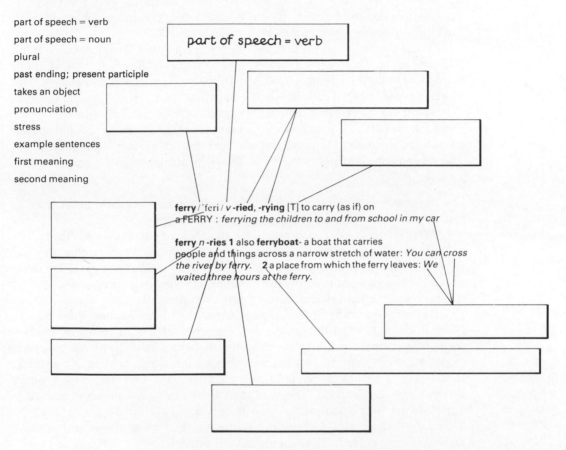

part of speech = verb

part of speech = noun

plural

past ending; present participle

takes an object

pronunciation

stress

example sentences

first meaning

second meaning

part of speech = verb

ferry / ˈferi / *v* **-ried, -rying** [T] to carry (as if) on a FERRY : *ferrying the children to and from school in my car*

ferry *n* **-ries 1** also **ferryboat**- a boat that carries people and things across a narrow stretch of water: *You can cross the river by ferry.* **2** a place from which the ferry leaves: *We waited three hours at the ferry.*

The point is that the students are being actively involved in learning what the dictionary conventions mean rather than telling them. The latter course of action will not have much impact and may be demotivating. The former, done over a period of time, will train them to understand dictionaries effectively.

In the exercise above students are having to deal with a variety of different information. We can get to this point by gradually training students to recognise symbols and conventions one or two at a time over a period of days or weeks. This can often form a follow-up to a reading or listening sequence. The teacher can ask the students to find out if a word they have encountered can be pluralised or not and ask them to find the information in their dictionaries, for example. This is a way of training them to recognise the symbols for countable and uncountable nouns.

177

(c) 'Write yourself in'[28]

This activity will help to make students more confident with their dictionaries. At the same time it is quite amusing.

Students are given words which they probably don't know. They have to look the word up in the dictionary and then write a sentence using the word and the pronoun 'I' or 'We'. If one of the words they look up is 'janissary', a sentence like 'I don't understand the meaning of "janissary"' is not allowed, whereas a sentence like 'We think janissaries were probably extremely handsome but very rough' is acceptable. (Janissaries were Turkish soldiers in former times.)

'Write yourself in' can be turned into a team game. Team A is given a different list of words from Team B. The members of Team A look up their words and write their sentences. Team B guesses the meaning. Team A scores a point only if Team B gets the meaning.

There are many other dictionary games, such as 'Call my Bluff' (originally a BBC TV game) where a team looks up the correct definition of an obscure word and then invents two incorrect but plausible definitions. The other team has to guess which is the right definition.

(d) Word consensus

It is important to make dictionary use a part of normal classes rather than just a rather exotic extra. This procedure does just that.

After students have read a text ask them to list the five words they would most like to know the meaning of. When they have done this they have to compare their list with a colleague's. The two have to agree on five words they most want to know the meaning of. Now pairs are joined together and the new groups have to agree on their lists.

By this stage many of the original words have been explained by the other student(s). What the groups now end up with is a list of words which they all really want to know the meaning of – words that they want to adopt (see 9.4.2.) Tell them to find the meanings of the words in their dictionaries. In the case of a word having multiple meanings make sure the whole group agrees on the correct one. They can then write example sentences much like those for the 'Write yourself in' activity above.

These dictionary training activities represent only a small proportion of the ones that can be used. Time spent on such activities will not be wasted for in giving students a key to their dictionaries we are giving them one of the most useful tools that they are likely to be able to use.

9.7 Conclusions

In this chapter we have looked at the difference between teaching language structure and teaching vocabulary. We have identified problems of selection with the latter which are not so prevalent with the former. We have seen how counts of frequency alone are not enough to determine what words should be taught.

We have seen that knowing a word means more than just knowing its meaning. Even that is problematical, since meaning includes sense relations and context, for example. To know a word we also need to know about its use, how it is formed and what grammatical behaviour it provokes or co-exists with.

We have discussed the methodology of vocabulary teaching, placing special stress on the desirability of getting students to 'interact' with words. Rather than just learn them, students should manipulate words and be involved with them. For this reason we placed special emphasis on discovery activities.

We have looked at activities designed to present and practise vocabulary, showing – in the largest section – how discovery techniques can aid vocabulary acquisition.

We have discussed the importance of monolingual dictionaries – and how they do not suffer from the same limitations as bilingual dictionaries do. We have looked at ways of training students so that their dictionaries can be a useful resource for them.

Above all, in this chapter, we have seen how vocabulary teaching and learning need to be emphasised in order for students to be competent language users.

Discussion

1 What do you think are the most appropriate ways of teaching vocabulary at different levels? How useful are discovery activities at beginner levels?
2 Which is more important for language learners: structure or vocabulary? Why?
3 Is it possible to train all students to use dictionaries? Why? Why not?
4 How important is it to learn idioms? Do idioms ever change?

Exercises

1 Look at your textbook. Find vocabulary exercises and say what aspect of vocabulary they are dealing with (see 9.3.1 – 4).
2 What words relating to the family would you teach to a group of elementary students? How could you teach them?
3 What metaphorical or idiomatic use of language can you identify with the following words:

die   dream   heart   dog

4 Which of the following words would you *not* teach beginners? Why?

orange   table   car   pilot   pocket   girlfriend   companion   spaghetti undertaker   angry   conductor

References

1 Much of the content of this chapter is heavily influenced by work which I have been doing on vocabulary material with Richard Rossner. I have made use of many of his insights here, though the final result is entirely my own responsibility.
2 See especially the excellent Gairns and Redman (1986) written for language teachers, and the more theoretical Carter and McCarthy (1988) which explores some of the issues behind how words work and how they are learnt and acquired. McCarthy (1991) looks at vocabulary and how it is treated in teaching materials and practice.
3 See Channell (1988) who states that '... there is justification for teaching approaches which make vocabulary learning a separate activity.' (page 94). Widdowson goes further and writes 'I think we arrive at a

recognition of the need to shift grammar from its pre-eminence and to allow for the rightful claims of lexis.' (1989:136).

4 See R Hindmarsh (1980).

5 The Cobuild Dictionary (see J Sinclair (1984)).

6 See D Willis and J Willis (1988).

7 See, for example, the Longman Mini-Concordancer (1989).

8 The Longman Dictionary of Contemporary English, New Edition (1987).

9 See Gairns and Redman (1986) pages 90 and 91, for example.

10 See J Channell (1988) who emphasises the importance of word stress in the learning of words.

11 From M Swan and C Walter (1984).

12 From J Soars and L Soars (1986).

13 From S Redman and R Ellis (1989).

14 From B Seal (1987).

15 From J Soars and L Soars (1987).

16 From R Rossner (1988).

17 From J Harmer (1990).

18 The extract is from 'Gibraltar' by Ian Jack. *Granta* magazine no. 25 (1988).

19 From J Harmer and R Rossner (1990).

20 From J Shepherd and F Cox (1991).

21 From G Wellman (1989).

22 From J Harmer and R Rossner (1991).

23 From S Redman and R Ellis (1989).

24 I am grateful to Della Summers and Sue Maingay for first involving me with dictionary design and dictionary use and for encouraging me to pursue the subject.

25 'Expensive Mary' was written by Nick Dawson.

26 Training manuals for dictionary use do exist, for example A Underhill (1980) and J McAlpin (1989). On dictionary use in general see R Gairns and S Redman (1986) pages 79–82, R Ilson (ed). (1985) and J Whitcut (1984).

27 Taken from M Swan and C Walter (1987).

28 From S Elsworth (1988).

29 From J Morgan and M Rinvolucri (1986).

10 Receptive skills

In this chapter we will look at material designed to train students in reading and listening skills. In 2.5 we called these *receptive skills* and we emphasised the point that reading and listening involve active participation on the part of the reader or listener. We said that many students can cope with a higher level in receptive skills than they can in language production and we discussed the value of listening and reading material (where it has been adapted for students) as roughly-tuned input (see 4.3).

10.1 Basic principles

We will look at some basic principles that apply to both reading and listening, for despite the fact that the activities are performed with different media (written and spoken text) there are underlying characteristics and skills which apply to both when being practised by native or non-native speakers of the language in question. We will look at *content*, *purpose and expectations* and *receptive skills*.

10.1.1
Content

In our daily lives we read and listen to a great deal of language, and it is possible to divide this language into two broad categories: *interest* and *usefulness*.

Very often we read or listen to something because it interests us – or at least we think it will interest us. Magazine readers choose to read the article on, say, page 35 rather than the story on page 66 because they think the former will be interesting whereas the latter will not. Buyers in a bookshop often select books because they think they will like them, and the discerning radio listener tunes in especially to programmes that he or she expects will be stimulating. This category of interest, then, includes reading and listening for enjoyment, pleasure and intellectual stimulation, etc.

Sometimes, however, it is not the fact that a text might be interesting which causes someone to read it: it is rather the usefulness of the text which prompts this action. If you wish to operate a coffee machine for the first time it is a good idea to read the instructions first so that you don't get cold soup instead of hot coffee. No one would suggest that the instructions you read are intrinsically interesting, but then neither are directories, maintenance manuals or rules and regulations. Nevertheless we have a desire to read or listen to these 'useful' texts because they will tell us something we want or need to know.

The two categories are not always independent of each other anyway. We may well read something that is useful and find that it is interesting – as students reading for their studies often do. The person who listens to the radio in order to learn how to build solar panels may do so with mixed motives. The instructions on the radio may have the joint characteristics of interest and usefulness.

10.1.2
Purpose and
expectations[1]

When dealing with listening and reading we need to address the same issues of purpose and desire that we discussed in relation to communicative tasks in 5.1 and 5.3.

In real life people generally read or listen to something because they want to (in the sense that we used 'want' in 5.1) and because they have a purpose in doing so. The purpose may be how to operate that coffee machine or to find out what has happened recently in an election (for the listener to the news) or to discover the latest trends in language teaching (for the listener to a talk at a language teachers' convention). In real life, therefore, readers and listeners have a purpose which is more fundamental than that involved in some language learning tasks which seem only to be asking about details of language.

Another characteristic of readers and listeners outside the classroom is that they will have expectations of what they are going to read or listen to before they actually do so. If you tune to a radio comedy programme, you expect to hear something funny (although this is sadly not always the case!) and the British citizen who picks up a newspaper and sees the headline 'Storm in the Commons' expects to read about a heated political debate in the House of Commons, the British parliament. The reader who picks up a book in a store will have expectations about the book because of the title, the front cover or the description of the book on the back cover.

People read and listen to language, then, because they have a desire to do so and a purpose to achieve. Usually, too, they will have expectations about the content of the text before they start – except when they turn on the radio at random, for example.

The concepts of desire, purpose and expectations will have important methodological implications for language learning as we shall see in 10.2.3 and 10.3.

10.1.3
Receptive skills[2]

Readers or listeners employ a number of specialist skills when reading or listening and their success at understanding the content of what they see or hear depends to a large extent on their expertise in these specialist skills. We can look at six of these skills, some of which we will be focusing on in this chapter.

(a) Predictive skills

Efficient readers or listeners predict what they are going to hear and read; the process of understanding the text is the process of seeing how the content of the text matches up to these predictions. In the first instance their predictions will be the result of the expectations they have – which we discussed above. As they continue to listen and read, however, their predictions will change as they receive more information from the text. One of the main functions of the *lead-in* stage when teaching receptive skills (see 10.3) will be to encourage predictive skills, and the examples of materials and techniques in 10.4.1. and 10.5.2. are especially designed for this purpose.

(b) Extracting specific information

Very often we read something or listen to it because we want to extract specific bits of information – to find out a fact or two. We may quickly look through a film review just to find the name of the star. We may listen to the news, only concentrating when the particular item that interests us comes up. In both cases we may largely disregard the other information in the review or the news bulletin. We will be aware of this information and may even at some level take it in, but we do so at speed as we focus in on the specific information we are searching for. This skill when applied to reading is often called *scanning* and we will concentrate on the skill of extracting specific information in 10.4.2. and 10.5.3.

(c) Getting the general picture

We often read or listen to things because we want to 'get the general picture'. We want to have an idea of the main points of the text – an overview – without being too concerned with the details. When applied to reading this skill is often called *skimming* and it entails the reader's ability to pick out main points rapidly, discarding what is not essential or relevant to that general picture. Listeners often need the same skill too – listening for the main message and disregarding the repetition, false starts and irrelevances that are often features of spoken language (see 10.5).

(d) Extracting detailed information

A reader or listener often has to be able to access texts for detailed information. The information required can be of many kinds. Exactly what does the writer mean? What precisely is the speaker trying to say? Questions like 'How many?' 'Why?' 'How often?' are often answered by reference to this kind of detail. Sometimes the detail we are looking for is the writer's or speaker's attitudes; how do they feel about the situation/person they are describing? What, precisely, is their intention? In our need to teach purposeful reading and listening with an emphasis on skimming and scanning (in reading) we should not forget the importance of detailed reading and listening.

(e) Recognising function and discourse patterns

Native speakers of English know that when they read or hear someone say 'for example' this phrase is likely to be followed by an example. When they read 'in other words' a concept is about to be explained in a different way. Recognising such discourse markers is an important part of understanding how a text is constructed. We understand paragraph structure and paragraph organisation and we recognise devices for cohesion. We know which phrases are used by speakers to structure their discourse or give them 'time to think'. We need to make students aware of these features in order to help them to become more efficient readers and listeners.

(f) Deducing meaning from context

The other important sub-skill has already been dealt with. As we have seen in Chapter 9 (9.4.3 and 9.5.2), one of the things we can do for students is to help them to develop their ability to deduce the meanings of unfamiliar words from the context in which they appear.

All the skills mentioned here are largely subconscious in the minds of experienced and frequent readers – in other words, most literate adults. But reading or listening in a foreign language creates barriers for the learner (often through fear of failure or through simple frustration) which may make these skills and sub-skills more difficult to use. Our job, then, is to re-activate these skills which learners have in their own language but which may be less effective when they are faced with English. If we can make students feel less anxious and thus remove some of the barriers, that alone may dramatically improve their receptive abilities.

10.2
Methodological principles for teaching receptive skills
10.2.1
Receptive and productive skills

Our discussions in 10.1 have important implications for the teaching of receptive skills which we can now consider. We will look at *receptive and productive skills, authentic and non-authentic texts, desire and expectations, receiving and doing* and *teaching receptive skills.*

We said in the introduction to this chapter that students can generally deal with a higher level of language in receptive skills than in productive skills. This, after all, is the point of roughly-tuned input for students who might have difficulty with completely authentic writing and speaking. It should be remembered here that being able to understand a piece of text does not necessarily mean that students have to be able to write or speak like that! Rather their job will be to interact with the text in order to understand the message, and this seems possible even where the text contains language which the students are not able to produce. All over the world there are students who can read English (often for scientific or academic purposes) but who are unable to speak it very well.

Receptive skill work, then, should involve students in reading or listening where they are able to process the language sufficiently at least to extract meaning, whether the language has been roughly-tuned for them or whether – for more advanced students – the language is completely authentic (see below).

10.2.2 Authentic and non-authentic text	One aspect of reading and listening that concerns many teachers and methodologists is the difference between authentic and non-authentic texts. The former are said to be those which are designed for native speakers: they are 'real' texts designed not for language students, but for the speakers of the language in question. Thus English-language newspapers are composed of what we would call authentic English, and so are radio programmes for English speakers. A British advertisement is an example of authentic English, so is a chapter from a novel written for an English-speaking audience.

A non-authentic text in language teaching terms is one that has been written especially for language students. Such texts sometimes concentrate on the language they wish to teach and we end up with examples like this:

John: How long have you been collecting butterflies?
Mary: I've been collecting them since I entered secondary school.
John: How many butterflies have you collected?
Mary: I've collected about four hundred foreign ones.
John: Are there any rare ones among them?
Mary: Yes, there are some. I got them in Thailand.
John: My hobby is playing football.
Mary: How long have you been playing it?
John: I've been playing it since last year. I can play it pretty well now.
Mary: Another hobby of mine is cooking.
John: Will you cook me a meal?
Mary: Yes, of course.

There are a number of clues which indicate at once to us that this language is artificial. In the first place, both speakers use perfectly formed sentences all the time. But conversation between people is just not like that! Especially noticeable is the fact that when one speaker asks a question using a particular grammatical structure, they get a full answer using the same structure. For example, the answer to 'How long have you been collecting butterflies?' would, in real life, probably be something like 'since secondary school .. no .. yes just after I started', rather than the perfect grammar we get here.

Another clue to this text's inauthenticity is the fact that the language is extremely unvaried (see 5.3). The repetition of the present perfect continuous ('Have been doing') and simple ('have done') shows what the purpose of this text is – to teach or revise those structures.

Other clues are John's sudden change of subject and the constant repetition of the verb 'play'. The conversation just doesn't 'sound right'.

All over the world language teaching materials use such devices. Their aim is to isolate bits of language so that students can concentrate on it. Such material should not be used, however, to help students become better listeners or readers. The obviously artificial nature of the language makes it very unlike anything that they are likely to encounter in real life. Whilst some may claim that it is useful for teaching structures, it cannot be used to teach reading or listening skills.

Should we, therefore, only use authentic material for teaching reading and listening? On the face of it this seems like a good idea, but what effect will it have on students? Imagine giving a group of elementary students a page from Shakespeare or an editorial from a quality Sunday newspaper. They would probably not understand it and they would become very demoralised. And that demoralisation would undermine the very reasons for giving students reading and listening material. There are three reasons:

(a) Being better readers, being better listeners

Clearly the most obvious reason for giving students reading and listening material is to encourage them to be better readers and listeners! In the broadest sense, it is clear that the more reading and listening we give them (and which they suceed with) the better they will become at reading and listening in English.

(b) Acquiring language

Students who read and listen a lot seem to acquire English better than those who do not. In other words, one of the main advantages of reading and listening for students is that it improves their general English level. Some of the language in the texts they read and listen to is acquired by them – provided, of course, that the input is comprehensible (see 4.1.3 and 4.3). Indeed we could go further: without a lot of exposure to reading and listening material students who learn languages in classrooms are unlikely to make much progress.

(c) Success

Students are frequently made nervous by reading and listening material. It looks incredibly difficult to them and it is incredibly difficult. When teachers present students with texts they cannot understand, the effect is extraordinarily demoralising. But when teachers choose the right kind of material (and use appropriate teaching techniques) and the students are successful, then the benefits are obvious. In other words, if we can say to our students that they have read (or listened to) something difficult but that they have managed to understand it then they have every reason to feel triumphant. And because they have been successful the barriers to reading and listening are slightly lowered. A frequent diet of successful reading makes students more confident when they read in English: successful listening classes make students better able to cope with listening to English.

We have now seen how obviously non-authentic material would not necessarily make our students better listeners or readers, especially since they would not be acquiring real language. But we have also seen how students would become unsuccessful and demoralised if they were presented with language that was simply too difficult for them (as authentic material can be). Both extremes are obviously not useful for our purposes.

What we need, therefore, are texts which students can understand the general meaning of, whether they are truly authentic or not. But texts – whether authentic or not – must be realistic models of written or spoken English. If teachers can find genuinely authentic material which their students can cope with that will be advantageous; if not they should be using material which simulates authentic English. In simple terms the texts should be roughly-tuned[3] rather than finely-tuned (see 4.3).

An example may show this distinction. The following reading material for intermediate students[4] may not use completely authentic records of what four real people actually said, but we recognise their words as being pretty much like the real thing.

Who's speaking?

These four people were asked to talk about what they eat.
Can you guess who is speaking?

Maria de Lisséo
Alexander Smythe
Carol Simpson
Dominic Rider

1 I eat a great deal of foreign food; Italian, French, Lebanese . . . that sort of thing. Strangely enough, I think I'd rather have ordinary, well-cooked English food. My favourite is still steak! I prefer it rare. I'm also very fond of good red wine, particularly Burgundy.

2 I'm just not very interested in food. I usually have only a cup of tea and a bowl of cornflakes for breakfast, and often skip lunch. For dinner, I often buy a tin of soup or perhaps a frozen hamburger, and heat it up. Occasionally I get something from a Chinese takeaway, or one of those fried chicken places. I never touch alcohol. It doesn't agree with me.

3 Food is still one of life's mysteries for me. It's all my parents' fault. They're awfully conventional in their tastes. My mother insists on cooking things like roast beef or lamb and boiled potatoes with some carrots or brussels sprouts. In fact, the kind of food I have to eat is so disgusting that I'd rather not talk about it, if you don't mind.

4 I absolutely adore fish, particularly white fish, such as sole or haddock, cooked in a little white wine, with some garlic and lemon. Recently, I've been experimenting with Japanese recipes, particularly raw fish. Oh, and I love fresh vegetables such as courgettes, broccoli and asparagus, and fresh green beans. But I hate them overcooked. Oh, and I'm terribly fond of pasta . . . but it must be freshly made!

The authors of this material have roughly-tuned the language and content to suit their students, but they have not sacrificed the feel of the language. Their simulated authenticity will be helpful to students who are practising reading.

What is being suggested, therefore, is that material designed to foster the acquisition of receptive skills must at least simulate authenticity. The need for language control at lower levels must not be used as an excuse for extreme artificiality.

10.2.3
Purpose, desire
and expectations

In 10.1.2 we said that people usually read or listen to something because they have a desire to do so and some purpose to achieve. Furthermore they generally have some expectations about what they are going to read or hear before they actually tackle the text.

The methodology for teaching receptive skills must reflect these facts about real life, and the tasks we ask students to perform must be sufficiently realistic and motivating for the students to perceive a useful purpose for text study. We will not get students to interact properly with spoken and written material unless we ensure that their desire to read or listen has been awakened. Especially where the subject matter of the texts may not be immediately appealing to them we have the responsibility to make students interested and to encourage them to tackle the text with positive anticipation.

Our methodological model in 10.3 will reflect these points about creating a desire to read and allowing students to develop expectations, and the material in 10.4 and 10.5 will be designed to get students to read and listen for a purpose.

10.2.4
Receiving and
doing

The purposes for which people read and listen are, of course, extremely varied. However, we can say that when people read or listen they do something with what they have just seen or heard. We discussed this point in some detail in 5.5 where we saw how skills are not performed in isolation but integrated with other skills. As a general methodological principle, therefore, we would expect students to use what they have read or heard in order to perform some task. When they have done work on comprehension skills, in other words, we would expect them to react to, or do something with, the text. This might take the form of giving opinions about what they have just read, following instructions, writing a postcard, summarising the content of the text or having a conversation based on the text.

Many of the materials we will look at in 10.4 and 10.5 will have just such a follow-up task which is called in 10.3 a *text-related task*.

10.2.5
Teaching receptive
skills

The job of the teacher is to train students in a number of skills they will need for the understanding of reading and listening texts. We can divide these skills into *type 1* and *type 2* skills.[5] Type 1 skills are those operations that students perform on a text when they tackle it for the first time. The first thing students are asked to do with a text concerns its treatment as a whole. Thus students may be asked to look at a text and extract specific information. They might read or listen to get the general picture. They might read or listen to perform a task, or they might be attempting to confirm expectations they have about the text. Type 1 skills are those that we detailed in 10.1.3, (a), (b) and (c), and it is suggested that such tasks form the basis for the first activities that students are asked to perform when learning receptive skills. Type 2 skills are those that are subsequently used when studying reading or listening material and they involve detailed comprehension of the text (after students have performed type 1 skills); the study of vocabulary to develop guessing strategies; the identification of discourse markers and construction and an investigation into the speaker's or writer's opinion and attitude. Type 2 skills, then, are generally concerned with a more detailed analysis of text and for this reason are generally practised after type 1 skills have been worked on (see 10.1.3 (d), (e) and (f)).

10.3 A basic methodological model for the teaching of receptive skills

We can now look at a model for teaching the receptive skills which is based on the discussion of methodological principles in the first part of this chapter. Just as in our model for introducing new language (see Figure 9 on page 58) this model is not designed to be followed slavishly but is intended to provide general methodological guidelines.

The model has five basic stages which are:

Lead-in: Here the students and the teacher prepare themselves for the task and familiarise themselves with the topic of the reading or listening exercise. One of the major reasons for this is to create expectations and arouse the students' interest in the subject matter of the spoken or written text (see 10.2.3).

T directs comprehension task: Here the teacher makes sure that the students know what they are going to do. Are they going to answer questions, fill in a chart, complete a message pad or try and re-tell what they heard/saw? This is where the teacher explains and directs the students' purpose for reading or listening (see 10.2.3).

SS listen/ read for task: The students then read or listen to a text to perform the task the teacher has set.

T directs feedback: When the students have performed the task the teacher will help students to see if they have completed the task successfully and will find out how well they have done. This may follow a stage in which students check their answers with each other first. (See 8.1.1 (c) and examples in 10.4 and 10.5.)

T directs text-related task: The teacher will then probably organise some kind of follow-up task related to the text. Thus if the students have answered questions about a letter the text-related task might be to answer that letter. The reasons for text-related tasks have been argued in 5.5 and 10.2.4.

The five stages are concerned with type 1 skills. In other words the students perform one skill operation on the text and then move on to a text-related task. This procedure may vary, however, in two particular circumstances.

When the students have performed tasks for type 1 skills the teacher may then ask them to re-examine the text for type 2 skill work. Thus if the first task involved getting the general picture (see 10.4.4) the teacher might return to the text (after directing feedback) for a type 2 skill task such as inferring attitude or deducing meaning. This takes place before the students move to a text-related task.

If the students perform very unsuccessfully in their first comprehension task (type 1) the teacher may redirect them to the same task to try again. This will take place before the text-related task.

These procedures are represented diagrammatically in Figure 18. The solid lines (_____) represent a course of action that will generally be taken. The four stages of type 1 skill work and the three stages of type 2 skill work (if the type 2 option is taken up) are examples of this. The broken lines (– – – –) represent optional courses of action. Thus the text-related task is optional (although we have stressed that it is a good idea) and so is the re-reading of/listening to the text for type 2 skills or for repair work on type 1 skills. The latter case explains the (1) in brackets.

In general, then, this is the model we will follow when looking at materials for reading and listening in 10.4 and 10.5.

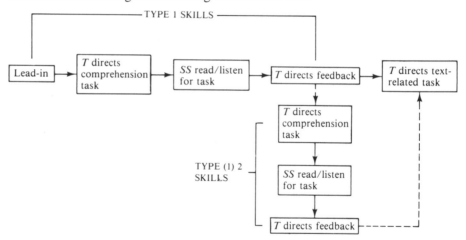

Figure 18 A methodological model for the teaching of receptive skills

10.4
Reading material

Before looking at examples of reading material we will make some general comments about reading in the classroom.

Reading is an exercise dominated by the eyes and the brain. The eyes receive messages and the brain then has to work out the significance of these messages. Unlike a listening text, a reading text moves at the speed of the reader (except where the reader is trying to read an advertisement that flashes past a train window). In other words it is up to the reader to decide how fast he or she wants to (or can) read a text, whereas listeners often have to do their best with a text whose speed is chosen by the speaker. The fact that reading texts are stationary is clearly a huge advantage.

It is often difficult to convince students of English as a foreign language that texts in English can be understood even though there are vocabulary items and structures the student has never seen before. But this is the case, not only for non-native speakers, but also for some speakers of English as a first language. Skills such as extracting specific information (see 10.1.3 (b)) can be satisfactorily performed even though students do not understand the whole text; the same is true for students who want to 'get the general idea' of a text. It is considered vitally important to train students in these skills (e.g. the ability to understand what is important even though the reader cannot understand everything) since they may well have to comprehend reading in just such a situation in real life.

The same is of course true for listening, but because the reading text is static students are often tempted to read slowly, worrying about the meaning of each particular word. And yet if they do this they will never achieve the ability to read texts in English in anything but a slow and ponderous way. Certainly they will continue to have difficulty in quickly scanning (see 10.1.3 (b)) or skimming (see 10.1.3 (c)) unless the teacher insists on these skills being performed rapidly. In other words the teacher should insist on the comprehension task being performed in a limited amount of time: if this is regularly done the teacher will find the amount of limited time necessary becoming less and less.

We will now look at a number of examples of reading materials both published and unpublished using a variety of types of exercise.[6] We will look at *reading to confirm expectations, reading to extract specific information, reading for communicative tasks, reading for general understanding, reading for detailed comprehension* (*information*) and *reading for detailed comprehension* (*function and discourse*).

10.4.1
Reading to
confirm
expectations[7]

In the following example of a reading exercise the students are involved in reading in order to confirm their expectations about the information they think the text will contain. This technique places great emphasis on the lead-in stage (where students are encouraged to become interested in the subject matter in the text), encourages students to predict the content of the text (see 10.1.3 (a)), and gives them an interesting and motivating purpose for reading.

The Empire State Building[8]

The students are going to read a text about the Empire State Building. This text is designed for intermediate students. The subject is not necessarily interesting in itself to some of the students, and so much of the teacher's job will be to arouse that interest.

The teacher puts the following chart on the board:

Things you know	Things you are not sure of	Things you would like to know

The students then say what things they know about the Empire State Building, and the teacher writes them on the chart in note form.

In the same way the next two columns are filled with notes which reflect facts which the students are 'not sure of' and things which they don't know. The chart might begin like this, for example:

Things you know	Things you are not sure of	Things you would like to know
very tall *USA*	*in New York?* *tallest building?*	*how many floors?* *when built?*

When the students have come up with sufficient facts to put in the chart they are told to read the following text as quickly as possible: their only task is to confirm (or not) the information on their chart. This is the *T direct comprehension task* stage.

THE EMPIRE STATE BUILDING

NEW YORK CITY is situated at the mouth of the Hudson River on the East coast of the USA. It is made up of five boroughs with a combined population of over 17 million people. The heart of New York City is the island of Manhattan, where, in the Midtown and Downtown districts, the buildings 'scrape the sky'.

One of these sky-scrapers is the Empire State Building on Fifth Avenue, between 33rd and 34th Street. Like the Statue of Liberty and Brooklyn Bridge, it is instantly recognised as a symbol of New York - a symbol which captures the power, energy and excitement of one of the world's most-loved and most- hated cities.

When the 102-storey structure was built in 1931, it was the tallest building in the world. From the top, on a clear day, you can see over a 50-mile radius. Its towering height and distinctive Art Deco style made the Empire State Building an instant success with the public.

Its record as the world's tallest building has since been beaten - the World Trade Centre in New York and the Sears Tower in Chicago are both taller - but the Empire State Building remain uniquely fascinating.

At night it is floodlit with coloured lights. Some people love the lights but others complain that their favourite New York building has been turned into the biggest Christmas tree in the world.

EMPIRE STATE FACTS

★ The Empire State is 'steeped' above a certain height, rather like a pyramid, to prevent it from blocking light and air from the neighbouring area.

★ There are 6,500 windows nearly seven miles of elevator shafts and enough floor space to shelter a town of 80,000 people.

★ The building was first cleaned in 1962. It took thirty people six months to complete the job. They were all experienced at high altitudes, including one who was a former paratrooper.

★ In the famous film 'King Kong', the giant gorilla, King Kong has his final battle from the top of the Empire State.

192

When the students have done this (and checked their work in pairs or groups) the teacher leads them through the points on the board again and asks whether the text confirmed what they knew, or answered any of their uncertainties. This is the *T directs feedback* stage.

For a text-related task students could role play an interview between a reporter and someone who works at the Empire State Building; you could tell them that it is the year 1931 and that they should write an article for a magazine describing this new wonder; the students could describe a famous building in their city or area.

The 'reading to confirm expectations' technique is highly motivating and successful since it interests students, creates expectations, and gives them a purpose for reading. The text-related tasks we have suggested will produce a great deal of spoken or written language.

10.4.2
Reading to extract specific information

We will look at three examples in which students are asked to read a text to extract specific information, a skill we said was important (see 10.1.3 (b)). A vital feature of this type 1 skill is that students should see the questions or tasks they are going to answer or perform before reading the text. If they do this it will be possible for them to read in the required way; they should scan the text only to extract the information which the questions demand (see 10.4): they do not have to worry about parts of the text they have difficulty with but only those that they need to extract the required information. We can now look at our examples.

(a) Small ads: open-ended questions[9]

The example on page 194, from an intermediate coursebook, gives students practice in a universally useful skill – scanning the small ads in a newspaper to find what you are looking for.

The teacher may start by asking students what is advertised in newspapers, asking them how often they consult small ads in their own language. Now they are told that they are going to look at some advertisements in English.

The teacher now asks the students to find the information in questions 1 to 15 as quickly as possible.

A way of making this activity even more enjoyable is to divide the class into groups. Each group has five pieces of information to find. Which group can find their information first?

As a text-related task students can ring the advertisers or write letters to one of the people who are advertising for friends. If students are living (temporarily) in the UK you might want to go through some of the special language used here (e.g. '3 dble beds/excellent clean condition', etc.).

2 Fast reading practice. Look at the small ads
and see how quickly you can answer the questions.

1. What does the cheapest metal detector cost?
2. A man in South Essex is looking for a friend. How old is he?
3. Will Christine improve your mind or your body?
4. Which costs more – a 400-year-old cottage near Winchester or a 5-bedroom house in Wales?
5. Why is today a special day for Paul?
6. How much will two bottles of Chateau Latour 1964 cost you?
7. What town do you write to for bath, body and face oils?
8. Where can you buy things for a party?
9. How long will it take you to learn to make a guitar?
10. Does the lady who is bored with the cat prefer tall or short men?
11. How much will it cost you to give somebody a pound of smoked salmon and a bottle of champagne (with a message)?
12. You can buy something that was produced on the day you were born. What?
13. Somebody is offering a baby bath for sale. How much for?
14. Does the nice 42-year-old woman smoke?
15. How many nationalities has Olga got?

BILLIARD TABLES bought and sold. Mr Villis. (02805) 66 (Bucks).

GIFT CHAMPAGNE. We post a bottle with your message. From £14.50 incl. Orders or details 0642 45733

CHRISTINE'S beauty treatment and body therapy.. 402 6499, 0473 4004

SMOKED SALMON
8oz sliced £5.75, 1lb sliced £11, 2lb 4oz side £16.90, 2lb 8oz side £19.50, 400gms offcuts £5. Prices include UK 1st class postage. Cheques with order. Cornish Smoked Fish Co. Ltd, Charlestown, St. Austell, Cornwall.

400-YEAR-OLD thatched cottage between Winchester/Basingstoke : 3 dble beds, sec gdn & extras. £110,000. (0962) 88109

CHATEAU LATOUR, 1964. 24 bottles, £75 each. Phone (0227) 9848 evenings.

GOING IN TO BUSINESS? Send £7.45 inc p&p for 'The Beginners Guide to Success in Business.' Comquip Ltd, 189 Highview, Meopham, Gravesend, Kent. (0732) 22315.

SILVER CROSS detachable coach Pram (navy), shopping tray, excellent clean condition, £30; Carry Cot, £5; Baby Bath, £2.50; Atari system, joystick and paddle sticks, in good working order, needs a new mains adapter, £40; 5 Atari Cassettes, £10 each, very good condition, ideal Xmas presents. — Apply 34 Kynaston Road, Didcot, Oxon. evenings. 415702

C-SCOPE METAL DETECTORS. The ideal family gift to treasure from £39.99 to £449.50. Tel. Ashford (0233) 2918 today for free colour brochure.

BEAUTIFUL farm estate, total 700 acres. Diplomats 4 bed 1832 house. £220,000 ono. 0639 73082

5 BEDROOMED HOUSE in quiet mid-Wales village. 1 acre of land, fishing and shooting available. £42,000. Tel : 059 787 687 (after 6 p.m.)

W. ANGLESEY. 2 dble beds. S/d bung. Lge with patio drs to 1½-acre garden, kit/b'fast room, bathroom. Dble glaz/ins. GCH. Garage & util rm, summer hse, grn hse. Scope for extensions. £29,500 o.n.o., quick sale. Tel 040 741031.

MAKE A GUITAR
12 week courses. Details : Totnes School of Guitarmaking, Collins Rd, Totnes, Devon. 0803 65255.

HAVANA CIGARS
And other fine cigars at wholesale prices. Send for list to James Jordan Ltd, Shelley Hall, Shelley, Huddersfield. Tel.: 0484 60227

THE TIMES (1814-1985). This Xmas give someone an original issue dated the very day they were born. £12.50 or 2 for £21. Tel 01-486 6305 or 0492 3314

PARTYMANIA, everything for your party in one "funtastic" store. — 179 Kingston Road, Oxford 513397, own parking. 37685

HAVE A very happy birthday Paul.

NICE WOMAN, 42, seeks close, affectionate friendship with independentish man. Non-smoker, sense of fun, creative. Enjoys walks, talks, sensuality. Photo please. London area. Box (50) 2059. N50 3

OLGA: RUSSIAN/FRENCHWOMAN from Lille, seeks an Englishman, tall, 50s, open-minded, with whom she can have a close, but stable relationship. Box (50) 2051. N50 7

OXFORD: lively divorcee, mid forties, bored with solitude and the cat, seeks male, preferably tall, to share local pleasures and pastimes, music, the arts etc. Box (50) 2050.

VERY PERSONABLE, attractive, charming, amusing, considerate graduate, professional – 40 – own lovely coastal home, seeks lady – friendship/marriage – personality more important than age. All nationalities welcome. Box (50) 2052. N50 6

WARM, ATTRACTIVE, humorous woman, 35 lover of music, literature, cinema, theatre and leftish politics, seeks man of similar inclinations, to share it all with. London. Box (46)1899. N49 8

SENSITIVE, TALL, caring, unattached man, 55, likes people, music, walking, seeks intelligent, helpful n s woman, mid forties. South Essex Box (49)2011. N49 13

GIVE HER a luxurious Christmas with a special gift set of soothing bath, body and face oils. Send £9.50 to Claydon Aromatherapy, 107 Marine Parade, Worthing BN11 3QG.

LADIES NARROW SHOES. AA and narrower, sizes 2½-11½. Also wide EE. SAE Muriel Hitchcock Shoes, 3b Castle Mews, Arundel BN18 9DG.

(b) *QE2*: yes/no questions[10]

In this text, designed for elementary classes, students read about the cruise liner the *QE2*.

For the lead-in stage the teacher and students discuss different types of holiday, eventually coming round to the subject of luxury cruises. The teacher then tells the students that they are going to read a text about the *QE2*, one of the most luxurious liners in the world.

The students are asked to read the eight yes/no questions – only the questions. They are then told to read the text as fast as they can in order to answer those questions. They do not have to understand every word. The objective is only to find the answers to the questions, and they should do this as quickly as possible.

A   Read these questions. Then read the passage to find out whether your answer is 'Yes' or 'No'.

1 Is the ship in the picture small? . . . . .
2 Are there many ships like the QE2? . . . . .
3 Do most people prefer to travel by sea? . . . . .
4 Is the QE2 expensive? . . . . .
5 Can the ship carry 2,950 people? . . . . .
6 Can the passengers swim on the ship? . . . . .
7 Do they sell drinks on the QE2? . . . . .
8 Can boys and girls watch films on the ship? . . . . .

The ship in the picture is the Queen Elizabeth II, usually called the QE2. It is a large, modern passenger ship. There are not many ships like the QE2 now. Most people prefer to travel by air and not by sea. The QE2 is very slow and expensive compared with a modern jet plane. But some people do not like to travel by plane, and the QE2 is. . .well, different.

The ship is really an enormous floating hotel, almost a small floating town. The five-day voyage from Southampton, England to New York is a real holiday.

The QE2 can carry 2,000 passengers, and it has a staff of 950 running the ship and looking after the passengers. The ship has three restaurants, eight bars, a ladies' hairdresser's[1] and a men's barber's[2] shop. In addition, there are four swimming pools, two cinemas (they show many films for adults but there are some films for children, too), a casino, two libraries, a hospital, a bank, and a gymnasium. There are also some shops[3]. Yes, it is like a small city. But there are no cars, buses or trucks, and there is no smog; the air is clean and there is peace and quiet.

When the students have finished answering the questions they can check their answers with each other. The teacher then conducts feedback, finding out how well they did and explaining any misunderstandings. It might be sensible to find out how many students got how many answers correct and which ones these were.

As a text-related task students are told that they are themselves taking a cruise on the *QE2* and they should write a postcard to an English friend of theirs. The students and the teacher might discuss the kind of things they could say in such a postcard (particularly the use of the present simple and the present continuous – often found in this kind of writing). After students have written their cards, the more interesting ones can be read out to the class or circulated among the students.

(c) Across Canada: transferring information[11]

As a lead-in to this text for lower intermediate students the teacher can ask the students if they have ever given any money to charity. Why did they do it? What is the most deserving cause they can think of? etc.

The teacher then asks the students to look at the page, and before reading anything asks them what they think the text(s) will be about. This gives them a chance to exercise the predictive skill we mentioned in 10.1.3 (a).

The students are now asked to look at the chart (see Reading 1) and told to find information in order to complete it. Once again they are told not to try to understand every word. This is a scanning exercise.

When students have compared their answers the teacher can get them to fill in a chart on the board – or the feedback can be given orally.

The students will be asked to read the text(s) again, answering more detailed questions (see 10.4.5).

For a follow-up task students could be asked to role play an interview with Steve Fonyo; they could write a newspaper article about him. Another possibility is for them to discuss what they thought of these charity runs, and then to design their own fund-raising activity.

Across Canada

Reading

1

Copy and complete the chart about *either* Terry Fox *or* Steve Fonyo. (You can get information from the text and/or the press releases.)

> Name:
> Disease:
> Date of start of run:
> Age at start of run:
> Distance covered:
> Amount of money raised:

2

Answer the following questions.

1 Where did Steve Fonyo begin and end his run?
2 How many differences can you find between Steve Fonyo and Terry Fox?

Terry Fox

Steve Fonyo

Terry Fox was a college athlete who lost a leg due to bone cancer. At the age of 21, on a cold February day, he set out to run across Canada. He wanted to raise money for the Canadian Cancer Society, but on September 1st, he was forced to give up. He had raised more than 23 million dollars and had become a national hero. He died the following June.

Steve Fonyo lost a leg during his childhood due to cancer. He never completed high school. But at 19, Steve Fonyo still managed to complete a run all the way across Canada, passing through all the major cities.

Below are some of the press releases made during Steve's run.

ST. JOHN'S, NEWFOUNDLAND

MARCH 31

STEVE FONYO, THE 19-YEAR-OLD CANCER VICTIM, TODAY DIPPED HIS ARTIFICIAL LEG INTO THE ATLANTIC ON THE START OF HIS RUN ACROSS CANADA. FONYO'S "JOURNEY FOR LIVES" IS STARTING IN FREEZING CONDITIONS AND TERRIBLE SNOWSTORMS.

THUNDER BAY, ONTARIO

NOVEMBER 29

TODAY STEVE FONYO ARRIVED AT THE SPOT WHERE TERRY FOX HAD TO GIVE UP HIS RUN IN 1981. A WOODEN BOARD THERE READS "TERRY FOX. 3,339 MILES." AFTER READING THE INSCRIPTION, FONYO SAID HE WOULD NOT RUN AGAIN UNTIL TOMORROW.

VICTORIA, BRITISH COLUMBIA

JUNE 3

STEVE FONYO TODAY DIPPED HIS ARTIFICIAL LEG INTO THE PACIFIC OCEAN IN FRONT OF A CHEERING CROWD. HIS ARRIVAL AT THE SEASHORE MARKED THE END OF HIS 5,000-MILE RUN ACROSS CANADA ON HIS "JOURNEY FOR LIVES." IN 425 DAYS HE HAS RAISED $9 MILLION FOR CANCER RESEARCH.

The three examples shown here have demonstrated the use of *scanning* as a type 1 skill – the way it is frequently used in real life. It is also perfectly possible, of course, to read a text for general understanding first and then look for details (see 10.4.5).

We have looked at three examples of exercises designed to train students to extract specific information. Obviously there are many more possibilities.

10.4.3
Reading for
communicative
tasks

In this section we will look at three examples in which the reading of a text is designed to foster a communicative interaction of some kind.

(a) Find the story: jumbled text[12]

A popular reading technique is the reassembling of a text that has become disordered. In solving the puzzle students will be working in a rather different way: the process of reading – the process of solving the puzzle – becomes an end in itself. This example from an intermediate coursebook concerns Jill Robinson, a journalist, whose father bitterly opposed her going to university. The students have already read part of the story. Now they have to put the following bits together to make the end of it.

Find the story

Here is the rest of Jill Robinson's story, in seven fragments (a – g). Part a is the beginning. But the others (b – g) are *not* in the correct order. Read out parts b to g in what you think is the correct order.

Questions

1 What explanation does Jill give for her father's attitude to her?
2 Describe what happened when she learned that he had died.
3 How have her feelings changed since her father died?

a Of course, now I can understand it all more clearly. Father and I belonged to widely different generations, held different expectations; a revolution in attitudes to

b it would be hypocritical to travel 300 miles to pretend to mourn when I had not even bothered to see him for four years. I could not grieve for him at all. Everything I had achieved, I told myself, I had done in the

c I realised; and maybe I could have eventually forgiven him. But would he ever have forgiven me?

d to please myself, or to spite him; that in fact I attained my academic goals mainly because of his opposition. Perhaps I owe him more than

e opportunities that had been denied him.
   A neighbour sent me the announcement of his death in the local paper. The funeral was to be the day after I received the news. I thought

f face of his opposition, I thought I owed him absolutely nothing, not even the courtesy of attending his funeral.
   Now I sometimes wonder whether my determination to succeed sprang from a desire

g women had occurred between his day and mine. But at the time, all I could feel was bitter resentment, because he was not proud of me (as I thought he should be), but deeply jealous that I had

The students can do this activity in pairs and then the teacher can ask different pairs to read the story out loud in the (correct) order.

As a text-related task the teacher can ask the students whether they think Jill was right not to go to the funeral. What do parents and their children argue most about? How important is education? This kind of text lends itself naturally to discussion.

(b) The last cigarette: student questions

In this activity some of the students read a text so that they can answer their colleagues' questions. The teacher starts the session by asking students the following question:

> Which of the following would you find most difficult to give up if you were asked to do so?
>
> alcohol   smoking   meat   chocolate   men/women   (something else)

They can discuss this in pairs or groups before talking about it with the whole class – probably in a light-hearted manner.

The teacher now tells the class that they are going to read a text called 'That Last Cigarette' about giving up smoking. Half of the class are given the text and told to read it so that they will be able to answer their colleagues' questions. The other half are put into a group to decide what questions they would like to ask in order to help a friend of theirs give up smoking (for example 'when should you smoke your last cigarette?').

This is the text that half the class read:

That Last Cigarette

Having decided your timing, you are now ready to smoke that last cigarette.
Before you do so just check on the two essentials:
1 Do you feel certain of success?
2 Your frame of mind. Have you a feeling of doom and gloom or a feeling of
   excitement that you are about to achieve something marvellous?
When you feel quite ready, smoke that last cigarette. Do it alone and do not
smoke it subconciously. Concentrate on every puff, concentrate on the taste
and smell, concentrate on the cancerous fumes going into your lungs,
concentrate on the poisons gunging up your arteries and veins, concentrate
on the nicotine going into your body and, when you put it out, just think
how marvellous it will be not to have to go on doing it. The joy of being
freed from this slavery. It's like coming out of a world of black shadows into
a world of sunshine.

From *The Easy Way to Stop Smoking* by Allen Carr (Penguin 1985)

They now put down the text and try to answer their colleagues' questions on the basis of what they have read. They may have to answer 'I don't know' if the text has not given them any answers to the others' questions.

The reading here is purposeful and communicative. Those who read know that they will have to answer real questions (in contrast to pre-written textbook material) in order to communicate. Clearly if this technique is used more than once it is important to be sure that both halves of the class have a chance to read.

(c) The Ten Tors Expedition: pooling information[13]

In this activity from a book for elementary students different students read different texts in order to complete a task by sharing their information (this is related to the concept of the information gap (see 7.1.2): we will expand on the concept of jigsaw listening (and reading) in 10.5.4).

The students are divided into two groups, A and B. Group A reads the following article:

TEN TORS ENTRY LIMITED TO 2,400

MORE THAN 2,000 young walkers are taking part today and to-morrow in the 24th annual Ten Tors Expedition on Dartmoor.

The massed start at Okehampton Camp provides a spectacular sight as the 2,400 walkers, all aged between 14 and 19, and wearing brightly-coloured safety clothing, set off to cover some of the wildest and most beautiful moorland in the Westcountry. More walkers wanted to enter this year but the number has been restricted to 400 teams of six to protect the countryside and for safety.

The Ten Tors is an adventurous event demanding endurance and team work. The walkers come from a wide variety of organisations with boys aged 15 and 17 covering 45 miles. Young men aged 18 and 19 hike 55 miles and girls walk 35 miles, although some can take longer routes.

Each team has 24-routes to choose from, but they must visit 10 tors in a certain. order and they have to carry enough food to last for the two days as well as their tents and bedding. Times for completing the course can vary widely, but it is expected that the main group will return to the camp by 5 p.m. on Sunday.

Hundreds of Service men and women have given up their weekend to help to run the event. There will also be support from the Dartmoor Rescue Group, the police, the St. John Ambulance Brigade, volunteer doctors, nurses and others.

The expedition is organised by the Army's South West District Headquarters at Bulford Camp. There will also be support from the Royal Navy, the Royal Marines, and the Royal Air Force. A special one-day event is also being run for handicapped people. These will be tackling routes cross country or on army roads with support from volunteer helpers.

---

and answers some simple comprehension questions.

Group B reads a different text and answers simple comprehension questions in the same way. This is the text:

Beaten by Dartmoor

One boy was burned and harsh weather forced more than 450 other youngsters to drop out of the 24th annual Ten Tors expedition on Dartmoor at the weekend.

Ronald Wheeler, aged 15, a member of the Eastbourne Sea Cadets team was burned when a gas cylinder he was using in a tent exploded after his team had set up camp at Rough Tor, near Postbridge.

He was taken by a Wessex helicopter to the Royal Naval Hospital, Plymouth, where he is expected to stay for two days.

A young man, who had been flown on Saturday back to the medical centre at Okehampton Camp, suffered from hypothermia, left the centre yesterday after treatment.

The other casualties were mainly youngsters with blisters and twisted ankles.

The army, which organises the expedition, says the Ten Tors is a test of endurance. Exeter Schools' combined caded force was first home in the 35-mile section, a group from Exeter called Operation Dartmoor was first home in the 35-mile section, and RAF Halton was first home on the 55-mile route.

The class is then divided into pairs with one member of each pair coming from Group A and the other from Group B. They tell each other about their articles and then use their shared information to complete the following task.

E2 Work together to complete this summary.
The Ten Tors Expedition takes place on......................
every............... The competitors walk in teams of
.............people. They wear ....and they must
carry...................................and....................with them.
They walk...........................or 35...........................
according to their age.
In 1983.....................started the course but more than
...............couldn't finish because the......................was
very bad. One boy had to go to hospital by
..................when a gas cylinder.................in his tent.
There were a lot of.................with...................on their
feet an...................ankles. The 'winners' were the
...................combined cadet force, the group called
............................from Exeter, and RAF........................

There are many possible follow-up tasks here; students could write their own newspaper article about the Ten Tors expedition. They could use the information to write an item for the radio news. They could do the same for feats of endurance which are performed in their country.

The three examples here have shown how reading can be used as more than a comprehension question-answering exercise. There are, of course, many other ways of making reading come alive and of getting students interactively involved in the task.

**10.4.4
Reading for
general
understanding**

We will look at three examples of this kind of reading, where students are skimming to 'get the general picture' (see 10.1.3 (c)).

(a) Famous people: matching[14]

In this example from an American English textbook for false beginners students are simply asked to identify the main features of a four-part text.

The teacher could start by asking students the names of film stars/directors that they know about. What do they know about them?

Following this lead-in students are asked to match the names and descriptions on the basis of the reading text.

Read on your own
Famous people from the movies

This woman is a popular actress. Her name is Sonia Braga. She was born in Parana, Brazil. People in other countries know her because of movies like *I Love You, Kiss of the Spider Woman*, and *Gabriela*.

Akira Kurosawa is a great film director. His more well-known films include *Rashomon* and *Ran*. His films are usually about important events in Japan's history.

Joan Collins is originally from England, but she is very popular on American television now, especially in "Dynasty." In that series, she is a rich and beautiful woman – but not a very nice one!

This man is very funny. His name is Eddie Murphy. He's an American comedian and movie star. He is still young (born in 1961), but he already has a movie contract for fifteen million dollars ($15,000,000).

▶ Match the names and the descriptions of these people.

1	Sonia Braga	a)	a director of films
2	Akira Kurosawa	b)	a British actress in a TV series
3	Eddie Murphy	c)	a movie star from South America
4	Joan Collins	d)	a young actor from the United States

When students have compared their answers the teacher can ask them to talk about actors they know in the same way. They can bring their own pictures (from magazines) to class and write a paragraph about the actor concerned. These could then be stuck up on a board for all the students to look at.

(b) The developing world[15]

The following example comes from a textbook for upper intermediate students preparing for the Cambridge First Certificate exam. They are going to write an essay on the topic of hunger, but first they must read the following paragraphs. All they have to do is match the pictures with the correct paragraphs.

GIVE BACK THE LAND

STOP USING MONEY AGAINST THE POOR

PUT FOOD FIRST

CONTROL THE CORPORATIONS

AIM FOR SOCIAL JUSTICE

PARAGRAPH

1 Debt has been crippling the Third World over the last five years. Countries can be forced to sacrifice as much as half their export earnings as repayments on debts to Western banks. And, before the West offers new loans, it insists on drastic cuts in welfare spending which hit the deprived hardest. Debt repayments should never amount to more than ten per cent of a country's export earnings.

2 Hunger only affects the poor — there are no hungry countries, just bigger or smaller numbers of hungry people within countries. The government's commitment to social justice isn't the icing on the cake — it is the cake itself. The only way to end hunger is to reduce poverty and inequality, and make feeding people a priority.

3 Much of the world's cultivable land is owned by people with large farms — particularly in the Americas. Left to itself, this situation will worsen, not get better, since it is the large farmers who can borrow and afford mechanization and fertilizer. Land reform is not only essential for reasons of justice — it also increases food production, since smallholders farm much more efficiently than the big landowners. But sharing out the land will not work if inequality persists elsewhere in society.

4 The world is now a supermarket for the rich world's consumers — and the managers of that supermarket are the multinational agribusiness corporations. These companies control production prices, often holding small farmers under contract for their export crops. This way they can buy harvests at controlled prices while leaving the risks of bad weather and plant disease on the shoulders of the individual farmer.

5 Developing countries are still locked into a farming system created for the benefit of the rich world. Their best land and resources are used to grow cash crops for export rather than food. The trend away from crops for local consumption must be halted and farmers paid more for their harvests.

As a follow-up task (before writing their essays) students could use the information in the paragraphs to make an imaginary speech to the United Nations about world debt. The use of pictures in this way can be very rewarding. Any narrative text can be accompanied by pictures which students have to put in the correct order, for example.

(c) General comprehension: general questions

In all the discussions about reading so far, we have missed out a vital question which students should be asked. It occurs in the following extract, however:[16]

The Ainu people of Japan tell this story.

The Fire Goddess

One day, the Fire Goddess's husband went for a walk and never returned. After many months, the Fire Goddess looked over the world. She saw her husband living with the

out. The Rain Goddess's dress began to burn. She cried, "Please stop. I'm sorry!"

The Fire Goddess stopped the flames. She left the house without her husband.

The husband returned with many gifts, but the Fire Goddess said nothing to him. After that, he stayed at home.

Did you like this story?   ☐yes ☐no
Think of a story about fire or rain.
What is the name of the story? _____

Rain Goddess. She was very angry and went to talk to them.

She said, "Rain Goddess, let us compare our powers. If I lose, you can keep my husband." She took out her fan. It was painted with pictures of sunlight and fire.

The Rain Goddess took out her fan. It was painted with pictures of clouds and rain.

The Fire Goddess shook her fan and sunlight came out. The Rain Goddess became very hot. She shook her fan. Rain came out.

The Fire Goddess shook her fan. Fire came

The fire goddess

The question 'Do you like this story/text?' is important for any reading (or listening) text. It is one of the general questions that can always be asked.

In an article in the *ELT Journal* Michael Scott and his colleagues described a 'standard exercise' which could be used by their students with any reading text (Scott et al. 1984). Working in Brazil they designed a series of questions in Portuguese which could be answered by students about any text they read. The questions were detailed and there were many of them, but their usefulness was assured. Any students, even though their spoken English was very poor, could go to a text in English and tackle it with the help of this general reading 'kit'.

The students that Scott and his colleagues were teaching were involved in English for Special Purposes at university level. But the principle is equally good for general English classes, even where the nationalities are mixed. In the latter case we will have to content ourselves with simple questions in English.

Here are five standard questions for general understanding which aim to achieve the same kind of effect as Scott's standard exercise for students of general English and which can be used with most reading texts:

1 What is the text about?   4 What is the writer's intention?
2 Who was it written by?   5 Do you like it?
3 Who was it written for?

Students can look through a text in pairs and discuss the answers to these questions. The answers are not always obvious. How would students answer the questions, for example, with the following text?[17]

The Church with a missile on top

Where can you find a school with a team called *The Rockets*? Where can you take your children to a Missile Park—full of old guided missiles? And where can you find a church which actually has a missile on top?

The answer is El Paso, an American city of 489,000 inhabitants. This is the centre of the American missile programme, and all kinds of missiles, both nuclear and non-nuclear are tested in the area. Missiles are everywhere in El Paso. People collect them and put them in their gardens. Their ashtrays are made from bits of old missiles, and farmers buy old missiles for their cows to drink water from!

If you live near El Paso, though, life can be a bit frightening! In 1947, for example, a rocket was fired and it flew north. Then, for some reason, it changed direction and flew back over El Paso. 'It made a noise like an express train,' said one old inhabitant of the city. The missile flew over the border and landed in the Mexican town of Juarez. Recently the Americans wanted to simulate a nuclear explosion. They used chemicals to make a mushroom cloud. It looked very realistic, but many people had not been warned about the simulated explosion. They saw the cloud and thought it was the start of World War III!

If you visit the area and feel nervous, please don't worry. You can always relax with a drink at the 'Missile Inn' hotel. The best drinks are in the 'Rocket Bar'.

Reading for general comprehension is a skill that involves absorbing only the main points of the text. The reader is not looking for specific points, but rather for whatever is necessary to get an overall understanding of the text. We have shown three different examples of general comprehension.

10.4.5
Reading for detailed comprehension: information

So far the skills we have asked the students to perform have been of the type 1 kind. We can now look at type 2 skills which concern work that the students do after they have read in one of the ways so far mentioned.

(a) Across Canada: open-ended questions

In 10.4.2 (c) students were asked to complete a chart about the incredible cancer victims Terry Fox and Steve Fonyo. When that has been done the teacher can ask them to look at the text again to answer these questions:

1 Where did Steve Fonyo begin and end his run?
2 Where did Terry Fox begin and end his run?
3 Why did Steve Fonyo stop running at Thunder Bay on November 29?
4 How many differences can you find between Steve Fonyo and Terry Fox?

The students can ask and answer the questions in pairs before the teacher leads feedback and then organises a text-related task of the kind we have mentioned on page 189. Notice that the answers to these questions are not essential for an overview of the text; they are the details which we expect students to be able to access on the second reading, not on the first.

(b) Murder: detailed questions[18]

The teacher might start this lesson by asking what students know or don't know about Sherlock Holmes. If students are unaware of this greatest of all fictional detectives then the teacher might explain something about him.

As a type 1 task students are asked to read the following passage (at the upper intermediate level) to answer the questions *Who was murdered? Who does Inspector Lestrade think did it? What is Sherlock Holmes' opinion of Lestrade's conclusions?*

'An extraordinary case, Holmes,' said Inspector Lestrade, smiling, 'but quite simple, really. We made an arrest immediately.'

'I see,' said Sherlock Holmes, lighting his pipe. 'Tell me about it.'

'Well,' Lestrade began, 'first the people. Old Sir Clarence Forbes married his second wife – the present Lady Forbes – just a year or two ago: very attractive, long dark hair, and young enough to be his daughter. He has a son, too, George, who's 22, and a bit of a disappointment to the old man. Which is why he made this rather strange will.'

Holmes raised his eyebrows. 'Go on.'

'Well, he clearly wants his son to get married and settle down,' continued Lestrade. 'The will says that when he dies half his fortune is to go to his wife, and half to the son – but only if the son is married.'

'And if not?'

'Then it all goes to the wife.' Lestrade paused. 'Well, to cut a long story short, the son is – or was – about to get married. To a local girl called Anna Young. The wedding was to be next month.'

'Was?' asked Sherlock Holmes.

'Yes. This morning Anna Young was found dead – shot through the head – in Lady Forbes' dressing room. The gun was in her hand, and there was a suicide note by the body. It said "Forgive me. I can't live with my guilt any more."'

'And what guilt was that?' Holmes asked.

'I'm coming to that. According to George Forbes, Anna had once had an affair with the family chauffeur – a man called Grimes. And it turns out that Lady Forbes wanted to get all Sir Clarence's fortune for her self. She threatened to tell Sir Clarence about this affair if George didn't cancel the wedding. And there's no doubt that Sir Clarence would have stopped the wedding if he had known.'

'And the chauffeur?'

'Oh, he's out of it. He was out in the car all morning and didn't return till after lunch. Anyway, nowadays he's more interested in Lady Forbes – and she apparently doesn't discourage him. There was a bit of trouble between him and George the other day. They had a quarrel, and Grimes hit George and broke his glasses. Sir Clarence is out of it too – he was out in the car

with Grimes when the murder took place.'

'And why,' asked Holmes, 'do you say it was murder and not suicide?'

'Well for one thing the gun was in the dead girl's right hand, and we know she was left-handed. But the big mistake was the suicide note. We checked the handwriting, and do you know whose writing it was? Lady Forbes'! Of all the stupid mistakes to make.'

'So who have you arrested?'

'Lady Forbes! Who else? She denies everything, of course. She claims that she heard the shot while she was in the bath – next to the dressing room – and that she put a towel round her and rushed out to find Anna on the floor. But she's guilty, all right. She thought her threat to tell Sir Clarence wouldn't work, and decided to stop the wedding properly – by killing Anna Young. She had plenty of time to fake the suicide, too.'

'Hmm,' said Holmes. 'Tell me, Lestrade. Am I right in thinking that Anna Young was dark-haired?'

'Why, yes,' replied Lestrade, in a surprised voice. 'But – how did you know that? That's got nothing to do with . . .'

'I'm afraid, my friend,' said Holmes, 'that you've arrested the wrong person.'

(With apologies to Sir Arthur Conan Doyle)

The object of this reading activity is for students to solve the murder and help Holmes to prove Lestrade wrong. But in order to do so they need to understand the text in detail. Here are questions to help them do it.

1 a) Explain the terms of Sir Clarence Forbes' will.
  b) Why did he make his will like this?

2 a) What was Anna Young's secret?
  b Why did she want it to remain a secret?
  c) Why did Lady Forbes not want it to remain a secret?

3 a) What two indications were there that Anna's death had been suicide?
  b) What two reasons did Lestrade have for deciding that her death had in fact been murder?

4 a) According to Lestrade, what motive did Lady Forbes have for murdering Anna?
  b) Can you see a weakness in his reasoning?

5 What alibis did the other three suspects have?

6 Complete the following sentences
  a Lestrade accused Lady Forbes . . .
  b) Lady Forbes denied . . .
  c) Lady Forbes threatened . . .
  d) Lady Forbes claimed . . .

7 Why was Lestrade surprised by Sherlock Holmes' questions about the dark hair? Give two reasons.

Who was the murderer? This activity can be pursued by students working in detection teams and should provide considerable amusement for them.

Most texts lend themselves to detailed comprehension work. It can give students a valuable opportunity to study written English in detail and thus learn more about the topic and about how language is used. The same is true of the next category of reading skills.

10.4.6 Reading for detailed comprehension: function and discourse

We have said that it is important for students to understand the way in which texts are structured, and to recognise the functions that are being performed. Three examples will show how this can be done and how students can be made aware of the discourse structure that goes into writing – and which they must be able to decode if they wish to understand the text fully.

(a) Coelacanths: context questions

In this example students are asked to recognise the function of cohesive devices in a text much as we saw in 7.2.3. The idea is to train them to recognise the way in which such devices refer to information elsewhere in the text.

The students have read the following text for the performance of type 1 skills (after an appropriate lead-in, etc.):

They are then asked to explain what the following words in the text refer to:

1	they	(l.3)	5	them	(l.7)
2	them	(l.4)	6	they	(l.7)
3	its	(l.4)	7	its	(l.8)
4	this	(l.6)	8	we	(l.9)

> **Coelacanths** are some of the weirdest creatures on this earth - or at least in the sea, for they are big ugly fish. They first inhabited the planet over four million years ago, making them its oldest living beings. Coelacanths are only found in the Indian Ocean at quite extraordinary depths. This means that few people have actually seen them. Still, they provide the world's inhabitants with one of its oldest living species and a throwback to a time long before we occupied the planet.

Notice that whereas numbers 1–7 refer back to things within the text, item 8 refers out to the reader's understanding of who 'we' are.

(b) Polenta: identifying function

In the following exercise students are asked to recognise the writing functions and see how the same function can be performed with two distinct language types.

Students work with type 1 skills on the following recipe:

POLENTA

Polenta is finely ground Indian corn meal; it makes a filling but excellent dish and this is the recipe as it is cooked by northern Italians with large families to feed.

1 lb of polenta will feed 6 hungry people. First prepare a very large heavy pan full of boiling salted water; when the water boils pour in the polenta, little by little, stirring all the time to eliminate lumps and adding more salt and pepper. It will take about 30 minutes to cook, and when ready is the consistency of a thick purée (rather like a purée of dried peas) and is poured out on to a very large wooden board, where it should form a layer about a quarter of an inch thick. Over it is poured a hot and rich tomato or meat sauce (see sauce bolognese for spaghetti), which is topped with grated Parmesan cheese. The board is placed in the centre of the table and everybody helps himself. Whatever is left over is trimmed into squares about the size of a piece of toast, and grilled over a very slow charcoal fire; the top crust of sauce and cheese remains undisturbed and the under side, being nearest the heat, is deliciously browned.

They are then asked to do the following exercise:

Re-write the recipe for Polenta by filling in the blanks:

Prepare _____ .
Pour _____ . Stir _____ .
Add _____ . Cook for _____ .
Pour onto _____ . Pour _____ . Top with
_____ . Trim what is left _____ . Grill
_____ .

209

The original recipe is a mixture of instructions using imperative forms ('First prepare a very large heavy pan . . .') and descriptions of the procedure using passive forms ('(it) is poured out onto a very large wooden board.'). This re-write asks students to convert the whole text into a series of instructions, thereby changing some of the functional value of parts of the text, but not its underlying aim. The exercise is revealing about the use of these two language forms and the uses to which they are being put.

Two text-related tasks suggest themselves here. The first is for the students to write a recipe for one of their favourite dishes in English, and the other is to make Polenta.

(c) Mean people: identifying paragraph structure [19]

The upper-intermediate material in this example is designed to make students aware of how paragraphs start with topic sentences, and by asking students to match different paragraphs with their topic sentences it brings home that relationship. After students have discussed various human vices, partly through looking at a cartoon strip, they are asked to read the following text:

1.

We all know about Paul Getty I, the richest man in the world. He's the one who, in his 72-bedroomed country mansion, used to have a pay-phone for his guests. He's also the one who refused to pay the ransom for the release of Paul Getty III, his grandson, until the poor boy's ear was cut off — and even then, the money paid was a loan to Paul Getty II at an interest rate of four per cent.

2.

A magazine recently asked its readers to write in with their tales of miserliness done to or by them. Obviously, this is a subject close to many people's hearts. Many readers said they could hardly bear to remember the tight-fisted habits of their parents, while others reported that years of stinginess had either broken up their marriages or had made their lives a misery.

3.

One man bought his wife a dustpan for a Christmas present. When his workmates asked him about the brush to go with it, he replied, 'Oh, she's getting that for her birthday.'

4.

Every year on her birthday her husband would give her the same birthday card, until one year she hit upon the idea of burning it (one wonders what took her so long). What did her husband do? He bought the cheapest substitute he could find, which happened to be a card for belated birthday greetings, so his wife suffered the added insult of receiving the card late.

5.

There's the woman who for birthdays gives delightful home-made cards, with the message written on a separate piece of paper. With the card she'll enclose a short note asking for the card back in a few days' time.

6.

His wife wrote, 'He's always charging the family for the things he does around the house. He grows vegetables in the back garden, but I have to pay for them out of my house-keeping money. When he gives our daughter a lift to work, he'll ask her for the bus fare and a little bit more because it's a door-to-door service.'

7.

Putting out the pilot light on gas cookers and fires is commonplace. Some people refuse to let others open the freezer without their permission. One man unashamedly wrote in to say how he cuts down on his heating bill. His wife never has the central heating on during the day while he's out at work because he's told her that gas is twice as expensive in the day-time — so the heating conveniently comes on at six o'clock in time for his return.

8.

You might marvel at the man — a Frenchman at that — who ordered half a bottle of wine and eight glasses, or shake your head at the couple who boasted they could make a tin of beans last a week, but there is something very upsetting about putting bacon rashers end to end so that each portion can be measured to the nearest millimetre.

9.

She has decreed that family and friends must limit themselves to three sheets of paper per visit to the lavatory.

10.

There were tales of people who scrape salt from dirty plates back into the salt-cellar, retrieve cloves from eaten apple pies, save lemon slices from dirty glasses and preserve them in water to be re-used later, or put used paper tissues to dry on the radiator. Life with a Scrooge is not a lot of fun.

Their task is as follows:

2 The *topic sentences* (in this case, the first sentence of each paragraph) have been removed. They are listed here. Match them with the correct paragraph. Write the corresponding paragraph number in the box by the topic sentence.

☐ a. When it comes to counting the pennies, how about this charming man?

☐ b. Many of the stories were to do with the giving of presents.

☐ c. Incidentally, the woman who used to measure the bacon so carefully, rations other aspects of her family's life.

☐ d. The meanness of the rich is legendary.

☐ e. One woman's attempts to reform her husband's meanness were a complete failure.

☐ f. Common ideas of hospitality do not inhibit mean people, then, and nor do considerations of hygiene.

☐ g. Fuel economies are a wide-spread form of penny-pinching.

☐ h. Stories about stinginess over food were plenty.

☐ i. But the meanness of more humble people is no less breathtaking.

☐ j. Giving with one hand and taking with the other is a common trick.

The teacher can go on to show the typical relationship between topic sentences and those that follow – which tend to expand or exemplify the opening line(s).

As a follow-up task students can choose one of the people from the article and create dialogues about situations they find themselves in.

10.5 Listening material

The teaching of listening skills will follow the methodological model in 10.3 in the same way as for the teaching of reading skills. But training students in listening skills presents problems for both teacher and student which are not found with reading material.

Listening as a skill certainly shares many similarities with reading, but the differences are there, too. Most importantly, the text itself is different.

A written text is static. It can be consumed at the speed of the reader, and read again and again. Not so spoken text: if it is on audio or video tape it can certainly be repeated, but it still happens at its speed, not the listener's. Of course in conversation a listener can ask the speaker to repeat what is being said, but the same is not true of a lecture you are listening to, or the radio programme that flashes past.

Spoken language differs markedly from written text. Most people when they write do so with an eye to grammatical correctness. A good piece of writing develops an argument or a point of view (or story, etc.) logically because the writer is aware of the need for clarity (see 5.6). Introductory sentences begin paragraphs and one sentence is finished before the other is begun. Even more importantly, writers can amend, re-draft and correct what they have written before releasing their final version.

We can compare this idealised view of writing with a piece of natural dialogue, even though the setting is structured. In this extract[20] an actress in a popular British soap opera is being interviewed about what it feels like to be constantly in the public eye.

Interviewer: Do ... has this ever ... does this cause you any any problems? I mean do you get, do you get a lot of attention that you don't want from the media?

Sue: Um yeah, you know, sort of knocking on my door, eight o'clock in the morning saying er ... tell you a funny story ... I mean I haven't had a lot of hassle from the press.

Both speakers seem to be having trouble – or at least to be unsure of what they are trying to say, and yet on tape their conversation is, perhaps surprisingly, understandable. It is when you read what is actually said that it looks so messy! In a foreign language, however, some of the speech phenomena demonstrated here can act as a barrier to comprehension. What are the speech phenomena in this short extract?

The interviewer starts by trying to ask a question which he then quickly decides to reformulate. Perhaps he wanted to ask 'Do the media ...?' but then changes his mind to ask about past experiences before changing his mind again to ask about the general present rather than the past. On two occasions he repeats words or phrases unnecessarily ('any ... any', 'do you get, do you get') before finally getting a coherent question out. Such repetition is redundant.

Sue Tully, the actress, behaves in a similar fashion. She starts off by using common hesitation devices – to give herself thinking time, perhaps – ('Um yeah, you know ..') then she starts to speak almost in note form before deciding to tell a story, an idea which she quickly abandons before putting a view which appears to contradict her first response to the question. As the interview progressed, however, she did develop a coherent attitude to the question, telling a funny story and complaining that while she didn't mind media attention she objected to them harassing her family and friends.

All these speech phenomena, *hesitation*, *reformulation*, *redundancy*, and *topic change* are a natural part of spontaneous speech. Much of this behaviour seems to show the speaker 're-drafting' what they are going to say rather in the same way as a writer does. The difference is that we don't have to read the writer's first drafts!

It is part of our job when training students in listening skills to help them to disregard these phenomena and to concentrate instead on the main message of what is being said. They do this in their own language, and are not sidetracked by speech phenomena – at least as far as comprehension is concerned. We must make sure they can do the same in English, although clearly in acceptable stages. We would not play the Sue Tully interview to our beginners' class with any confidence that they would understand it! (see 10.2.2).

The major problem that teachers and students encounter when tackling listening material, however, is not these speech phenomena, but rather the actual way in which listening material is presented to students. The most common form of doing this is through the use of the tape recorder. There are many good reasons for this: there is no limit to the variety of voices that tapes can contain. Tapes are small, and modern cassette players are easily portable. There is more and more good taped material available for students of English.

Using tape recorders can be a nerve-racking experience, however. In the first place it is hardly natural for thirty or forty people to sit in silence listening to a tape, especially when the people in the back row find it difficult to hear. Students often feel very threatened in this situation particularly since, if they begin not to understand what they are hearing, they gradually lose the thread, while the tape continues on relentlessly. And of course disembodied voices in a foreign language are much more difficult to cope with – as anyone who has used a telephone in another language they are not especially competent in will tell you.

Some of these drawbacks (though not all) can be answered through the use of video tapes (see 10.5.1) but audio tapes are still the most common way of giving students listening practice. Not only are they cheaper and more portable, but they also focus the students' attention exclusively on spoken English – rather than on visual contact, gesture, surrounding events, etc.

Many objections to the use of listening material are met, also, by individual access to tape recorders where there is teacher supervision – for example in a language laboratory or in a learning centre. The number of schools and institutes that have such facilities is limited, however.

The difficulties inherent in the use of listening material in the classroom lead us to a number of conclusions about how such material should be handled.

(a) Lead-in

We must be sure to give as clear a lead-in as possible, because the students' expectations are vital here. If they have some idea of what is coming they are less likely to put a 'panic barrier' between themselves and the tape recorder. It is vital, too, that they should be interested in what they are going to hear since they are unlikely to be very successful without the commitment that such interest will bring.

(b) The use of visual material

It is often extremely useful to give students a visual setting for the tape they are going to listen to, some pictorial back-up that will create expectations and reassure the listeners.

(c) Listening tasks

It is important that listening tasks should be designed to help students to listen more effectively rather than as traps for them to fall into. When students look at the tasks they have to complete before listening to a tape, they should be able to predict the content of what they are going to hear – at least in part.

(d) The equipment

It is important to make sure that both machine and tape are in good condition before taking them into class. Nothing is more demoralising than a tape that cannot be understood because of poor quality. Tapes can become damaged, and tape recorders can have poor speakers or tone controls.

In 10.5.2 to 10.5.7 we will look at a number of different types of listening material using a variety of listening tasks. We will look at *listening with video, listening to confirm expectations, listening to extract specific information, listening for communicative tasks, listening for general understanding,* and *listening for detail (information and discourse structure).*

10.5.1
Listening with
video[21]

Video tapes have many of the problems we have already discussed for audio tapes, but of course the major advantage is that students can (sometimes) see people speaking and can have a visual context for what is being said.

The principles for using video are very much the same as those for using listening, and there is an especial need for teachers to set motivating and challenging tasks. This is partly due to the very nature of video material which is, after all, so like television. Students, like all of us, see television as a form of relaxation, yet teachers are trying to use it as a positive learning aid. The problem is not insurmountable and television has a long and respectable history in first language education, but it is worth bearing in mind when setting viewing tasks.

Apart from general principles, however, there are some video-specific techniques that we can mention here:

(a) Silent viewing

One of the commonest techniques with video material is silent viewing. This acts as a powerful predictive exercise. The teacher plays the video tape with the sound turned off. The students speculate about what the characters are saying. Only then do they watch the tape with sound to check whether their predictions are right.

(b) Freeze frame

The teacher might create expectations by freezing a frame on the screen. The students can predict what the characters will say.

(c) Sound only

Video is sometimes used very much like audio tape. Students listen to the sound only (the teacher can turn the contrast down or cover the screen with cardboard). Their listening task may be to say where the conversation is taking place and who the speakers are, for example. Then they watch the extract to see if they were right.

(d) Jigsaw viewing

We have already seen jigsaw reading in action (10.4.3) and we will see its use with listening material (see 10.5.4). With video, one technique is to let half the class watch without sound and the other half hear without a picture. They can then compare notes and build a complete picture of what happened before watching the video with both picture and sound. A variation of this[22] is for half the students to sit with their backs to the screen while the other half tells them what is happening while the video is being shown. When the first half then watch the video they can see how accurately it has been described to them.

Video material can contextualise listening material in a very beneficial way. There is still a place for audio cassettes, however. They provide a focus for the spoken language without the distractions that pictures can sometimes bring.

10.5.2
Listening to
confirm
expectations

Just as we can ask students to read to confirm expectations (see 10.4.1) so we can ask students to listen for the same reason. The technique has the same advantages for listening as it has for reading: the students' expectations and interest are aroused, and they have a definite purpose for listening.

(a) The Empire State Building

In 10.4.1 we saw how a text about the Empire State Building could be used for reading to confirm expectations: the teacher elicited information from the students about what they knew/didn't know/weren't sure of concerning this building.

In this example the teacher would start in exactly the same way, using the same procedure to elicit information from students. The text used in 10.4.1 (a) can serve as a model for a talk the teacher could give and which would serve as a listening text. The teacher would modify the original written version so that it would sound more like a real talk. It could be done like this:

Now you all know about New York, don't you? It's on the east coast of the States .. at the mouth of the Hudson River actually .. and its five boroughs have a population of .. of .. er .. seventeen million people. That's right! Seventeen million people ......

The teacher feedback and text-related task can be the same as in 10.4.1 (a).

(b) EastEnders[23]

In this activity for upper intermediate classes teacher and students have been discussing soap operas. Students have told each other which ones are most popular in their country and whether they like them. In groups they look at a photographic still from a soap opera and speculate on what it might be about. Then, probably again in groups, they make a list of the topics which soap operas tend to deal with.

The teacher now tells the students that they are going to listen to the first half of an interview with Sue Tully who acts in Britain's most popular soap opera, *EastEnders*. She is going to describe the programme. The students have to answer the following questions:

1 Look at your list of soap opera topics. Which of them does Sue Tully mention? Which of them does she not mention?
2 What was the big storyline in the first year of *EastEnders*?

This is what the students hear:

File Two. EastEnder, Part One.

Sue: Basically, it's um it's life in the East End of London i.e. um the Cockney, the Cockney way of life but that isn't what, you know, the most important thing about the programme; that isn't the the reason for its success. The reason for its success is it deals with social . . . social problems that other soap operas have never dealt with before. I mean our aim isn't to shock but it's just that we can't, we believed that we couldn't do a realistic situation drama about the East End without incorporating topics like drugs, homosexuality, um divorce, adultery all those things that other soap operas have only skimmed on or done . . .
Interviewer: Prison . .
Sue: . . . very nicely . . .
Interviewer: . . . prison and breaking the law
Sue: Prison, nervous breakdowns – I mean it's not just all gloom and doom . . . um . . . There is a lot of humour um and there is a lot of love and warmth in the programme as well; er so really if anyone says what is EastEnders about? it's not about Cockneys, I mean, because the situations that we deal with are characteristic of a lot of, um, inner city communities all over Britain, and I'm sure, in other cities in the world. But it's just that we we cover them with an edge on how a Cockney and how a Cockney community reacts and deals with those problems.
Interviewer: What part do you play?
Sue: I play um a girl called Michelle Fowler; well no, Michelle Holloway – she got married last year. Um she was Michelle Holloway to start with, she was in a family. She lived in the same house with her mother and father and her grand . . . grandmother. The son run away and then the mother had another baby and then she got pregnant by the local landlord – this is Michelle got pregnant, not my mum – um by the landlord of the local pub, er, which nobody knows about; no one knows who the father is – that was the big storyline um in the first year. And after she had the baby she married a a local lad who she'd known for a few years.
Interviewer: Is she at all like you?
Sue: Um, she speaks like me, that's where it ends. No she's not at all like me; I mean, my circumstances are . . . if, if maybe if I hadn't gone into acting there probably would have been more similarities but because my life is changed and my circumstances have changed so much over the past couple of years, um, no, there are . . . the only similarities between me and Michelle is our accent.
Interviewer: Do you like her?
Sue: Yeah I like her. I think she's very brave, very courageous to have the baby and very strong to keep the secret of who the father is because um the consequences of everyone knowing who the father was would just be so catasroph . . . catastro . . . blblblbler er strophic . . . stropha . . .
Interviewer: Cata-something or other
Sue: I'm such a good speaker! Yeah, cata-something or other; um, so she's got the strength to keep such a big secret with her and she she believes that she'll keep it with her for the rest of her life.

They can now compare their lists with Sue Tully's. They should do this in groups before the teacher leads feedback.

The students will now be asked to listen to the tape again to find out more about Michelle's family and background. Then they can move on to a follow-up task. One possibility is to give them some information about a fictitious family situation and ask them to create their own soap opera scenes, like this:

Follow-up: Write your own 'soap opera'

6 Kevin runs a pub in the country, but he has problems.

- Kevin's wife has just given up smoking and shouts at him all day.
- Kevin's daughter is having an affair with his wife's best friend's husband.
- Kevin's son Michael has just got a place at university but he doesn't want to go; the police have just arrested him for shoplifting.
- the doctor has told Kevin that he must take a rest.

Kevin is suddenly taken ill . . .

Give the soap opera a name and then conduct a script conference in which you decide what happens to each of the characters mentioned here in the next two episodes.

By making their own list and comparing it with Sue Tully's students have not only created their own expectations, but they have become personally involved in the act of listening; do their perceptions of soap operas match her description?

When students listen to confirm expectations they have a clear view of what it is they are going to listen to. This helps them to cope with the material and achieve success.

**10.5.3
Listening to extract specific information**

The skill of listening to extract information is as important as it is for reading. Thanks to the speech phenomena we mentioned in 10.5 and the other difficulties associated with tape recorder use it can be extremely difficult.

The two examples we are going to look at both involve filling in charts, but there is no reason, of course, why other question types should not be used.

(a) Weather forecast[24]

This first example is an exercise in listening to extract specific information at its most simple and direct. Students are told that they are going to listen to a weather forecast. They are then given this listening task:

The teacher will make sure that they understand the meaning of the words 'cold, cool, raining, drizzle' and that they know what 'temperature' and 'outlook for tomorrow' mean. Students will be reminded that all they have to do to complete the task is to note which of the words and numbers written in front of them appear on the tape. This is what they hear:

3 ⌨ LISTENING

Listen and note the weather words and temperatures you hear.

WEATHER REPORT

TODAY'S WEATHER:
cold   cool   dry   raining   drizzle

TEMPERATURE (°C):
0   2   4   6   8   10

OUTLOOK FOR TOMORROW:
foggy   cloudy   sunny   windy

TEMPERATURE (°C):
0   2   4   6   8   10

Good afternoon from the Weather Centre. This is the report on the weather for today at 14.00 hours. It is cool and mainly dry but with some drizzle in places. There is a ground temperature of 4°Celsius. The outlook for tomorrow. Temperatures will fall to about 2°Celsius. The day will be mainly cloudy but with some sunny periods. Thank you for calling the weather line.

The task is simple but the listening extract itself is fairly complex with some difficult constructions and some extra vocabulary. But notice that the extraction of the specific information (in this case the actual words and figures) is easily achievable and helps to train students in this type of listening skill.

In the material from which this extract comes, students go on to describe the weather in different cities using the vocabulary here. Another possibility would be to ask them to write their own weather forecast.

(b) The road accident[25]

This listening material is for lower intermediate students. They are going to hear three different versions of a road accident and they must work out what actually happened.

To start with, the students are shown the following map and charts:

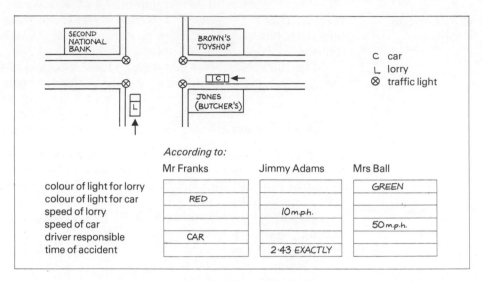

According to:	Mr Franks	Jimmy Adams	Mrs Ball
colour of light for lorry			GREEN
colour of light for car	RED		
speed of lorry		10 m.p.h.	
speed of car			50 m.p.h.
driver responsible	CAR		
time of accident		2·43 EXACTLY	

The teacher explains that there has been an accident, and makes sure that the students understand the information that they have to listen for (e.g. driver responsible/time of accident, etc.). Notice that some of the entries have already been made; this will help the students since they have less detail to concentrate on.

The students hear three short conversations. Here are the first two:

Conversation 1

POLICEMAN: Now, Mr Franks. I'd just like to read your statement back to you and then you can sign it.

MR FRANKS: Fine.

POLICEMAN: 'I was standing in front of the Second National Bank building at about 2.40 p.m. I saw a small red car approaching the junction of Churchill Avenue and York Road. It was coming towards me along Churchill Avenue at about 40 miles per hour. The traffic lights on York Road changed to green and a delivery lorry began to move forward at about 5 m.p.h. The driver of the car didn't see that his traffic light had changed from amber to red and ran into the side of the lorry.'

MR FRANKS: That's correct. I'll sign it.

Conversation 2

POLICEMAN: Now, Jimmy, did you get a good view of the accident?

JIMMY: Oh, yes. I was standing outside Brown's toyshop and I saw it all quite clearly.

POLICEMAN: Do you know what time it was?

JIMMY: Yes, I checked my watch. It's a quartz watch, you know. It was 2.43 exactly.

POLICEMAN: Good. Now, how fast was the delivery lorry moving?

JIMMY: Well, quite slowly – about 10 miles an hour. It was coming up York Road and I suppose the driver realised the lights were going to change. But they were still red when he went over them.

POLICEMAN: I see. What about the car?

JIMMY: It was a red Volkswagen. It was coming along Churchill Avenue at about 30 miles per hour. The driver braked when he saw the lorry crossing the Avenue.

POLICEMAN: Did you see what colour his traffic light was?

JIMMY: Yes, it changed to amber just before he crossed it.

During the feedback session the teacher can check with the students that the charts have been filled in correctly as a result of the three conversations. As a follow-up task students can be asked to work in groups in which they have to write the policeman's report to his superior about what he thinks really happened. This will involve the students in a discussion of the three different accounts after which they will have to reach a consensus before writing the report.

Of course this material could also be used for jigsaw listening (see 10.5.4 (c)).

| 10.5.4 Listening for communicative tasks | The three examples in this section ask students to listen in order to perform some kind of communicative task which is as much like real life as possible (given the artificial nature of listening in the classroom), and which, in the third example, involves students working together to solve a problem. |

(a) Filling in forms

The simplest kind of listening material of this kind involves filling in forms of one kind or another. Teachers and their colleagues can easily record their own dialogues for this as in the following example for beginners.

The students might be shown a picture of a woman going into a parachute club to register as a new member – or some other place where people sign up for something. Now they are shown the following chart:

```
PENTONVILLE PARACHUTE CLUB

Last name:  _____
First names: _____
Address:  _____
          _____
Telephone:_____
Age:      _____
```

They are told to listen to the tape and complete it with information they hear. The dialogue is on page 220.

Woman: Hello. What's your name?

Mattie: Mattie Schwartzenhof.

Woman: Oh right. Could you spell that, please?

Mattie: Of course. M-A-T-T-

Woman: No, your surname. Schwatz ... er ..

Mattie: Oh. OK. S-C-H- ...

Woman: Please ... er ... Write it down here?

Mattie: Sure.

Woman: Thanks. What's your address?

Mattie: In Miami or in London?

Woman: Oh, here in London, please.

Mattie: OK. That's 24 Kilburn Road.

Woman: And your phone number here in London?

Mattie: 071-657-7573

Woman: OK, and how old are you?

Mattie: Well, let's say 32.

Woman: OK. Well, thanks very much Ms Schwar .. Schwartz .. er

Mattie: Call me Mattie.

Woman: Phew. Thanks Mattie!

When the teacher and students have checked that they have filled in the chart correctly they can organise a follow-up task in which students interview each other to fill in similar personal details. To make it more fun the teacher can prepare a series of role cards so that students are not repeating information about themselves which they have already used in smaller chunks for language practice.

(b) Directions[26]

Understanding directions is clearly a vital skill and in this example at the elementary level students have to listen to the tape in order to find a spot on a map.

Students are involved in a nine-part murder mystery and they start by recapping the story. Then they look at the picture. What can they see? They discuss who the person is and where she is.

Listening

Murder at Walton Hall: a radio drama in 9 parts

The story so far... Inspector Wade and Sergeant Pride have visited Walton Hall to ask questions about the murder of Mrs Walton. Mrs Walton was poisoned. Bruce Carter, Sally Walton's boyfriend, has accused Anne, the maid, of Mrs Walton's murder.
Part 3: A Telephone Call

1

Study the map. Now listen to the cassette and put a cross (X) where you think Stan's house is.

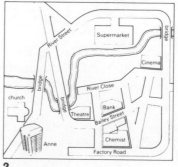

2

Using the map in exercise 1 have phone conversations in which student **A** rings up student **B** and asks for directions. Mark **B**'s house on the map.

Now the teacher asks the students to look at the map. They must realise that Anne is in the phone box and they must try and find out where Stan's house is. This is what they hear:

ANNOUNCER:	Murder at Walton Hall.
ANNOUNCER:	Part 3. A Telephone Call.
STAN:	377023. Hello.
ANNE:	Hello, Stan. It's me. Anne.
STAN:	Anne?
ANNE:	Yes, Stan, it's me!
STAN:	Well. . . hello.
ANNE:	Can I come and see you?
STAN:	What, now?
ANNE:	Yes, now. I've got to talk to you.
STAN:	But you've never been to my house before.
ANNE:	I know. But I've got to talk to you.
STAN:	What about?
ANNE:	I can't talk on the phone. Can I come over? Please!
STAN:	All right. All right. You'd better come.
ANNE:	Oh thanks, Stan. How do I get to your house?
STAN:	Where are you now?
ANNE:	At a phone booth next to the bridge — there's a church opposite.
STAN:	OK. Right, now listen. Go across the bridge and keep going until you reach the crossroads. Take the first turning on your right and cross the second bridge. OK so far?
ANNE:	Yes. Yes, I think so.
STAN:	So you're over the second bridge. Go down the second turning on your left until you get to River Close. Then turn right and go along River Close for about 50 metres and it's on your right, opposite the cinema.
ANNE:	So it's first on the right. . . over the bridge. . . second right.
STAN:	No, no, no. First right, second left. . . *left*. Hello? Anne? Can you hear me, Anne? Are you there?

(The tapescript here omits the sounds of an approaching car and the clear evidence that Anne has been interrupted – that's why she doesn't finish the conversation.)

The students see if they agree where Stan's house is. The teacher can then ask students what they think has happened to Anne and why. As a follow-up task they can have similar phone conversations in which one student gives directions and the other has to guess where the location is. Once again the students can check each others' maps to see if they have the same information. The teacher can help if necessary.

(c) Jigsaw listening[27]

Jigsaw listening is the term popularised by Marion Geddes and Gill Sturtridge[28] to describe an activity in which different students get different information from different listening passages which they then have to share in order to perform some kind of task. In other words three students may each listen to a taped conversation. The conversation they listen to is different in each case (each person listens to only one conversation) thus giving each student a different piece of the 'jigsaw'. The students then join together to use their 'pieces' to put the jigsaw together. In many ways the idea is similar to the story construction activities we looked at in 8.1.4(c) and 8.2.3(b) except that here the original input comes from listening material, not pictures or written sentences.

In this example, called 'The meeting' students are told that there is to be a business meeting in Birmingham next week that four men are going to attend. Some of them will be travelling by train.

The class is then divided into three groups. Each group is going to hear one telephone conversation in which two of the men discuss arrangements for the meeting. Using this information they should answer the following two questions and fill in the following chart using information from the railway timetable that is given to them:

1 When *exactly* is the meeting?
2 Where *exactly* will the meeting be?

NAME	Time of departure	Place	Time of arrival	Place
1 2 3 4				

WEEKDAY TIMETABLES			
		MANCHESTER	08.10
LONDON (Euston)	09.10	Stoke-on-Trent	09.42
Watford	09.26	Stafford	10.19
Coventry	10.17	Wolverhampton	10.39
BIRMINGHAM (New St)	10.45	BIRMINGHAM (New St)	10.59

These are the three conversations that the groups hear:

Conversation 1

BRADWELL: 340 1148. Jack Bradwell speaking.
WHITE: Oh hello Jack. It's Don. Don White here.
BRADWELL: Oh hello Don. How are things up in Birmingham?
WHITE: Oh not too bad. Listen ... I'm just phoning about the meeting. It's next Thursday.
BRADWELL: Aha ... yes, yes. I've got my diary here, let's have a look. Er ... yes, next Thursday the 14th.
WHITE: That's right. Now it'll be here in Birmingham at 11.15 on Thursday in the Rose Hotel.
BRADWELL: Good. Let's see, there's a train leaving just after 9 o'clock. I'll get that. That'll give me thirty minutes to get from the station to the hotel. Where is the Rose Hotel by the way? Is it the one opposite the park?
WHITE: Oh no ... that's the Red Rose restaurant. Don't go there. No, the Rose Hotel is just around the corner from my office here. it's opposite the library.
BRADWELL: Right. See you on Thursday. Bye Don.
WHITE: OK. Bye Jack.

Conversation 2

STEVENS: Hello. Tony Stevens speaking.

WHITE: Oh hello Tony. It's Don White here. How are you?

STEVENS: Oh hello Don ... fine ... fine. What's the weather like in Birmingham?

WHITE: Oh not too bad. Now look Tony, it's about the meeting next Thursday here.

STEVENS: Ah yes ... yes ... it's for 11.15 isn't it?

WHITE: That's right. Now it's at the Rose Hotel at a quarter past eleven. Now you know where it is don't you?

STEVENS: Oh yes ... of course I know the Rose. Right. Thursday the 14th at 11.15 at the Rose. I'll catch the 10.17 from here and that gets in around 10.45.

WHITE: Right ... OK. Now listen, look out for Jack Bradwell ... He's coming up on the same train from London.

STEVENS: Right. I'll see him on the train then.

WHITE: Oh there's just one more thing Tony. Can you telephone Bob Gordon for me and make sure he knows where and when to come?

STEVENS: Of course I'll do that now. Oh, by the way, I'm just going off on a business trip so you won't be able to contact me again before next Thursday.

WHITE: All right. Well I think everything's all right.

STEVENS: Fine. I'll ring Bob Gordon now. See you in Birmingham on Thursday. Bye.

WHITE: OK, yeah, thanks. Cheers Tony.

Conversation 3

GORDON: Bob Gordon speaking.

STEVENS: Hello Bob. It's Tony Stevens here. How are things?

GORDON: Fine. How about you?

STEVENS: Oh not so bad. Listen, I wanted to talk to you Bob about next Thursday. I hope you haven't forgotten.

GORDON: No ... no. I've got it in my diary ... just looking it up. Thursday the 14th ... meeting in Birmingham. Don't know when or where though.

STEVENS: Right, well Don White asked me to tell you. It's in Birmingham at a quarter past eleven in the Rose.

GORDON: D'you mean the Rose Hotel or the Red Rose restaurant opposite the park?

STEVENS: The one opposite the park. I've never heard of the Rose Hotel. Er ... now you've got the time right? 11.15. OK?

GORDON: Yeah ... fine. 11.15. I may be a few minutes late. There's a train from here at 8.10. I'll take that one. Which train are you getting?

STEVENS: I'm catching the 10.17. It gets in at about 10.45.

GORDON: OK. See you Thursday then. Cheers Tony.

STEVENS: Bye Bob.

In each group the students have now filled in their table as far as possible and they will have listened for the answers to the questions. The teacher will have stressed that they must find out when and where *exactly* the meeting is to be.

The teacher then rearranges the class. A student is taken from each group and now forms part of a new group of three. The whole class is divided up into groups of three in this way, so that each student comes from one of the original groups. In each new group of three each student will have listened to a different conversation. They are then given the following 'discussion stage' questions:

DISCUSSION STAGE

1 Find out from the other groups the names of the other people attending the meeting. Complete the table.
2 Check with the other groups that everyone knows when the meeting is and *exactly* where it is.
3 Who told each person where the meeting is?
4 If there are any problems what do you think will happen?

Clearly there will be problems when the students come to question 2 if they are alert. In the third conversation Stevens told Gordon that the meeting was to be in the Red Rose restaurant whereas both White and Bradwell are going to meet at the Rose Hotel. Students can then discuss what they think will happen: will Bradwell meet Stevens on the train and correct Stevens's mistake? What will Gordon do if he arrives at the Red Rose restaurant and finds no one there?

'The meeting', then, works as a listening exercise: students listen for the answer to two questions in order to fill in a table/chart (which we suggested was a useful and realistic skill). But the jigsaw activity is also communicative in the sense that students communicate information to each other as a result of what they have heard.

Getting three different groups using three different tape recorders may, of course, cause difficulty. We will look at the use of tape recorders in 10.5.8.

Exercises that involve the students in doing something with what they hear (such as the four examples above) are extremely beneficial because they reflect real listening and are highly motivating.

10.5.5
Listening for general understanding

In the following two examples students listen to conversations in order to get a general idea of what the main points are. Once again, the ability to get the general picture without getting too stuck on individual words and phrases is something that students can be trained for.

(a) Anna's doubts[29]

In this video example for elementary students, students watch one of the central characters in a video story talking about her new friend, Jeff, and her son Terry.

The teacher starts by asking students to recall the story so far. Ask them if they think Anna likes Jeff. How does she get on with her son?

'There are secrets. It's just a feeling I have.'

Tell students that they are going to watch the video in which Anna will talk about her worries. Their viewing task is simply to answer these two questions:

1 How did Anna feel before Jeff came into her life?
2 What does she feel about Jeff now?

They are told not to worry about anything else; can they just get a general idea of the answers to these questions?

This is what Anna says on the video:

THE STORY

Anna, in monologue, tries to explain and justify her feelings of doubt and mistrust for Jeff.–She admits that there is a lack of openness in her relationship with him.

FILM TRANSCRIPT

ANNA: Before Jeff came into my life, I thought I was secure I had my work and Terry, my son, I thought I was really safe.–But then Jeff walked into my house that day and I knew I wasn't.–I knew I was hiding.–He surprised me, I surprised myself.–I suddenly realised how cautious I had become since the divorce.–Seeing Terry with him, so open, so at ease, made me realise how much I had changed.
———After Jeff came to stay, we spent some time together, Terry, Jeff and I.–Then I relaxed a little, still I felt I had to be careful, still I felt I needed more time.–Perhaps I was wrong.–I know Jeff sensed that I was holding back but I couldn't help myself.–I don't want to be hurt again, and I don't want Terry to be hurt.–Jeff is important to him too, I must think of that.–And somehow I feel Jeff is holding something back.–He avoids talking about himself and his home in New Zealand.–There are secrets.–It's just a feeling I have.
ANNA:

225

For a follow-up task students can role play an interview with Anna and ask her how she feels and why. They could role play a conversation with Jeff in which someone tells him what she has said and he reacts. This would involve the students predicting what will happen in the future – something they will be able to check against future episodes.

(b) David Attenborough[30]

Once again, in this example for intermediate students, students are simply asked to get the general gist of quite a long interview.

The students have discussed various areas of the world and the teacher now introduces the topic of the environment. Students are asked to get into groups and make a list of the three main causes for worry about the earth's environment. When they have done this the class can discuss them.

Now that they have been introduced to the topic they are shown the following:

2 | **T.34** | You're going to hear an interview with David Attenborough.
Here is the introduction.

'David Attenborough knows the world better than most people. He's spent much of the last seven years globe-trotting for his hugely successful television programmes *Life on Earth* and *The Living Planet*.

But his next series might well be named *The End of Life on the Dying Planet*. David Attenborough is very gloomy about much of what he's seen.'

David Attenborough talks about the places mentioned on page 69. What do you think is happening in these places that makes him 'gloomy'?

Listening for gist

Listen to the interview.
What *is* making David Attenborough gloomy about each place?
Is there a common cause?

John and Liz Soars   Headway
Student's Book   Intermediate
Page 70

They are told to listen for the answers to the gist questions and not to worry about difficulties they have, especially since this is quite a long tape extract. This is what the students hear:

"Groundwell" Broadcast 13.4.84, Radio 4
"Released by Arrangement with BBC Enterprises Limited"

I = Interviewer
A = David Attenborough

I David Attenborough is very gloomy about much of what he's seen. What's depressed him most has been the huge speed and scale of change that human beings are inflicting on the world. A powerful symbol of that change is the simple act of felling trees.

A In the Himalayas, for example, people cut down forests simply because there are an awful lot of people who need firewood to keep warm. And so they cut down huge hillsides, in a few years . . . are stripped of their forests.

I This leaves fertile Himalayan hills naked, unprotected from the heavy rains. The trees were umbrellas, but now the rain washes out the good soil, which ends up as mud a thousand miles away in the channels of the river Ganges.

A When the next rains come, instead of the forests on the hillside holding the rains and letting it out a bit at a time as though it were a sponge, the forest isn't there, so the rain water runs straight off and when it goes down in a huge flood; and it gets into the channels which are clogged with mud, so it then floods, so then the whole area is under water, people lose their farm land and people drown.

I So cutting down trees in Nepal drowns people in Bangladesh. In Africa the gathering of wood is making the desert grow.

A In parts of the Sudan, the desert in just 15 years has advanced sixty miles. And it's a . . . it's a . . .

devastating statistic and . . . what's more, it's a heart-breaking one, because how can you go to these people and say, 'You mustn't cut down that tree in order to cook your food'?

I But is it universally so bad? Or are some environmentalists just getting into a flap about isolated, extreme examples? David Attenborough used to wonder that, too.

A I remember very well flying over the Amazonian jungle for hour after hour after hour and not a sign of the hand of man beneath me, just this green carpet of trees. And I said to myself, 'It can't be true, it can't be true that this will disappear by the end of the century'. And so I looked into the question as to how people made these estimates. I mean, I thought, was it one of these things where you suddenly multiplied one statistic by 500,000 and you get an extraordinary answer? The fact of the matter is that those statistics are based on surveys by satellites with infra-red cameras which actually measure the change of a patch of green leaves into a patch of bare ground. And even on that level the rate at which the jungle is being . . . er destroyed amounts to about 29,000 square miles in a year.

I That's an area the size of the whole of Scotland disappearing every year. Trees are a vital part of the water cycle, and of course they give us the oxygen that we breathe. And cutting down the rain forests kills the plants beneath the trees as well, plants which help us fight disease.

A Forty per cent of our drugs, our medicines, are derived from plants and most of those come from the tropical rain forests, and

most of those come from the Amazon.

I Those plants also help fight the diseases that threaten our food. The funguses and moulds that attack wheat, for example, are continually growing stronger. But they only evolve to match specific varieties of wheat. So plant breeders beat the funguses by changing the varieties.

A What does a plant breeder need to change a variety? Answer – new genes. Where do they come from? Answer – wild plants. That happens with all our food plants. With rice, with potatoes, with wheat, with barley, all that applies. And if we lose those wild strains, we could well be . . . devast . . . I mean the field could be devastated and mankind would starve.

I David Attenborough insists that none of what he's said is exaggeration. It's not just a distant problem somewhere on the other side of the world.

A What we're talking about is the survival of human beings, of men, women and children. It is happening now. The floods that we hear of in India and Pakistan, the starvation that we hear of in parts of Africa, these aren't accidents. These are direct consequences of what we are talking about. And the tragedy is that the people who suffer first are the deprived people, the people who are living on the edge of prosperity. And, but if we think that we are insulated from that, that it's always going to be them, we are wrong. They are the start. As sure as fate, they are coming our way.

I David Attenborough's thoughts after seven years of travelling around the world.

Students should be allowed to discuss what they think the answers to these questions are before the teacher leads feedback.

As a text-related task, students can discuss whether they are as pessimistic as Attenborough appears to be. How do they think people can be made to stop damaging the environment? Groups could design posters which are aimed at stopping people from causing their own environmental problems.

We have already noted that this listening extract is quite long, as is a lot of listening material at intermediate level and above. In 10.5.8 we will discuss some of the problems students have with listening and how to solve them.

The two examples we have looked at here were designed to encourage students – on their first listening – to concentrate on the general message rather than concentrating on detail. As such this is a type 1 skill. After this first listening, teachers will want to rewind the tape and have students listen again to pick up points of detail, including, for example, linguistic detail.

**10.5.6
Listening for detail: information and discourse structure**

A first listening will not be enough to ensure the students' understanding of a tape extract. Indeed, for students to be able to understand the information on the tape they will probably want to go back to it again and listen for more information, or for a greater understanding of the language used. The three examples here show how such detail can be accessed.

(a) English writer and lawyer[31]

In this material, at the advanced level, students listen to the tape at least twice. On the second reading they try to extract more detail than on the first.

Students have read the following paragraph about the English writer, John Mortimer.

● **John Mortimer** is primarily known as a playwright, novelist and journalist, from his many books and television plays and series, such as *Rumpole of the Bailey*, *Paradise Postponed*, and the award-winning *Brideshead Revisited*. Although the subjects he writes about and his characters are thoroughly English, his work is as popular in the United States as it is in his native Britain. Apart from being a writer, he was, until recently, an eminent lawyer and became famous in the 1960s for defending a large number of international writers whose works were banned on the grounds of obscenity. In this capacity, he is a QC or Queen's Counsel, a type of advocate found only in Britain and the Commonwealth. As the British terminology for various types of lawyers is often mystifying to foreigners, John Mortimer explains the differences.

After listening to the tape for the first time they listen again for more detailed information. This is the tape they hear:

John Mortimer First of all, you've got to realise that in England we have two different sorts of lawyers: one are called solicitors, and they're the people who prepare cases, sell houses, run businesses, do all those sort of things, but don't appear as advocates in the higher courts. And if you want an advocate to appear for you in a higher court, you have to have a barrister who is instructed by a solicitor. So the barrister is a particular breed of lawyer who is a . . . an advocate. And out of the barristers, the kind of . . . most expensive ones become something called 'The Queen's Counsels' which is rather a mysterious and ancient title. I suppose it means you're meant to help the Queen when she's in any trouble, but she never asked me to help her. And you wear a special sort of uniform. You wear a silk robe instead of an ordinary one, and by and large you have to have an ordinary barrister with you in a case, on the same side. So it becomes rather an expensive and a big deal to have a QC in a case, with the result that if you're a QC you only do rather elaborate and grand cases.

Tom Boyd You do so many different things. How do you apportion your time?

John Mortimer I'm not a barrister any more, so that's not a problem. I mean, I suppose on good days I start about five, but I never write after lunch, for the day is finished for me by lunchtime.

Tom Boyd Your work is well known and appreciated in the United States. Is it too English in character to appeal to the Continent?

John Mortimer I'm very surprised how successful it is in America. I mean, *Paradise Postponed* is an enormous success, and *Rumpole*'s a great success in America. And I think that the reason for that is that it's very English. I think the worst thing to try and be is a sort of Mid-Atlantic writer, you know, who offends nobody, and then you end up like a sort of tasteless dinner in the Hilton Hotel, which doesn't taste of anything. So I think that you should be as English as possible, but it probably *is* too English to appeal to Latin races, although it's read a lot in Nordic countries.

And these are the questions they answer for the second listening:

COMPREHENSION B

1 Name three things that John Mortimer says solicitors do.
2 What is special about the robe a Queen's Counsel wears?
3 What kind of cases does a Queen's Counsel do?
4 When does John Mortimer do his writing?
5 Name two works of John Mortimer that are great successes in the United States.
6 What does John Mortimer compare a Mid-Atlantic writer with? What does he mean?

As a follow-up students may compare the practice of law in England and their country. They could try to profile a writer that they know about or they could conduct a court case.

(b) Script dictation

One way of having students listen to a tape in a detailed way is to give them a script dictation. All this means is that they are given (some of) the tapescript with some of the words blanked out. All they have to do is fill in the words. This is especially useful for longer extracts, where teachers can focus on the parts that interest them especially.

It is easy to create script dictations. Let us imagine that students have already listened to the interview with David Attenborough (see 10.5.5 (b)) and answered the gist questions. The teacher now asks the students to try to fill in the gaps in the following extract before listening to the tape again:

Attenborough: In the Himalayas, for (1) _____ , people cut down forest simply (2) _____ there are an awful lot of people (3) _____ need firewood to keep warm. And so they cut (4) _____ huge hillsides, in a few years ... are stripped of their forests.
Interviewer: This leaves fertile Himalayan hills naked, unprotected (5) _____ the heavy rains. The trees were umbrellas, but now the rain

(6) _____ out the good soil, which ends up as (7) _____ a thousand miles away in the channels of the river Ganges.

The students now listen to the tape again with intense concentration. Are their language predictions correct?

Script dictations encourage students to listen in detail. They can be very useful in highlighting features which the teacher wishes to concentrate on. They are extremely useful in reminding students of the difference between tidy written prose and the way people speak.

(c) Hesitation phenomena

In 10.5.2 (b) students listened to part of an interview with Sue Tully, who acts in a British soap opera. Sue Tully demonstrates a number of features of informal spoken style, especially in her use of 'time-to-think' expressions and words. After students have listened to the two parts of the interview they see this:

Follow-up: Spoken style

4 When people are speaking they use noises, words and expressions to give them 'time to think'. What 'time-to-think' words or expressions is Sue Tully using in these extracts from the tapes?

a) 'Basically, it's um it's life in the East End of London, i.e. um the Cockney, the Cockney way of life but that isn't what, you know, the most important thing about the programme . . .'
b) 'I mean it's not just all gloom and doom . . .'
c) '. . . it's not about Cockneys, I mean, because the situations that we deal with are characteristic of a lot of, um, inner city communities all over Britain, and I'm sure, in other cities in the world.'
d) 'I mean if ever they . . . if ever I'm out somewhere and they take a photo of me it's very rare they put Sue Tully.'
e) 'Um yeah, you know, sort of knocking on my door, eight o'clock in the morning saying, er . . .'

What other words or expressions have you heard which perform the same function?

Notice that students are not asked to produce this kind of speech; the point of the exercise is to get them to recognise what its function is and to get to know typical British English ways of creating verbal thinking time.

10.5.7
Making your own
tapes[32]

Some teachers find it difficult to use commercially produced tapes either because the tapes don't quite suit the level or interests of their group or because they are unavailable or of poor quality. In such cases it makes sense for teachers to produce their own tapes. We will look at three possibilities.

(a) The dialogue

There is no reason why teachers and their colleagues should not write and record their own dialogues. They can either write a script and then record it or simply have a conversation around a given topic. Written dialogues can sound a bit stilted – they are some of the most difficult material to write – but, on the other hand, teachers can be sure that they are at the right level, in contrast to the freer topic-based discussion.

(b) The interview

One of the things it is fairly easy to do is to record interviews. These can be with interviewees as themselves or playing a role. Ideally the interviewee will be a native speaker, but where that is not possible a good speaker of English will certainly be OK. Other teachers in the same school or institute can be used; friends, families and neighbours can be pressed into service here.

(c) Stories and readings

Teachers can make their own tapes of story-telling or story reading. They could adapt a text in the way we suggested in 10.5.2 (a) or they could read something from a book. They could tell a story of their own.

Tapes which the teacher makes are often the most exciting ones for the teacher and the students to use. Two warnings need to be given, however. In the first place it is difficult to get good quality on some tapes and tape machines. The tape may be difficult to hear and it may sound very shoddy. Secondly, if students are only given home-produced tapes they may miss out on one of the main advantages of using taped material – the variety of speakers and voices that the students can be exposed to.

10.5.8
Dealing with listening problems

As we have already said, listening can cause problems. In general these can be summarised as *panic* and *difficulty*.

Students often panic when they see the tape recorder because they know that they are faced with a challenging task. Two things are guaranteed to increase that panic! The first is to refuse to play a tape more than once and the second is to expose an individual student's lack of success in the listening task.

It is almost always a good idea to play a tape all the way through on a first listening so that students can get an idea of what it sounds like. Often they will be able to complete the type 1 skill task – provided the teacher and the materials have given them enough help to do so. But often, too, they will have had considerable difficulty in following the extract, partly because they have not yet become accustomed to the voices or the 'sound' of the tape. It seems sensible, in such circumstances, to play the tape again, with very little comment – having first ascertained that it is necessary.

The teacher must obviously be prepared to repeat segments of tape for detailed work (e.g. script dictation – see 10.5.6 (b)) and must be able to get back to the beginning of the extract quickly. Students can become unnerved and irritated by your inability to find your place! It is worth making absolutely sure that you set the counter to zero before you start.

If students have listened to a tape to answer a comprehension task it can be very threatening for the teacher to point to individuals and ask them for their answers to questions – especially when they know that they don't know! That's why, with listening especially, it is a good idea to let students check their answers together in pairs or groups before organising a feedback stage. The individual's lack of success can be extremely demotivating: shared confusion is not nearly so damaging.

Some teachers and students find that listening to tapes is extremely difficult, especially when tapes are fairly long. And yet we may want to use fairly long extracts because they contribute to our overall teaching plan and because the topic is interesting. If the tape is proving difficult there are a number of things you can do to make it more manageable.

(a) **Don't play all the tape straight away.** Play half of it and then get students to predict what will happen next.

(b) **Give students the first third of the tapescript.** They can read it at home if they want. In class they discuss how the story is going to end or what is going to happen (if it is an interview programme, etc.).

(c) **Give one group a tape recorder** and give other groups different sections of the tapescript. Example: Group A has a tape recorder, Group B has the middle chunk of the story (in written form) and Group C has the end of the story (in written form). Group A listens to the beginning of the tape whilst at the same time Groups B and C read their tapescripts. When they have finished you reform the groups, creating new groups of three students (one from A, one from B and one from C). By pooling their information they can work out the whole story. Now you play the whole tape for everyone to listen to.

(d) **Preview vocabulary.** Choose a small number of key words that students might not be expected to know. Teach them to the students before they listen. Then get them to guess what the interviewee will say based on the words.

(e) **Use the tapescript.** In (c) above we saw one way of using the tapescript. In general it may be a good idea for the students to look at the tapescript after the first couple of listenings if they are having difficulty in coping with the tape. You could also cut the tapescript into paragraphs – or even smaller pieces – which they have to put in the right order as they listen to the tape.

(f) **Give students the interviewer's questions.** Especially with interviews it may be a good idea to give students the questions that the interviewer asks. This will help them to predict what the interviewee's answers will be. They can even role play the interview before they listen to it. Now they listen to the tape to see if their predictions were right, and because they have 'had a go' themselves they are prepared and interested.

These are just some ideas to make your listening more motivating and more successful, especially where there are difficulties.

10.6 Conclusions

We have discussed the teaching of receptive skills in some detail and we have stressed the importance of the teacher's role in creating expectations and enthusiasm for the text that is to be read or heard. We have discussed the use of authentic texts and stressed the need for authentic-like texts, even where students are at a relatively low level. We have provided a methodological model for the teaching of receptive skills.

In showing a considerable variety of listening and reading exercises we have explored some of the many ways to help students acquire the confidence to use their receptive skills with English text. Many of the comprehension question-types can easily be used by teachers with their own texts which they choose for their own classes.

We have discussed differences between video and audio material and we have discussed solutions to some of the problems (both linguistic and psychological) which students have with listening material.

Discussion

1 Do you think there are any kinds of authentic text which beginner students could cope with? If so, what kind of listening and reading tasks would be appropriate?
2 Which do you think are the most useful criteria for choosing listening and reading texts?
3 Are there any situations in which you would not use a lead-in stage?
4 Do you think that a teacher might start the treatment of reading/listening material with type 2 skill work?
5 What are the advantages in getting students to read quickly?
6 Think of your own speaking style in your first language. What speech phenomena do you particularly use?

Exercises

1 Look at the textbook you are using (or are familiar with). Find out if the textbook has material specifically designed for the teaching of reading or listening skills.
2 Find a reading text in the book you are using with students. How authentic is it? How interesting and/or useful is it?
3 Find a reading text that would be appropriate for the confirming type of exercise we saw in 10.4.1.
4 Write a conversation which could be used for a 'communicative task' type of listening.
5 Take a written text from any source and re-write it so that it could form the basis for a talk to be used for listening comprehension (see the example in 10.5.2 (a)).

References

1 Many of the points about expectations, interest, etc. are raised in N Coe (1978).
2 For more on the skills involved in listening and reading see J Willis (1981) pages 134 and 142.
On reading see F Grellet (1981) and an excellent short summary on methodology by R Williams (1986).
On listening see P Ur (1984) and M Underwood (1989).
3 It is worth pointing out that some 'authentic' material might be considered roughly-tuned! For example, a play uses authentic English but roughly tunes it to make it comprehensible to an audience: the dialogue may be naturalistic, but it is still artificial to some extent. What is special about a good play, however, is that we can recognise the dialogue as being similar to authentic spontaneous speech.
4 From R O'Neill and P Mugglestone (1989a).

5 Methodologists and teachers have frequently talked about *extensive* (i.e. general whole text) and *intensive* (i.e. detailed) skills. The reason for preferring the terms *type 1* and *type 2* skills is because in so doing we emphasise the methodological procedures involved and also because much of what has traditionally been called intensive skill work would automatically come at the first reading (or listening) of a text, thus making it, to some extent, extensive work.

6 For an excellent summary of different question-types and their uses see J Suarez (1979).

7 I first saw this technique demonstrated by Mick Wadham.

8 From B Abbs and I Freebairn (1989).

9 From M Swan and C Walter (1987).

10 The questions and text are from R Rossner et al. (1979b).

11 From J Harmer and H Surguine (1988).

12 From R O'Neill and P Mugglestone (1989b).

13 Taken from V Black et al. (1986).

14 Taken from R Maple (1988).

15 Taken from J Naunton (1989).

16 From M Helgesen et. al (1990).

17 From J Harmer (1988b).

18 The text and questions are taken from A Doff, C Jones and K Mitchell (1984).

19 The text is taken from J Soars and L Soars (1987).

20 The extract is from an interview in J Harmer and S Elsworth (1989).

21 Two excellent books on the use of video in language teaching are M Allan (1985) and J Lonergan (1984). Articles in J McGovern (1983) are also very interesting.

22 I first saw this technique demonstrated by Ingrid Freebairn.

23 See reference 20 for the source of this material.

24 The material is from B Abbs and I Freebairn (1990).

25 From R Rossner et al. (1980).

26 From J Harmer (1988b).

27 The material shown in this example is from M Geddes and G Sturtridge (1979).

28 See M Geddes and G Sturtridge (1978).

29 See B Abbs and Ingrid Freebairn (1985).

30 From J Soars and L Soars (1986).

31 From T Boyd (1988).

32 I have benefited from discussing teacher-created tapes with Gillie Cunningham. See also G Cunningham (1990).

11 Class management

In this chapter we will consider various aspects of class management including the role of the teacher, student groupings, and disruptive behaviour. We will show that class management skills are important since they help to ensure the success of the teacher and the activities which are used. The most effective activities can be made almost useless if the teacher does not organise them properly, and disruptive behaviour can spoil the best

classes if it is not checked. Teachers who do not use a variety of student groupings (pairs and groups, etc.) may be missing valuable opportunities to create a cooperative atmosphere in the class and to maximise student practice.

11.1
The role of the teacher[1]

In Part B of this book we have looked at a variety of activities that have ranged from tightly controlled accurate reproduction work (in Chapter 6) to free communicative activities (in Chapter 8); from controlled reading to extract specific information to the more communicative jigsaw listening and reading (in Chapter 10).

It will be clear that the way the teacher behaves in these different kinds of activities will change according to the nature of the activities.

Perhaps the most important distinction to be drawn here is between the roles of *controller* and *facilitator*, since these two concepts represent opposite ends of a cline of control and freedom. A controller stands at the front of the class like a puppet-master or mistress controlling everything; a facilitator maintains a low profile in order to make the students' own achievement of a task possible.[2] We will represent these extremes in the following way (see page 236):

235

Controlling ———————————————————————————— Facilitative

Figure 19

We will indicate where the different roles we are about to discuss can be placed on this cline. We will examine the roles of *controller*, *assessor*, *organiser*, *prompter*, *participant*, *resource*, *tutor* and *investigator*.

**11.1.1
The teacher as
controller**

As we have said, teachers as controllers are in complete charge of the class. They control not only what the students do, but also when they speak and what language they use. On our diagram this role is placed at the extreme end of the cline:

Controlling ✕———————————————————————————— Facilitative

Figure 20

Certain stages of a lesson lend themselves to this role very well. The introduction of new language, where it makes use of accurate reproduction and drilling techniques, needs to be carefully organised. Thus the *instruct-cue-nominate* cycle is the perfect example of the teacher acting as controller. All attention is focused on the front of the class, and the students are all working to the same beat (see 11.2.1).

The teacher as controller is closely allied to the image that teachers project of themselves. Some appear to be natural leaders and performers, while some are quieter and feel happier when students are interacting amongst themselves. Where teachers are addicted to being the centre of attention they tend to find it difficult not to perform the controlling role and this has both advantages and disadvantages.

We can all recall teachers in our past who were able to inspire us. Frequently this was because they possessed a certain indefinable quality which attracted and motivated us. Frequently, too, it was because they had interesting things to say and do which held our attention and enthusiasm. The same is true in language classes. Some teachers have a gift of inspiring and motivating us even though they never seem to relax their control. And at their best teachers who are able to mix the controlling role with a good 'performance' are extremely enjoyable to be taught by or observed.[3]

When teachers are acting as controllers, they tend to do a lot of the talking, and whilst we may feel uneasy about the effect this has on the possibilities for student talking time it should be remembered that it is frequently the teacher, talking at the students' level of comprehension, who is the most important source they have for roughly-tuned comprehensible input (see 4.3).[4]

We should not let these advantages fool us, however, into accepting the controller role as the only one that the teacher has. It is vital that control should be relaxed if students are to be allowed a chance to learn (rather than be taught). Even during immediate creativity (6.3) teachers will have begun to relax their grip, and during communicative speaking and writing (see Chapter 8) their role must be fundamentally different, otherwise the students will not have a chance to participate properly.

11.1.2
The teacher as
assessor

Clearly a major part of the teacher's job is to assess the students' work, to see how well they are performing or how well they performed. Not only is this important pedagogically, but the students quite naturally expect it, even after communicative activities (see below).

We must make a difference between two types of assessment: *correction* and *organising feedback*.

During an accurate reproduction stage, where the teacher is totally in control, student error and mistake will be corrected almost instantly (see 6.3.3). The teacher's function, we have suggested, is to show where incorrectness occurs and help the student to see what has gone wrong so that it can be put right.

A slightly less formal style of correction can occur where students are involved in immediate creativity or in doing a drill-type activity in pairs (asking and answering set questions, for example). Teachers will still want to correct, but we have suggested that such correction will be 'gentle' (see 5.4.2 and 6.3.3). *Gentle correction* involves showing students that a mistake has been made but not making a big fuss about it. Whereas, in the accurate reproduction stage, we insist on students saying the sentence, phrase or word correctly once they have been told about their mistake, with gentle correction the teacher says things like 'Well that's not quite right . . . we don't say "he goed . . .", we say "went".' The important point is that nothing more happens. The student doesn't have to repeat his or her sentence correctly; it is enough that a mistake has been acknowledged. This kind of gentle correction, used in the right way, will not seriously damage the atmosphere of pairwork or freer conversation.

We can represent these two kinds of correction in the following way on our cline:

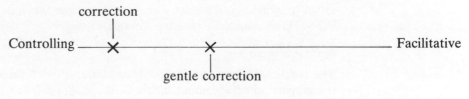

Figure 21

Organising feedback occurs when students have performed some kind of task, and the intention of this kind of assessment is for them to see the extent of their success or failure and to be given ideas as to how their (language) problems might be solved.

We must make a distinction between two different kinds of feedback. *Content feedback* concerns an assessment of how well the students performed the activity as an activity rather than as a language exercise. Thus, when students have completed a role play (see 8.1.7) the teacher first discusses with the students the reasons for their decisions in the simulation.

In the travel agent activity (see 8.1.7 (a)) teacher and students discuss why the pairs chose a particular hotel and if it was the most sensible choice. In other words, where students are asked to perform a task (including writing tasks – see 8.3) it is their ability to perform that task which should be the focus of the first feedback session. If the teacher merely concentrates on the correctness of the students' language then they will conclude that the task itself was unimportant.

Form feedback, on the other hand, does tell the students how well they have performed linguistically, how accurate they have been. When students are involved in a communicative activity the teacher will record the errors that are made so that they can be brought to the students' attention *after* whatever content feedback is appropriate.

There are a number of ways of recording errors and organising feedback:

(a) Pen and paper

The teacher can listen to what is being said and write down the errors that are made. This kind of record keeping can be done with a simple form, in the following way:

grammar	vocabulary	pronunciation	style and appropriacy

When the activity is over and the class have discussed it (during the content feedback stage) the teacher can write some of the more prominent and serious errors from the list on the board. In pairs students have to identify the errors and correct them. Alternatively the teacher can go to class armed with a number of small cards or pieces of paper. These can be given to individual students, detailing the errors they made and suggesting a cure. This is especially suitable for small groups.

(b) Tape recorder

The teacher might want to record the students' performance on tape. After the activity and the content feedback the students listen to it and discuss the errors. With very small groups the teacher can take the tape home and transcribe it. The next day individual students can be given their errors and a correct version. This is often done in a variation on Community Language Learning (see 4.1.5). With large groups teacher and students can listen to the tape together, though this is often not very successful.

(c) Video

Video is far more successful for whole class feedback than the tape recorder. It can be done in the following way:

First of all the teacher makes sure that the activity is filmed. When it is over, students can watch the video for content feedback, and then they can watch it again in order to concentrate on the language. One group can be detailed to watch/listen for any grammar mistakes, another group can be asked to listen for pronunciation problems, another for vocabulary problems, etc. That way students are actively involved in the feedback process.

Teachers should be aware, however, that feedback of this kind using audio or videotape will take a long time and only a small amount of the recording can be dealt with.

Two final points need to be made. Firstly it is important to stress again that feedback does not just include correcting language mistakes. It also means reacting to the subject and content of an activity. Secondly we have been discussing errors and mistakes, but feedback also means telling students what 'went right'. Where they have achieved a successful outcome, or where they have used good and appropriate language, they need to be told this. One of the groups of students watching the video playback (see (c) above) can be watching for anything which they think worked particularly well; when the teacher records language using pen and pencil, student successes should be written down as well as problems.

We can put the organising feedback function in the following place on our cline.

Controlling ———————————✕——————————— Facilitative

Figure 22

11.1.3
The teacher as organiser

Perhaps the most important and difficult role the teacher has to play is that of organiser. The success of many activities depends on good organisation and on the students knowing exactly what they are to do. A lot of time can be wasted if the teacher omits to give students vital information or issues conflicting and confusing instructions.

The main aim of the teacher when organising an activity is to tell the students what they are going to talk about (or write or read about), give clear instructions about what exactly their task is, get the activity going, and then organise feedback when it is over. This sounds remarkably easy, but can be disastrous if teachers have not thought out exactly what they are going to say beforehand.

Certain things should definitely not be done when organising an activity: teachers should never, for example, assume that students have understood the instructions. It is always wise to check that they have grasped what they have to do, and where possible, the students' native language can be used for this. Teachers should never issue unclear instructions; it is wise to plan out what you are going to say beforehand and then say it clearly and concisely. In lower level classes with monolingual groups, the students' language could be used for this if absolutely necessary. It is essential for the teacher to plan exactly what information the students will need. For example, if an information gap exercise is being used (such as those in 7.1.2) students must be told not to look at each other's material. If they do the exercise will be ruined. If students are reading for specific information (see 10.4.2) they must clearly understand that they are not to try to understand everything, but only read to get the answer to certain questions. If they do not understand this a lot of the point of the exercise will be lost. Lastly teachers must be careful about when they get students to look at the material they will be using for the activity. If they hand out material and then try to give instructions they will find that the students are looking at the material and not listening to the instructions!

In Part B of this book we have seen many activities and described how the teacher will organise them. Especially in Chapter 8 we have listed the stages the teacher should go through when organising communication activities.

The organisation of an activity and the instructions the teacher gives are of vital importance since if the students have not understood clearly what they are to do they will not be able to perform their task satisfactorily.

The organisation of an activity can be divided into three main parts. In the first the teacher gives a *lead-in*. Like the lead-in for presentation or for the treatment of receptive skills this will probably take the form of an introduction to the subject. The teacher and students may briefly discuss the topic in order to start thinking about it. This procedure is detailed in 8.1.7(d), for example. In 8.1.3(c) (the 'describe and draw' game) the teacher's lead-in might be very simple, e.g. 'You're going to test your artistic powers by drawing a picture. The idea of this exercise is to see how well you can talk about a picture and give instructions.' In the case of many of the reading and listening exercises we looked at in Chapter 10 the lead-in concerned a familiarisation with the topic (see, for example 10.4.1(a) and 10.4.2(a)).

When the lead-in stage has been accomplished the teacher *instructs*. This is where the students are told exactly what they should do. The teacher may (as in many of our examples in Chapter 8) tell the students they are going to work in pairs and then designate one member of each pair as A and the other as B. In the 'describe and draw' example the teacher then gives each student A a picture and says, 'Do not show this picture to B until the end of the game.' When all the A students have their pictures the teacher says, 'I want all the B students to draw the same picture as the one A has. A will give you instructions and you may ask questions. You must not look at A's picture until the game is complete.' At this stage, particularly in a monolingual class, it may be a good idea to get a translation of these instructions to make sure the students have understood. In certain cases the teacher may well organise a demonstration of the activity before giving instructions (see the information gap practice activities in 7.1.2).

Finally the teacher *initiates* the activity. A final check is given that students have understood, e.g. 'Has anyone got any questions ... no? ... good. Then off you go!' The teacher may ask the students to see if they can be the first to finish, thus adding a competitive element which is often highly motivating.

The *lead-in → instruct (demonstrate) → initiate → organise feedback* sequence can almost always be followed when the teacher is setting up activities – when the teacher is acting as organiser. For the sequence to have the right effect the teacher must remember to work out carefully what instructions to give and what the key concepts for the activity are (much as we work out what key concepts are necessary at the lead-in stage when introducing new language). The job is then to organise the activity as efficiently as possible, frequently checking that the students have understood. Once the activity has started the teacher will not intervene (where pair/groupwork is being used) unless it is to use gentle correction (see 11.1.2) or to prompt (see 11.1.4).

The teacher's role as organiser goes on our cline in the following way:

Controlling ————————————— X ————————— Facilitative

Figure 23

11.1.4
The teacher as prompter

Often the teacher needs to encourage students to participate or needs to make suggestions about how students may proceed in an activity when there is a silence or when they are confused about what to do next. This is one of the teacher's important roles, the role of prompter.

In 7.1.4 we looked at follow-up questions and real answers and we saw the teacher prompting the students to use these devices. The teacher encouraged the students to ask follow-up questions and was ready with suggestions about what those questions might be in case the students could not think of any themselves. We also said that in simulations the teacher might need to prompt the students with information they have forgotten.

The role of prompter has to be performed with discretion for if teachers are too aggressive they start to take over from the students, whereas the idea is that they should be helping them *only* when it is necessary.

The teacher's role as prompter goes on our cline in the following way:

Controlling ————————————————— X ——— Facilitative

Figure 24

11.1.5
The teacher as participant

There is no reason why the teacher should not participate as an equal in an activity especially where activities like simulations are taking place. Clearly on a lot of occasions it will be difficult for us to do so as equals (since we often know all the material and all the details, etc. such as with information gap exercises, jigsaw listening, etc.). In 8.1.7 we said that teachers might join simulations as participants, sometimes playing roles themselves.

The danger is that the teacher will tend to dominate, and the students will both allow and expect this to happen. It will be up to the teacher to make sure it does not.

Teachers should not be afraid to participate since not only will it probably improve the atmosphere in the class, but it will also give the students a chance to practise English with someone who speaks it better than they do.

The teacher's role as participant goes on our cline in the following way:

Controlling ————————————————————— ✗——— Facilitative

Figure 25

11.1.6
The teacher as a resource

We have stressed the importance of teacher non-intervention where a genuinely communicative activity is taking place in the classroom and this means that the teacher is left, to some extent, with nothing to do. There are still two very important roles, however. One is to be aware of what is going on as an assessor – although discreetly – and the other is to be a kind of walking resource centre. In other words the teacher should always be ready to offer help if it is needed. After all we have the language that the students may be missing, and this is especially true if the students are involved in some kind of writing task. Thus we make ourselves available so that students can consult us when (and only when) they wish.

We can see, therefore, that when the teacher is acting as a resource we are at the facilitative end of our cline:

Controlling ————————————————————————— ✗Facilitative

Figure 26

11.1.7
The teacher as tutor

We can talk about the teacher as a tutor in the sense of someone who acts as a coach and as a resource where students are involved in their own work, and call upon the teacher mainly for advice and guidance. This is the role the teacher adopts where students are involved in self-study or where they are doing project work of their own choosing (see 8.4). The teacher will be able to help them clarify ideas and limit the task, for example; the teacher can help them by pointing out errors in rough drafts; the teacher can also offer the students advice about how to get the most out of their learning and what to do if they want to study more.

This tutorial role – which approximates to a counselling function – is often appropriate at intermediate and advanced levels. It is a broader role than the others we have mentioned since it incorporates parts of some of the other roles, i.e. organiser, prompter and resource. It is, nevertheless, a facilitative role and therefore occurs to the right on our diagram:

Controlling ————————————————————————— ✗——— Facilitative

Figure 27

11.1.8
The teacher as investigator

All the roles we have mentioned so far have had to do with the teacher's behaviour as it relates to the students. But teachers themselves will want to develop their own skills and they will hope for a gradually deepening insight into the best ways to foster language learning.

Of course it is possible to go on teacher training courses and to attend teachers' seminars. These will certainly help teachers to come across new ideas and keep abreast of what is happening. But teachers can develop by themselves or with colleagues, too. The best way to do this is by investigating what is going on, observing what works well in class and what does not, trying out new techniques and activities and evaluating their appropriacy.

Teachers who do not investigate the efficiency of new methods and who do not actively seek their own personal and professional development may find the job of teaching becoming increasingly monotonous. Teachers who constantly seek to enrich their understanding of what learning is all about and what works well, on the other hand, will find the teaching of English constantly rewarding.

11.2
Student
groupings

In previous chapters we have often talked about activities where students work in pairs or in groups.

We will now consider briefly the relative merits and uses of various student groupings. We will consider *lockstep, pairwork, groupwork, the use of the mother tongue,* and *individual study.*

11.2.1
Lockstep[5]

Lockstep is the class grouping where all the students are working with the teacher, where all the students are 'locked into' the same rhythm and pace, the same activity (the term is borrowed from the language laboratory). Lockstep is the traditional teaching situation, in other words, where a teacher-controlled session is taking place. The accurate reproduction stage usually takes place in lockstep (although this is not necessarily the only way it can be done) with all the students working as one group and the teacher acting as controller and assessor.

Lockstep has certain advantages. It usually means that all the class are concentrating, and the teacher can usually be sure that everyone can hear what is being said. The students are usually getting a good language model from the teacher, and lockstep can often be very dynamic. Many students find the lockstep stage (where choral repetition, etc. takes place) very comforting. There are, in other words, a number of reasons why lockstep is a good idea.

There are also reasons, though, why the use of lockstep alone is less than satisfactory. In the first place, students working in lockstep get little chance to practise or to talk at all. Simple mathematics will show that if a ten-minute accurate reproduction stage takes place in a class of forty, and if each student response takes thirty seconds (including instructing and correcting) only half the class will be able to say anything at all. If this is true of controlled sentences, then the situation with language use is far more serious. In a class of forty only a very small percentage of the class will get a chance to speak.

Lockstep always goes at the wrong speed! Either the teacher is too slow for the good students (and therefore there is a danger that they will get bored) or the lesson is too fast for the weak students (in which case they may panic and not learn what is being taught). Shy and nervous students also find lockstep work extremely bad for the nerves since they are likely to be exposed in front of the whole class.

Most seriously, though, lockstep, where the teacher acts as a controller, cannot be the ideal grouping for communicative work. If students are going to use the language they are learning they will not be able to do so locked into a teacher-controlled drill. And if they are to attain student autonomy they must be able to do so by using the language on their own. Lockstep, in other words, involves too much teaching and too little learning!

This rather bleak view of lockstep activities does not mean we should abandon the whole-class grouping completely. As we have said, it has its uses. Where feedback is taking place after a reading or listening task clearly it will be advantageous to have the whole class involved at the same time both so that they can check their answers and so that the teacher can assess their performance as a group. Where pair and groupwork are to be set up clearly the whole class has to listen to instructions, etc.

11.2.2
Pairwork

We have mentioned pairwork before (e.g. for question and answer practice, information gap exercises, simulations, etc.) and students can be put in pairs for a great variety of work including writing and reading.

Pairwork seems to be a good idea because it immediately increases the amount of student practice. If we refer back to our imaginary class of forty students we can immediately see that at any one time (in an oral pairwork exercise) twenty students are talking at once instead of one. Pairwork allows the students to use language (depending of course on the task set by the teacher) and also encourages student co-operation which is itself important for the atmosphere of the class and for the motivation it gives to learning with others. Since the teacher as controller is no longer oppressively present students can help each other to use and learn language. The teacher will still be able to act as an assessor, prompter or resource, of course. With pairwork, then, students can practise language use and joint learning.

Certain problems occur with pairwork, however. Incorrectness is a worry, but as we have repeatedly said accuracy is not the only standard to judge learning by: communicative efficiency is also vitally important and pairwork encourages such efficiency.

Teachers sometimes worry about noise and indiscipline when pairwork is used particularly with children and adolescents. A lot depends here on the task we set and on our attitude during the activity. If we go and concentrate on one pair in the corner of the room to the exclusion of the others, then indeed the rest of the class may forget their task and start playing about! If there is a danger of this happening the teacher should probably remain at the front of the class (where without interfering in any way we can get a general idea of what is going on) and then organise feedback when the pairwork task is over to see how successful it was. We should try and make sure that the pairwork task is not carried out for too long. Students who are left in pairs for a long time often become bored and are then not only not learning, but also become restless and perhaps badly behaved. If the noise rises to excessive levels then the teacher can simply stop the activity, explain the problem and ask the students to continue more quietly. If this does not work the activity may have to be discontinued.

It is important, though, to remember that the type of pairwork the teacher will organise depends on the type of activity the class is working with. In Chapter 6 we saw many examples where students worked in pairs doing drills, or asking and answering questions using language that had just been presented. Sometimes they will merely be practising a learnt dialogue (see, for example, 6.6.3(a) where students have a brief pairwork session in which they repeat the dialogue before using it – later – as a model for their own conversations) or working together to agree on the answers to a reading exercise.

The point being made here is that it may be a good idea to familiarise students with pairwork at the beginning of a course by giving them this kind of very short, simple, task to perform. As students get used to the idea of working in pairs the teacher can extend the range of activities being offered.

A decision has to be taken about how students are put in pairs. Teachers will have to decide whether they will put strong students with weak students or whether they will vary the combination of the pairs from class to class. Many teachers adopt a random approach to putting students in pairs while others deliberately mix students who do not necessarily sit together.

There seems to be no research to give an answer to the ideal combinations for either pairs or groups (see 11.2.3).

Teachers should probably make their decision based on the particular class and on whether they wish to put special students together, whether they want to do it at random (e.g. by the letter of the alphabet which begins the student's name) or whether they simply put students sitting next to each other in pairs.

Pairwork, then, is a way of increasing student participation and language use. It can be used for an enormous number of activities whether speaking, writing or reading.

11.2.3
Groupwork[6]

Many of the activities in Chapter 8 were designed for students in groups (see for example 8.1.1(a), 8.1.4(c), 8.2.3(a), etc.) and teachers have been realising for some time now the advantages of organising the students into groups of five, for example, to complete certain tasks.

Groupwork seems to be an extremely attractive idea for a number of reasons. Just as in pairwork, we can mention the increase in the amount of student talking time and we can place emphasis on the opportunities it gives students really to use language to communicate with each other. When all the students in a group are working together to produce an advertisement, for example, they will be communicating with each other and more importantly co-operating among themselves. Students will be teaching and learning in the group exhibiting a degree of self-reliance that simply is not possible when the teacher is acting as a controller.

In some ways groupwork is more dynamic than pairwork: there are more people to react with and against in a group and, therefore, there is a greater possibility of discussion. There is a greater chance that at least one member of the group will be able to solve a problem when it arises, and working in groups is potentially more relaxing than working in pairs, for the latter puts a greater demand on the student's ability to co-operate closely with only one other person. It is also true to say that groupwork tasks can often be more exciting and dynamic than some pairwork tasks.

Of course the worries that apply to pairwork (like the use of the students' native language (see 11.2.4), noise and indiscipline) apply equally to groupwork: the problems do not seem insuperable, though, and the solutions will be the same as those for pairwork.

Once again the biggest problem is one of selection of group members. Some teachers use what is called a sociogram where, for example, students are asked to write down the name of the student in the class they would most like to have with them if they were stranded on a desert island. This technique certainly tells the teacher who the popular and unpopular students are, but will not help to form groups of equal sizes since popularity is not shared round a class in such a neat way.[7] At the beginning of a course a sociogram may not be appropriate anyway since students will often not know each other.

A lot of teachers form groups where weak and strong students are mixed together. This is often a good thing for the weak students (although there is a danger that they will be overpowered by the stronger members of the group and will thus not participate) and probably does not hinder the stronger students from getting the maximum benefit from the activity. Sometimes, however, it is probably a good idea to make groups of strong students and groups of weaker students.

The teacher can then give the groups different tasks to perform. It is worth pointing out here that one of the major possibilities offered by groupwork is just this fact: that where there are students of different levels and interests in a class, different groups can be formed so that not all the students are necessarily working on the same material at the same time.

Group size is also slightly problematical: in general it is probably safe to say that groups of more than seven students can be unmanageable since the amount of student participation obviously falls and the organisation of the group itself may start to disintegrate. But this is not always the case and a lot depends on the activity being performed. Where decisions have to be taken as a result of the activity it is probably a good idea to have an odd number in each group since in that way a split decision is impossible (see for example the activity in 8.1.1(b)). In more general tasks (e.g. designing material together or doing the first stage of jigsaw listening, etc.) the necessity for odd numbers in the groups is obviously not so great.

A major possibility for groupwork is the idea of *flexible groups*. Here students start in set groups, and as an activity progresses the groups split up and re-form; or they join together until the class is fully re-formed. An example of this type of flexible grouping is 8.1.4(c) where students start in groups of six and then re-form with each member of the original groups now being a member of another group. The activities in 8.1.1, however, in which students work to reach a consensus, start by having small groups of students. Gradually these groups are joined together. Thus if the class starts in groups of three, two groups will then be joined to make groups of six, then of twelve, etc. (see pages 122 and 123).

One other issue confronts us with groupwork, and that is the possibility of having group leaders. We have already said that different groups may be doing different tasks. There is nothing intrinsically wrong with the idea that while one group is doing a fluency activity, another group should be doing something like an accurate reproduction stage or a listening or reading activity. It may be advantageous in such cases to have one student acting as a group leader. The group leader could have two functions: one would be to act as the *group organiser*, making sure that a task was properly done, that the information was properly recorded or collected, etc., and the other could be as a *mini-teacher* where a student could conduct a drill or a dialogue, etc. In the latter case the teacher would have to make sure that the student was properly primed for the task. Certainly in mixed-ability groups (where students do not all have the same level of English) the idea of a student acting as a mini-teacher is attractive. In practice, though, even where groups are leaderless, students tend to take on definite roles. While one student is permanently commenting on what is happening (e.g. 'We seem to be agreeing on this point') another is permanently disagreeing with everybody! Some students seem to need to push the group towards a quick decision while others keep quiet unless they are forced to speak. This seems to be a matter of individual personality and few teachers are equipped to make reasoned judgements about exactly how to handle such situations. Ideally all teachers would take a training in psychology including a lot of work on group dynamics: if teachers have not done this, common sense and a degree of sensitivity seem essential.

Groupwork offers enormous potential. It can be used for oral work, tasks where decisions have to be taken, joint reading tasks, listening tasks, co-operative writing and many other things: it also has the great advantage of allowing different groups of students to be doing different things in the same classroom.

11.2.4
The use of the mother tongue

One of the biggest problems in the use of pairwork and groupwork is the use of the mother tongue by students in monolingual groups. It sometimes seems that they are unable or unwilling to take part in activities in English. How can a teacher try to discourage the use of the mother tongue? Should a teacher always discourage it?[8]

If students are speaking in their own language rather than English during an oral communicative activity then clearly the activity is fairly pointless. If, however, students are comparing their answers to reading comprehension questions, or trying to do a vocabulary-matching exercise in pairs then their occasional use of the mother tongue need not concern us. They are concentrating exclusively on English, and if a bit of their own language helps them to do this in a relaxed way that is all to the good. We have already said that teachers may want to have students translate the instructions they have given to check if the students have understood them (see 11.1.3). In other words, our attitude to the students' use of their own language will change, depending on the activity they and we are involved in.

It is important that students realise that our attitude to their language depends on the activity in question. If they don't know this they will not know why and when we are insisting on 'English only'.

There are three things we can do about the use of the students' language:

(a) Talk to the class

Have a discussion with the students (in their own language if they are beginners) about the use of their language. Get them to understand that whilst sometimes it is not too much of a problem, during oral activities it is not helpful. Ask them what they think the point of communicative activities is and get them to agree that it is essential for them to try and stick to the use of English in such activities even where it is difficult.

(b) During an activity

Encourage the students to use English. Go round the classroom helping students away from their language for this activity. Students will naturally slip into their language unless you remind them and prompt them.

In most classes the use of discussion and explanation, and the prompting of students during activities, ensures that English is used most of the time. With some groups, however, your efforts may not appear to be successful.

(c) Back to basics

With some groups your attempts to have them use English do not work; despite your explanations and promptings, students will not use English. In such cases tell them that as a consequence of this you are not going to use that type of activity any more. Use only tightly controlled activities for pairwork until you are confident that they will take part properly. Then become a little more adventurous and gradually move back in stages towards the use of freer activities in groups.

11.2.5
Individual study

Sometimes we must let students work on their own at their own pace. If we do not we will not be allowing the individual any learning 'space' at all.

Individual study is a good idea precisely because students can relax from outside pressure (provided there is no time limit or competitive element) and because they can rely on themselves rather than other people. Both reading and writing work can be the focus for individual study – although as we have seen in Chapters 9 and 10 there are many uses for pair and groupwork here as well.

Individual study is also frequently quiet! This attribute should not be underestimated. Sometimes we need a period of relative silence to reassemble our learning attitudes.

Of course language laboratories, listening centres, learning centres and individual computer terminals are ideal for students working on their own. Where such facilities exist, teachers should try and ensure that self-study is a planned part of the weekly programme. Where they do not exist, however, teachers should not forget the importance of individual study in their enthusiasm for pair and groupwork.

The use of different student groupings must be sensitively handled. While we, as teachers, may be clear on the value of groupwork, for example, students may resent always having to work with their peers.[9] There are occasions where a class needs to have a teacher controlling what is going on. The nature of the task has a lot to do with this as well, as do the students' reactions to each other. In other words, while we may rightly conclude that the use of different student groupings is vital in any language programme we should also use these groupings intelligently and appropriately in order to create positive learning for our students, not provoke negative reactions.

11.3 Disruptive behaviour[10]

At some stage of their lives all teachers encounter disruptive behaviour – a student or students whose behaviour gets in the way of the class. Such outbursts are frequently hostile to the teacher or the other students and they can be difficult to deal with.

Disruptive behaviour is not confined to one age group. Eleven-year-olds can become incredibly unruly and noisy, and adolescents may become completely unresponsive and unco-operative. Adult students are disruptive in different ways. They may publicly disagree with the teacher or try to become the class character to the detriment of their peers. There are lots of ways of disrupting a class!

One way of avoiding most disruptive behaviour (though not all) is by making sure that all your students of whatever age know 'where you stand'. Somehow you and they have to agree upon a *code of conduct*. With many adult classes this is an unspoken arrangement: with younger students it may need to be spelled out.

A code of conduct involves the teacher and students in forms of behaviour in the classroom. Certain things do not comply with such forms of behaviour – for example arriving late, interrupting other students when they speak, bringing drinks and food into the room, forgetting to do homework, not paying attention, etc. Where a code of conduct is established both teacher and students will recognise these acts as outside the code.

The teacher's role in the first few classes with a new group will be to establish the code through discussion and example. If this is done it will be easier to show students where they are going wrong later on. It is worth emphasising that the establishment of a code will be done differently, depending on the age of the students. With adults you may discuss the norms of behaviour that should apply, whereas with younger children you may be a bit more dictatorial – although here too the agreement of the class about what the code should be will greatly improve the chances of success.

Now that you have a code of conduct things should be all right. And yet students still behave badly. Why is this?

11.3.1 Causes of discipline problems

There seem to be three possible reasons for discipline problems: the teacher, the students and the institution. We will examine each of these in turn.

(a) The teacher

The behaviour and the attitude of the teacher is perhaps the single most important factor in a classroom, and thus can have a major effect on discipline. We can make a list of things that teachers should probably not do if they want to avoid problems:

Don't go to class unprepared: Students automatically identify teachers who are not sure what to do in the classroom. Particularly for those classes that might cause trouble, the teacher has to appear to be well prepared and knowledgeable about the subject.

Don't be inconsistent: If the teacher allows students to come to class late without taking action one week they cannot be reproached for doing the same thing again the week after. Teachers have to be consistent, in other words, about what the code of conduct is otherwise the students will lose respect for it.

Don't issue threats: Teachers who threaten students with terrible punishments and then do not carry them out are doing both the class and themselves a disservice. Hopefully threats are not necessary, but it is absolutely fatal to say that some action is going to be taken if it is not.

Don't raise your voice: One of the great mistakes of many teachers is to try and establish control by raising their voices and shouting. This almost always has disastrous consequences for it contributes to a general raising of the level of noise in the classroom. Very often a quiet voice is far more effective.

Don't give boring classes: We saw in Chapter 1 how important students found it that classes should be interesting (see page 6). It seems true that perhaps the greatest single cause of indiscipline is boredom. Interested students do not misbehave in the same way.

Don't be unfair: Teachers cannot allow themselves to be unfair, either to the class as a whole or to individuals. Teachers should always try to avoid having favourites or picking on particular individuals. Most teachers, of course, have students that they like or dislike more than others, but a major part of their job is not to show these preferences and prejudices in the classroom.

Don't have a negative attitude to learning: A teacher who does not really care and who is insensitive to the students' reactions to what is happening in the classroom will lose the respect of the students – the first step to problems of disruptive behaviour.

Don't break the code: If part of the code is that the students should arrive on time, then the teacher must too. If there is a ban on chewing gum then the teacher should not chew gum. If homework must be handed in on time then it must also be corrected promptly. A teacher who behaves in a way that is considered anti-social and which is disapproved of if imitated by the students will destroy the code of conduct, for it either exists for the group as a whole (including the teacher) or it does not exist at all.

(b) The students

A teacher who does everything to avoid trouble may still have problems because of the students: and all practising teachers know that while one group may cause no trouble, another may be difficult to handle.

There are, of course, a number of reasons why students behave badly and we can mention a few of these:

Time of day: The attitude of the students is often affected by when the class takes place. If the students are all tired after a long day of study they may find exacting classes too challenging. If the class takes place just before lunch students may tend not to pay too much attention as the lunch hour approaches. Early morning classes may cause students to be sleepy; classes after lunch are often full of drowsy students. The teacher must take these factors into account when planning the class (see Chapter 12).

The student's attitude: A lot depends on how the student views the class, the teacher, and the subject being learnt. Clearly, therefore, it is important for these to be seen in a positive – or at least neutral – light. For many reasons, though, students are often hostile to English classes and their teachers. Where a student starts with a negative attitude, however, much can be done: if the class is interesting – if students can become interested even against their better judgement – a lot of the problem will disappear.

A desire to be noticed: It is generally accepted that adolescence is a difficult time and that young adolescents often need to be noticed or have a desire to be recognised in some way. This is not just special to adolescents, however, and most teachers are familiar with students in their classes who demand attention and who are quite prepared to be disruptive in order to gain the recognition they need. It seems somewhat short-sighted, then, to label such bad behaviour as in some way wicked and punish it harshly. Much more important is the possibility of channelling this behaviour and involving the student; if recognition is what is needed then the teacher should try to make sure that it can be given within the context of the language class.

Two's company: Two students being disruptive together are far more effective than one! They may encourage each other in their anti-social behaviour and gradually influence the whole group. Action in such cases has to be taken fairly rapidly, and much can be achieved if students are reseated, if the troublemakers are separated, and if particularly disruptive students are made to sit at the front.

Students have a number of reasons for behaving badly: they cannot always be easily controlled and much will depend on the particular group and the particular teacher. In general, though, a bored student is a discipline problem, whereas an interested student who knows and understands the code is not.

(c) The institution

A lot depends on the attitude of the institution to disruptive student behaviour. Ideally there will be a recognised system for dealing with problem classes and students. It is to be hoped that the teacher can consult co-ordinators or department heads when in trouble, and that cases of extremely bad behaviour can be acted upon by such people.

If the institution does not have a recognised policy for dealing with discipline problems then it is up to the teachers to press for such a system.

Ultimately a student who causes a severe problem has to be handled by the school authority rather than by teachers on their own and it is, therefore, in the teachers' interest to see that there is a coherent policy.

Teachers should be careful about showing that they disagree with the policy of the institution (where they do) since this can have a bad effect generally on other classes in the same area. Teachers who disagree about things like the choice of textbook, for example, should not show this disagreement too openly to the students, but work with the administration to have the decision changed.

There are many causes of discipline problems, some of which we have looked at in this section. Generally we have been dealing with classes of children and adolescents, but many of the comments we have made apply equally well to adult classes for here too the teacher must have some kind of code of conduct and must take account, for example, of the time of day when the class takes place.

11.3.2
Action in case of indiscipline

There are a number of things a teacher can do when students behave badly, but in general two points can be made. Any 'punishment' that hurts a student physically or emotionally is probably dangerous and harmful in many ways. Its effect cannot be measured and it probably encourages in the student behaviour and psychology that we would want to avoid as educators.

The ability to control a group of students when things get out of hand depends to a large extent on the personality of the teacher, and some teachers certainly appear to find it easier than others. There are, however, a number of measures that can be taken.

(a) Act immediately

We have stressed the need for a code. When it is broken the teacher should act immediately. If the indiscipline involves anti-social behaviour in the classroom the teacher should take steps at once. Where it involves things like not bringing books to class the teacher should speak to the student either during or immediately after the class.

The longer a discipline problem is left unchecked, the more difficult it is to take action.

(b) Stop the class

Where the indiscipline involves disruptive behaviour the teacher should immediately stop the class. This is a clear indication to all the students that something is wrong. The teacher may then tell the students who are behaving badly what is wrong. Many teachers refuse to re-start the class until the student has settled down; they simply stop the class, make it clear that the student's behaviour is unsatisfactory, and wait until things improve.

(c) Reseating

An effective way of controlling a student who is behaving badly is to make the student sit in a different place immediately. Certainly where troublesome students are sitting together they should be separated. Often if students are moved to the front of the class they will behave better.

(d) Change the activity

Particularly where a majority of the class seem to be gradually getting out of control, a change of activity will often restore order. Thus a quick writing task will often quieten students down and at the same time provide good writing practice. The same effect can often be achieved by a reading task or a listening exercise.

In general, anti-social behaviour can usually be cured if students are given something to do which will involve them.

(e) After the class

Where one student is continually giving trouble the teacher should probably take that student to one side after the class is over. It will be necessary to explain to the student why the behaviour is anti-social. At the same time the student should be given a chance to say why he or she behaves in this way. The teacher can also clearly spell out the consequences if the disruptive behaviour continues.

(f) Using the institution

When problems become extreme it will be necessary to use the institution – the school or institute – to solve them. Many institutes will then seek the help of the child's parents (where children are concerned). This seems a reasonable thing to do since it is important for parents to be involved in their children's education. They can be contacted in cases of continual lateness, truancy, forgetting to bring materials and bad behaviour.

The institution, of course, has the final power of expulsion or exclusion; it is to be hoped that it is almost never used. The institution does also have the power to warn students of the consequences of their action, to change students from one class to another and to explain to students its attitude towards bad behaviour.

Teachers should not have to suffer serious problems on their own. They should consult their co-ordinators, department heads and principals when they need help.

There are, of course, other possible courses of action where indiscipline takes place; the options we have looked at avoid the possibility of either physical assault or humiliation: both are seriously wrong particularly for children and adolescents.

11.4 Conclusions

In this chapter we have discussed the subject of class management. We have seen that a teacher has a number of different roles and that the adoption of only one of these (e.g. teacher as controller) will be detrimental to a varied and interesting class. Teachers must be aware of the different roles they can adopt and know when and how to use them.

We have discussed student groupings and shown how lockstep on its own is not sufficient. We have shown the advantages and disadvantages of pairwork, groupwork and individual study and discussed their importance during the learning process, showing that it is during group-and pairwork that a lot of real learning (rather than teaching) takes place since the students can really use language to communicate with one another.

We have discussed the difficult problem of discipline and said that it involves a code of conduct designed so that learning can be efficient and effective. We have shown some reasons for indiscipline and we have also suggested some action that can be taken when the code of conduct is not adhered to.

Discussion

1 When do you think the teacher should act as a controller? Why?
2 Can you think of any other roles the teacher might adopt in the classroom apart from the ones mentioned here?
3 How much time do you think should be devoted to lockstep, pairwork, groupwork and individual study?
4 Why do you think groupwork is important?
5 Can you think of any other reasons why discipline problems might occur other than those quoted in 11.3.1?
6 Do you agree with the various courses of action in 11.3.2? What other action would you be prepared to take in cases of indiscipline?

Exercises

1 Take any two activities from Chapters 6–10 of this book and say what roles the teacher will be adopting for each activity and why.
2 Look at the textbook you are using (or one you are familiar with) and identify those activities which are intended for pair-and/or groupwork.
3 Take any activity from your textbook (or one you are familiar with) which is concerned with practice output or communicative output and say how you would organise the activity.
4 Take a reading and/or listening exercise from your textbook (or one you are familiar with) and say what you will do for the lead-in stage. What instructions will you give?
5 What items would you include in a 'code of conduct' for a class of thirteen-year-olds? Make a list and then decide how you would present the code to the class.

References

1 On the role of the teacher see A Wright (1987), and H Widdowson (1987) in more philosophical vein. A McLean's provocative views on the traditional role of the teacher (McLean 1980) are also worth reading. R Gower and S Walters (1983) Chapters 2 and 3 discuss the behaviour of the teacher and the management of a classroom.
2 K Blanchard et al. (1987) in their book *Leadership and the One Minute Manager* – written for corporation management in the USA – see the extremes in four stages: *directing – coaching – supporting – delegating* where delegating is directly opposite to the directing (or controlling) role.
3 See C Crouch (1989) for examples of successful 'performance teaching'.
4 See T Lowe (1985).
5 The teacher's role in lockstep can change. W Plumb (1978) shows examples of this.

6 On groupwork see D Byrne (1986) pp. 76–80, A Littlejohn (1987) and G Jacobs (1988).
7 D Byrne (see reference 6) suggests groups of roughly equal size.
M Long (1977) suggests that it is not necessary to have groups of equal size if the sociogram (or similar device) indicates unequal groups.
8 D Atkinson (1987) argues that we have ignored the benefits that mother tongue use can bring.
9 See J Reid (1987).
10 A number of the ideas in this section resulted from collaboration with Jean Pender and other colleagues at the Instituto Anglo–Mexicano de Cultura in Guadalajara.

12 Planning

In previous chapters we have come to conclusions about a general methodological approach (see Chapter 4) and we have looked at a number of ideas for various learning and teaching stages (see Chapters 5 to 10). We have discussed the need for the teacher to adopt different roles and for different student groupings (see Chapter 11). We are now in a position to consider how we can include such ideas in our own classes in less than a purely random way.

The best techniques and activities will not have much point if they are not, in some way, integrated into a programme of studies and few teachers would take an activity or piece of material into class without first having a reason for doing so. The best teachers are those who think carefully about what they are going to do in their classes and who plan how they are going to organise the teaching and learning.

In this chapter we will consider such issues and come to some conclusions about the guiding principles behind lesson planning. We are concerned about how to plan a class (whether it is of forty-five, fifty, sixty or seventy-five minutes' duration) taking into consideration what the students have recently been doing and what we hope they will do in the future. We will not consider an overall plan of study (for a term or a year), since decisions about the syllabus and general course content are often taken not by the individual teacher but by a school authority: we will confine ourselves to the teacher's role in planning (although in 12.1 we will make some comments about how such courses are generally described).

We will look at *planning, textbooks and the syllabus, planning principles, what teachers should know, the pre-plan* and *the plan*.

12.1 Planning, textbooks and the syllabus

All too often overall decisions about course content are not taken by teachers, but by some higher authority. Of course it will be necessary for a large institution to know that the same kind of teaching is taking place in all of its classes at the same level, but previous decisions about the exact syllabus and the textbook to be used can often tie teachers to a style of teaching and to the content of the classes if they are not careful.

Many institutions present the syllabus in terms of the main textbook to be used: by a certain date teachers are expected to have covered a certain number of units in the book. At the same time teachers are often provided with a list of supplementary material and activities that are available. Whether or not the course is tied to a particular textbook, its syllabus will generally have a list of language items at its core (see 3.6): the assumption being made is that these language items will be new for the students and should therefore be introduced to them in the order of the syllabus.

Where a textbook is involved there are obvious advantages for both teacher and students. Good textbooks often contain lively and interesting material; they provide a sensible progression of language items, clearly showing what has to be learnt and in some cases summarising what has been studied so that students can revise grammatical and functional points that they have been concentrating on. Textbooks can be systematic about the amount of vocabulary presented to the student and allow students to study on their own outside the class. Good textbooks also relieve the teacher from the pressure of having to think of original material for every class. Indeed there is a greater variety of published material for teaching and learning English than ever before.

But textbooks can also have an adverse effect on teaching for a number of reasons.[1] As we have already said they tend to concentrate on the introduction of new language and controlled work: a teacher relying too heavily on the textbook will often not be encouraged to provide enough roughly-tuned input or output practice (see Chapter 4). Textbooks also tend to follow the same format from one unit to the next. There are good reasons why this should be the case: they are thus easier to 'get to know' and to handle, both for teacher and student, and they are also easier to design and write. But this similarity of format generally involves a rigid sequence. Almost all textbooks at the elementary level start by introducing new language, for example, and they then follow a sequence of practice combining the new language with language the students already know. Reading and listening generally have a set place in the sequence and each unit looks more or less like those that come before and after it.

Discerning teachers with time to spare can move around the material selecting what they want to use and discarding parts of the units that seem to them to be inappropriate. Most teachers, though, are under considerable pressure both because they are obliged to complete the syllabus and because they teach a number of classes. They are also influenced by the attitude of the institution, their colleagues and the students who sometimes see the textbook not just as the provider of a syllabus but also as a programme of study and activities that has to be closely followed.

There are two major reasons why such an attitude may not be in the best interests of either students or teachers. In the first place teachers who over-use a textbook and thus repeatedly follow the sequence in each unit may become boring over a period of time for they will find themselves teaching the same type of activities in the same order again and again. In such a situation, even with good textbooks, students may find the study of English becoming routine and thus less and less motivating. Classes will start appearing increasingly similar and the routine will become increasingly monotonous. One of the cornerstones of good planning is the use of variety in teaching precisely to offset this tendency (see 12.2). The other main reason for worrying about textbooks is that they are not written for your class. Each group of students is potentially different from any other (see 12.3.3) and while most published books are written with a 'general' student audience in mind your class is unique. It may not conform to the general pattern, and the students need to be treated individually.

Another worry is whether the textbook has a balance of skills and activities that we said was desirable for the balanced activities approach (see 4.4). The need for balance is also a motivational consideration since, as we have said, a teacher who follows a programme of similar activities day after day will bore the students. In 12.2 we will study the need for variety in lesson planning in some detail. The balanced activities approach realises the need for balance, in terms of the different activities with which the students are faced, in order to provide them with an interesting and varied programme of study. And the best person to achieve the correct balance is the teacher who knows the students and can gauge the need for variety and what the balance should be. This is particularly true in the planning of activities during the pre-plan stage (see 12.4(a)).

It is not being suggested that textbooks are somehow destructive: the better ones are written by teachers and writers with considerable knowledge and skill and have much to recommend them; textbook writers are increasingly responding to the kind of worries expressed here, attempting to build flexibility and balance into their materials. But the textbook rarely has the perfect balance that the teacher is looking for. The textbook, in other words, is an aid (often the most important one there is) and not a sacred text. Teachers will have to work out the best ways to use their books; they should never let the textbook use them, or dictate the decisions they take about the activities in which the students are going to be involved. The contents of the pre-plan (see 12.4) will show how other considerations (apart from just textbook and syllabus) are incorporated into the planning process.[2]

12.2 Planning principles[3]

The two overriding principles behind good lesson planning are *variety* and *flexibility*. Variety means involving students in a number of different types of activity and where possible introducing them to a wide selection of materials; it means planning so that learning is interesting and never monotonous for the students. Flexibility comes into play when dealing with the plan in the classroom; for any number of reasons what the teacher has planned may not be appropriate for that class on that particular day. The flexible teacher will be able to change the plan in such a situation. Flexibility is the characteristic we would expect from the genuinely adaptable teacher.

We have already commented on the danger of routine and monotony and how students may become de-motivated if they are always faced with the same type of class. This danger can only be avoided if the teacher believes that the learning experience should be permanently stimulating and interesting. This is difficult to achieve, but at least if the activities the students are faced with are varied there will be the interest of doing different things. If new language is always introduced in the same way (e.g. if it is always introduced in a dialogue) then the introduction stages of the class will become gradually less and less challenging. If all reading activities always concentrate on extracting specific information and never ask the students to do anything else, reading will become less interesting. The same is true of any activity that is constantly repeated. Our aim must be to provide a variety of different learning activities which will help individual students to get to grips with the language. And this means giving the students a purpose and telling them what the purpose is. Students need to know why they are doing something and what it is supposed they will achieve. We have stressed the need for a purpose particularly with communicative activities (see 5.3) and receptive skills (see 10.1.2): but teachers must have a purpose for all the activities they organise in a class and they should communicate that purpose to their students.

In any one class there will be a number of different personalities with different ways of looking at the world. The activity that is particularly appropriate for one student may not be ideal for another. But teachers who vary their teaching approach may be able to satisfy most of their students at different times.

Variety is a principle that applies especially to a series of classes. Over a two-week period, for example, we will try and do different things in the classes. Variety also applies to a lesser extent to a single class period. Although there are some activities that can last for fifty minutes it seems generally true that changes of activity during that time are advisable. An introduction of new language that lasted for fifty minutes would probably be counter-productive, and it is noticeable how an over-long accurate reproduction stage tires students and fails to be very effective. We would not expect, either, to ask the students to engage in reading comprehension for a whole class. We might, however, be able to base a whole class on one reading passage, but only if we varied the activities that we could use with it. Thus we might get students to read to extract specific information; this could be followed by some discussion, some intensive work and some kind of written or oral follow-up. Children, especially, need to do different things in fairly quick succession since they will generally not be able to concentrate on one activity for a long stretch of time.

The teacher who believes in variety will have to be flexible since the only way to provide variety is to use a number of different techniques: not all of these will fit into one methodology (teachers should be immediately suspicious of anyone who says they have the answer to language teaching for this will imply a lack of flexibility).

Good lesson planning is the art of mixing techniques, activities and materials in such a way that an ideal balance is created for the class. In a general language course there will be work on the four skills (although a teacher will probably come to a decision about the relative merits of each skill): there will be presentation and controlled practice, roughly-tuned input (receptive skill work) and communicative activities. Different student groupings will be used.

If teachers have a large variety of techniques and activities that they can use with students they can then apply themselves to the central question of lesson planning: 'What is it that my students will feel, know or be able to do at the end of the class (or classes) that they did not feel or know or were not able to do at the beginning of the class (or classes)?' We can say, for example, that they will feel more positive about learning English at the end of the class than they did at the beginning as a result of activities that were enjoyable; we can say that they will know some new language that they did not know before; we can say that they will be able to write a type of letter that they were not able to write before, for example.

In answering the central question teachers will create the objectives for the class. Students may be involved in a game-like activity because the teacher's objective is to have them relax and feel more positive about their English classes. The students may be given a reading passage to work on because the teacher's objective is to improve their ability to extract specific information from written texts. New language may be introduced because the objective is that students should know how to refer to the past, for example.

We will return to these issues in 12.4 and 12.5 but first we will look at what the teacher should know before starting to plan.

12.3
What teachers should know

Before teachers can start to consider planning their classes they need to know a considerable amount about three main areas: *the job of teaching, the institution* and *the students*.

12.3.1
The job of teaching

Clearly well-prepared teachers need to know a lot about the job they are to do before they can start to make successful plans. There are six major areas of necessary knowledge.

(a) The language for the level

Clearly teachers must know the language that they are to teach. By 'know' we mean that teachers must be able to use the language themselves and also have an insight into the rules that govern its form and the factors which affect its use. This is obviously the result not only of the teacher's own knowledge of English but also of preparation and study where facts about language can be absorbed.[4]

(b) The skills for the level

Teachers need to 'know' the skills they are going to ask their students to perform. It is no good asking students to do a report if you cannot do it yourself!

(c) The learning aids available for the level

We need to know what aids are available and appropriate for the level we are teaching. These may include wall pictures, flashcards, flipcharts, cards, charts, tapes, tape recorders, video playback machines, overhead projectors, computer hardware and software, sets of books and materials and, of course, the board.

(d) Stages and techniques in teaching

We need to know and recognise different teaching techniques and stages. We need to know the difference between accurate reproduction and communicative activities so that we do not, for example, act as controller in both cases. We also need to be able to recognise stages in the textbook we are using so that we realise when an activity is controlled rather than free and vice versa. In particular, then, we must have a working knowledge of the issues discussed in Chapter 5 and the principles behind the teaching of receptive skills.

(e) A repertoire of activities

Well-prepared teachers have a large repertoire of activities for their classes. They can organise presentation and controlled output practice; they can direct students in the acquiring of receptive skills and organise genuinely communicative activities. This repertoire of activities enables them to have varied plans and achieve an activities balance.

(f) Classroom management skills

Well-prepared teachers will have good classroom management skills (see Chapter 11). They will be able to adopt a number of different roles, will be able to use different student groupings, and will be able to maintain discipline.

These areas are all vitally important for a teacher and they all imply a lot of work particularly where a level is being taught for the first time. Without these areas of knowledge a teacher is in a poor position to make decisions about lesson planning.

12.3.2
The institution

Teachers need to know a lot about the institution in so far as it is involved with their teaching. The following five areas of knowledge are crucial.

(a) Time, length, frequency

It sounds silly to emphasise that the teacher should know at what time, for how long and how often classes take place. Nevertheless this is clearly important since it will affect all planning.

(b) Physical conditions

Teachers need to know what physical conditions exist in the place(s) that they are going to teach. It is no good taking in an electrically powered tape recorder if there is no socket for a plug in the classroom! When planning it will be important to bear that kind of detail in mind as well as more major considerations like the condition of the chairs and blackboard, the brightness of the lighting, the size of the room, etc.

(c) Syllabus

It is clearly important to be familiar with the syllabus the institution has for the levels that are being taught. We will have to be sure in general terms that we can cover the majority of the syllabus where possible. It is impossible to plan within an institution without such knowledge.

(d) Exams

It is also extremely important to know what type of exams (if any) the students will have to take and when, since clearly a major responsibility of the teacher will be to try and ensure that the students are successful in tests and exams.

(e) Restrictions

Teachers should be aware of any restrictions imposed by the institution upon their teaching: apart from the obvious restrictions of physical size and shape of the classroom, there are also the limitations of class size, availability of aids and physical conditions (see (b) above).

Clearly a knowledge of all these things is vital if the teacher is to make plans that are realistic in the circumstances.

12.3.3 The students	Teachers need to know a considerable amount about their students. We have already made the point that each class is unique (see 12.1) and as a result, each class will need to be treated differently. Nowhere is this more true than in planning, where we select the activities that will be suitable for our students. In order to do so we obviously need to know a lot about them.

Teachers need to know *who the students are*, *what the students bring to the class* and *what the students need*.

(a) Who the students are

It is obviously necessary for teachers to know about the following things:

Age: How old are the students? Are they children? Adolescents? In each case they will need to be treated differently (see 1.3) from each other and from an adult class. Are they all more or less the same age?

Sex: Are they all girls/women? Is there a mixture of the sexes? Are they all men? In an ideal world the sex of the students should make no difference to the activities and content of the lesson. In practice, however, there are still countries where a teacher may well feel that what is suitable for one sex is not suitable for the other.

Social background: It is important to know if your students are rich or poor; whether or not they are used to luxury or are oppressed by it. What kind of behaviour is usual in the social class to which they belong? In a classless society where wealth was adequately shared this might not be so important. Such societies do not exist, however! Especially where a small minority of the students come from a different social background to the rest of the class it will be vital to take this fact into account when planning the content of your class.

Occupation: Clearly the occupation of your students will help you to make decisions about your planning. Where a teacher is fortunate enough to have thirty students who all have the same occupation (see 1.1(d)) the task will be considerably easier since assumptions can be made about what things the students know and what activities they are used to. Certainly this is the case with secondary school classes, etc., but with adults there is usually a variety of different occupations represented by the students.

Of these four items the most difficult to ascertain will be the students' socioeconomic background. Teachers might well prepare a confidential questionnaire at the beginning of the term/semester to help them get an idea of such information.

(b) What the students bring to the class

Teachers need to know how the students feel about learning English and what they 'know'. Again there are four major areas for them to investigate:

Motivation and attitude: How do the students feel about learning English? Are they generally positive about coming to class? Do they feel friendly or hostile towards the culture that English represents for them? What is their attitude to teachers and to their English teacher in particular? Clearly special efforts will have to be made with hostile students having negative attitudes and teachers might well place a greater emphasis on motivating the students than on anything else, at least for a time.

Educational background: Closely tied to motivation and attitude is the educational background of the students. Clearly the content of the class will be different if the students are postgraduates than if they have never got beyond primary education. At the same time the educational experiences of the students are important. Some students who have been previously unsuccessful may need more encouragement than usual. The style of their previous learning is also important. Students who have been rigidly disciplined in a classroom where the teacher is the only person speaking may find the sudden insistence on communication and interaction difficult to take (and vice versa). Again the teacher may think it a good idea to issue a questionnaire – or at least talk to the students informally – at the beginning of the term/semester.

Knowledge: Teachers will want to know about various aspects of the students' knowledge. For example we will obviously want to know how much English each student knows. At the same time, though, we will want to know how well the students perform in their own language: can they write academic papers, do they write informal letters fluently?, etc.

Another important major area of knowledge concerns the world in general. How much do students know about current affairs? Are there parts of the world about which they appear to be largely ignorant? Are there large areas of knowledge they do not have? It is vital to know this since much planning will be unsuccessful if we assume knowledge of current events, etc. which the students do not have. It might be worth adding here that teachers are often scathing about their students' apparent ignorance; if this is the case they should try and work out what world knowledge *they* are unfamiliar with. It is a salutory experience.

Interests: Teachers will want to know what the students' interests are (and we will be lucky if we can find a majority interest in various subjects). Often we will take planning decisions on the basis of student interest rather than anything else (see 12.4): it should not be forgotten that interest is a primary ingredient of motivation.

(c) What the students need

We have said that different types of student will need to be treated differently (see 1.3): we also saw that people learn languages for a variety of different reasons (see 1.1). Particularly in the light of why our students are studying language we must analyse what their needs are.

If we are teaching a group of medical students who are unlikely to have to use oral English in their professional lives, but who need to be able to read medical textbooks in English, we might at once identify the ability to read scientific texts (medical, in this case) as the students' need and therefore design a course consisting exclusively of exercises and texts designed only to give students this ability. If our students are training to be travel guides, on the other hand, we might identify their biggest need as being the ability to give quick oral descriptions and answer factual questions in English (as well as the ability to 'organise' people and give directions, etc. in English). The point being made is that where possible teachers or co-ordinators should find out exactly what it is their students really need English for[5] and use this knowledge to make decisions about course design. What skills should have greater emphasis? Is there a need for communicative oral activities or should the emphasis be on writing? The analysis of student needs helps to answer these questions and provide a sound basis for course decisions.

The fact that a student need has been identified, however, does not necessarily mean that all decisions about course design and planning can be taken immediately. Two more considerations are important; student wants and methodological principles.

The fact that the medical students' need is to be able to read medical texts in English does not necessarily mean that all they want to do for all and every English class is read medical texts. They might want to learn some oral English, be able to write informal letters, etc. The travel guide's needs may be largely oral but the students might also want to be able to read English novels. In other words, needs and wants are not necessarily the same and the job of the course designer and lesson planner is to try and reach a compromise between the two. Thus the main theme running through our course for medical students might be the reading and understanding of medical texts. But this might be integrated with oral work about the texts, or might even run side by side with work on oral social English. What is being suggested is that we will have to pay attention to what the students want even where it seems to conflict with student needs.

Even where wants and needs are compatible and well-established, however, there may be good reasons for using material which is not especially directed towards those needs. We have already stressed the concepts of variety and flexibility in lesson planning and they are no less important with specialist classes than for the 'general' class. Even where students are studying English for a specific purpose (ESP, see 1.1(d)) teachers will want to include a variety of motivating activities. The initial enthusiasm of students who are studying ESP can easily be destroyed unless the teacher remembers general planning principles.

The majority of students, however, will be studying English for a reason that makes their needs difficult to identify (see 3.6.4). In such cases we will teach the four skills, making our decisions about how much weight to give each skill (and the language to be used) as best we can.

A detailed knowledge of the students, then, is essential when planning what activities to use and what subject matter to teach. It is important for the students to be interested in the subject, but it is also important that they should be able to cope with its level of difficulty (not just of the language, but also the content): where there are clearly definable student needs it is important for the students to see that the teacher has taken account of these needs and is organising classes accordingly – although we should bear in mind our comments about needs and wants and the importance of general planning principles.

Knowing the students (who they are, what they bring to class and what their needs are) will give the teacher a good idea of how to provide a programme of balanced activities that will be most motivating and most beneficial to the students.

12.4
The pre-plan

Teachers who are knowledgeable about the institution, the profession and the students, are ready to start making a plan. Before actually writing down the exact contents of such a plan, however, we will need to think about what we are going to do in a general way so that our decisions are taken on the basis of sound reasoning. This is where the *pre-plan* is formed.

The idea of the pre-plan is for teachers to get a general idea of what they are going to do in the next class or classes. Based on our knowledge of the students and the syllabus we can consider four main areas: *activities*, *language skills*, *language type*, and *subject and content*. When we have ideas of what we want to do as a result of considering these areas we can decide whether such ideas are feasible given the institution and its restrictions. When this has been done we have our pre-plan and we can then move towards the final detailed plan. The concept of the pre-plan and how it operates is summarised in figure 28.

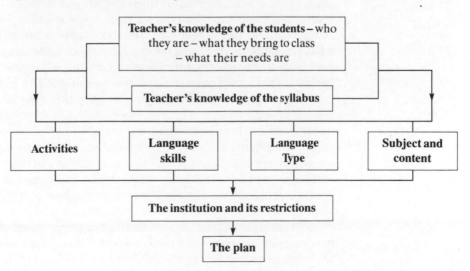

Figure 28 The pre-plan

We will now consider the four major elements of the pre-plan:

(a) Activities

'Activities' is a loose term used to give a general description of what will happen in a class. It is important to realise that here we are not talking in any way about items of language; we are talking about what, generally and physically, the students are going to do.

A game is an activity; so is a simulation. The introduction of new language is an activity; so is parallel writing or story reconstruction. Listening is an activity and so is an information gap task; 'The hot seat' (see 7.1.4(c)) is an activity, so is an oral composition.

An activity is what teachers think of when they are asked. 'What are you going to do in class today?'. Rather than give details they will often say, 'Oh, I've got a nice group-writing task and then we're going to do a song.'

When teachers think of what to do in their classes it is vital to consider the students and what they have been doing recently. If, for example, they have been doing largely controlled work (e.g. presentation and controlled practice) then the teacher may well take a preliminary decision to plan a freer activity. Only subsequently will he or she decide what skill or skills this might involve. If recent work has been very tiring, challenging, and over-serious the teacher may make an immediate decision to include an activity whose main purpose is to give the students an enjoyable time. If, on the other hand, the last two classes have largely consisted of communicative activities the teacher may decide to include language input or controlled work.

Teachers should make decisions about activities independently of what language or language skills they have to teach. Their first planning thought should centre round what kind of class would be appropriate for the particular group of students on a particular day. It is in this consideration of activities as a starting point for lesson planning that the teacher can ensure a motivating balance of the type we have discussed (see 4.4 and 12.1).

It will also be necessary to consider activities not only on the basis of what the students have been doing recently but also in terms of the class period itself. In other words we must consider what activities to include in a period of, say, sixty minutes, and how to balance the different activities within that period of time. We have already said (see 12.2) that a lengthy session of accurate reproduction would probably be de-motivating and unsuccessful. Where presentation is included in a class we will want to make sure that students are not only involved in a lockstep accurate reproduction stage, but are also involved in other motivating activities. In general our aim will be to provide a sequence that is varied and does not follow one activity with a completely similar activity and then follow that with one that is the same.

The decision about what activities are to be included in a plan is a vital first stage in the planning process. The teacher is forced to consider, above all, what would be most beneficial and motivating for the students.

(b) Language skills

Teachers will have to decide what language skills to include in the class. Sometimes, of course, this decision will already have been taken when the activity has been selected (e.g. listening). In the case of more general activities, though (e.g. communicative activity, roughly-tuned input, etc.) we will then decide whether we wish to concentrate on one skill or a combination of skills. Even where the choice of activity has determined the skill to be studied (e.g. listening) it will still be necessary to decide what sub-skills the class are going to practise. In Chapter 10 we looked at a number of different ways of listening: when planning, the teacher will select which of these types of listening is most appropriate.

The choice of language skills to be practised and studied will be taken in accordance with the syllabus. The latter will often say what skills and sub-skills should be taught during the term or year and it will be the teacher's job to cover these over a period of time. Teachers will also make their choice on the basis of their students' needs. They will also bear in mind what the students have been doing recently, just as they do when thinking of activities.

(c) Language type

Teachers will have to decide what language is to be focused on during the class. There is, of course, a great range of possibilities here. We may decide that we want the language to be used to be 'general and unpredictable'. This would be the case if we were going to organise a 'reaching a consensus' activity or perhaps a simulation (see 8.1.1 and 8.1.7). We might decide, however, that we want to focus on yes/no questions using 'was' and 'were'. These are the two extremes (completely free language and completely controlled). Teachers may choose to concentrate on a language area: we might want our students to 'talk about the past' using a variety of past tenses or in general to concentrate on 'inviting'. Much will depend on the language in the syllabus.

The choice of language type is a necessary decision: all too often it is the first decision that teachers make and thus classes take on the monotonous controlled aspect that we discussed in 12.2. Here it is only one of four major areas the teacher has to think of when drawing up the pre-plan.

(d) Subject and content

We have considered what kind of activity would be suitable for our students and we have decided on language skills and type. The last and in some ways most important decision still has to be made. What kind of content will our class have? We may have decided that a simulation activity is appropriate but if the subject of that simulation does not interest the students in any way the choice of activity is wasted. Although we have said it is the teacher's job to interest students in a reading passage, for example, it will surely be more motivating to give the students a reading passage that they would find interesting with or without the teacher.

Teachers who know who their students are and what they bring to class will be in a much better position to choose subject and content than a teacher who does not. And this knowledge is vital since one of language's main functions is to communicate interest and ideas.

These four areas, then, form the basis of the pre-plan. It should be noticed that two of them are not in any way concerned with decisions about language, but are based on what will interest and motivate the students. This reflects everything we have said about language use since language is a tool for doing things, not just an abstract system.

Teachers who concentrate on activities and subject and content will benefit the students far more than those who only concentrate on language skills and type.

When we have a general idea of what we are going to do in our class as a result of considering the four areas in the pre-plan we will then consider the institution and the restrictions it imposes. If we have decided that we want to take a song into class we must make sure that this is possible: is a tape of the song available and are the tape recorders in good working order? Is the activity we would like to take into class suitable for the number of students we have to teach? How should we organise the activity for that number of students? Will we be able to do all the things we want to in the time available, and if we can how should we order the class? What should come first?

Experienced teachers consider all these details without, perhaps, consciously realising they are doing so. The new teacher, or the teacher starting a job in a new school or institute will have to bear all these points in mind.

We now have a clear idea of what we are going to do in our class: we are ready to make a detailed plan.

12.5
The plan

The plan we are going to consider is extremely detailed and it should be understood that most experienced teachers do not write down what they are going to do in such a complicated way. The detail in our plan and in the specimen plan in 12.5.1 is felt to be necessary, however, for two reasons. Firstly, the inexperienced teacher needs a clear framework of reference for the task of planning, and secondly the form of the plan forces the teacher to consider aspects of planning that are considered desirable.

There is one particular situation in which a detailed plan is beneficial and that is when a teacher is to be observed: by providing a plan such a teacher clearly shows why he or she is doing things in the classroom, and where an activity is not totally successful, the observer can see how it would have gone if it had been performed or organised more efficiently.

The plan has five major components: *description of the class*, *recent work*, *objectives*, *contents* and *additional possibilities*. When we have discussed these we will look at a specimen plan.

(a) Description of the class

Teachers may well carry this part of the plan in their heads: the more familiar they become with the group the more they will know about them.

The description of the class embraces a description of the students, a statement of time, frequency and duration of the class, and comments about physical conditions and/or restrictions. We will see how this works in the specimen plan on page 270.

(b) Recent work

Teachers need to have in their heads – or on paper – details of recent work the students have done. This includes the activities they have been involved in, the subject and content of their lessons and the language skills and type that they have studied. Only if all this is known (or remembered) can teachers make reasonable planning decisions about future classes (see especially 12.4(a)).

(c) Objectives

We will write down what our objectives are for the class. We will usually have more than one since there will be a number of stages in the class and each one will be there to achieve some kind of objective.

Objectives are the aims that teachers have for the students and are written in terms of what the students will do or achieve. They are written in general terms (e.g. 'The objective is to relax the students'), in terms of skills (e.g. 'to give students practice in extracting specific information from a text') and in terms of language (e.g. 'to give students practice in the use of the past simple tense using regular and irregular verbs, questions and answers'). The written objectives will be more or less specific depending on how specific the teacher's aims are.

The objectives, then, are the aims the teacher has for the students. They may refer to activities, skills, language type or a combination of all of these.

(d) Contents

By far the most detailed part of the plan is the section in which the contents are written down. Here we spell out exactly what we are going to do in the class. The 'Contents' section has five headings:

Context: Here we write down what context we will be using for the activity. Context means 'what the situation is: what the subject of the learning is'. The context for introducing new language might be a flight timetable; the context for an oral composition might be a story about a man going to the zoo. The context for a simulation might be 'The travel agency'.

Activity and class organisation: Here we indicate what the activity will be (see 11.4(a)) and we say whether the class will be working in lockstep, pairs, groups or teams, etc.

Aids: We indicate whether we will be using the blackboard or a wall picture, the tape recorder or the textbook, etc.

Language: Here we describe the language that will be used. If new language is to be introduced we will list some or all of the models. If the activity is an oral communicative activity we might only write 'unpredictable'. Otherwise we may write 'advice language', for example, and give some indication of what kind of language items we expect.

Possible problems: Many activities can be expected to be problematic in some way. We can often anticipate that the new language for a presentation stage may cause problems because of its form. The introduction of the past simple may cause problems because of the different verb endings: question forms are often difficult because of word order, etc. We should be aware of these possible problems and have considered ways of solving them. Certain activities have complicated organisation. Again we should be aware of this and know how to overcome it.

(e) Additional possibilities

Here we write down other activities we could use if it becomes necessary (e.g. if we get through the plan quicker than we thought or if one of our activities has to be stopped because it is not working well).

All these details, then, form the major part of the plan.

We can now look at an example of the kind of plan we have been discussing.

12.5.1
A specimen lesson plan[6]

We will now look at a specimen lesson plan which closely follows the model we have described. It is designed for an adult class that has been studying for about two hundred hours – the students are near the beginning of their sixth term.

In order to show how the plan operates most of the activities will come from earlier chapters of this book. The reading material comes from a textbook at this level which it is assumed the students are using as a class text (see page 192). The recent work is based on the syllabus of the textbook.

Where page numbers and other references are given the teacher should refer to earlier sections of this book.

Specimen plan

A – Description of the class

Level: *Intermediate*
Students between the ages of 16–25. 21 women, 9 men (6 secretaries, 5 housewives, 10 university students, 3 teachers, 1 doctor, 1 businessman, 4 secondary students).
The class takes place from 7.45–9.00 p.m. on Mondays and Wednesdays. The students are generally enthusiastic, but often tired: concentration sometimes suffers as a result. Students have completed approximately 200 hours of English.

B – Recent work

- Students have been studying the passive – discovery activities followed by language practice.
- Writing complete passive sentences about e.g. the world's first postage stamp, the VW Beetle, etc.
- Listening work (listening for detailed comprehension).
- Writing notes based on the listening.

C – Objectives
(*for details see*
'Contents' *below*)

1 To create interest in the topic of buildings: to promote discussion.
2 To raise expectations and create involvement in a reading task.
3 To read to confirm expectations.
4 To study relevant words.
5 To prepare a description of a famous building.

D – Contents

Objective 1: (*Estimated time: 15 minutes*)	
(a) *Context*:	Students' own lives – buildings.
(b) *Activity/class organisation*:	Discussion (buzz groups) in small groups. SS are asked to agree on the five most famous buildings in the world and say how they make them feel.
(c) *Aids*:	None.
(d) *Language*:	All and any.
(e) *Possible problems*:	Students may not have much to say. The teacher will be prepared to prompt if necessary – or shorten the activity if that seems appropriate.

Objective 2: (*Estimated time: 10 minutes*)	
(a) *Context*:	'Creating expectations' about the Empire State Building.
(b) *Activity/class organisation*:	Whole class contributes suggestions to T who writes them up in 3 columns on the board (see 10.4.1 (a) page 191).
(c) *Aids*:	Board; chalk or board pen, etc.
(d) *Language*:	All and any; 'buildings' vocabulary.
(e) *Possible problems*:	Students don't know anything about the Empire State Building! T can prompt with 'Is it tall?' 'Where is it?', etc.

Objective 3: (*Estimated time: 25 minutes*)	
(a) *Context*:	A text about the Empire State Building (see page 192).
(b) *Activity/class organisation*:	Students read individually and then check in pairs to see if the questions/doubts written on the board have been settled by the information in the text. T then leads the feedback session and discusses with the whole class.
(c) *Aids*:	The text (in the textbook): the 'expectations' chart on the board.
(d) *Language*:	All and any – especially vocabulary related to buildings.
(e) *Possible problems*:	The 'expectations' questions may not be answered in the text. T will have prepared a series of type 2 questions for detailed comprehension (or will find them in the book being used) e.g. 'How many boroughs make up New York City? Where exactly is the ESB situated in Manhattan? When was it built?', etc.

Objective 4: (*Estimated time: 10 minutes*)	
(a) *Context*:	Words about different kinds of building.
(b) *Activity/class organisation*:	In pairs students have to put 'buildings' words (e.g. block of flats, skyscraper, house, bungalow, hut, palace, cottage, semi-detached, detached, terraced, etc.) in order of height, overall size, privacy, worth, etc. T then discusses their conclusions.
(c) *Aids*:	Wordlist/textbook.
(d) *Language*:	As in (b) above); discussion language. 'Buildings' words.
(e) *Possible problems*:	Students don't know any of the words. Maybe they know all of them. T assesses the situation and is prepared for more explanation or to cut the activity short and move on.

Objective 5: (*Estimated time: 15 minutes*)	
(a) *Context*:	Buildings – the world/students' lives.
(b) *Activity/class organisation*:	T and SS talk about paragraph organisation of a text about a famous building (e.g. Para 1: identify building, say where and when it was built; Para 2: describe the building and its distinctive features; Para 3: say what people think of the building, why it is famous, what happens/happened there, etc.). Students get into groups to plan a composition about a particular building. They are then asked to write the composition for homework.
(c) *Aids*:	The board and/or handout and/or textbook with notes/hints about paragraph organisation. SS's notebooks, etc.
(d) *Language*:	As in (b) above. T will try to elicit passives and building vocabulary when discussing organisation.
(e) *Possible problems*:	SS might not know much about any famous building! T has some information about other famous buildings, e.g. Eiffel Tower, Taj Mahal, etc. to help out just in case.

E – Additional possibilities

1 Find the differences (see 8.1.4 (a)). The teacher gives each pair two pictures of urban landscapes – with different buildings, etc. They have to find at least ten differences between their pictures without looking at each other's.
2 Describe and draw (see 8.1.3 (c)). In pairs one student tells another student to draw a building (of the first student's choice). Then they do it the other way round.
3 A co-operative writing exercise (see 8.2.3 (a)) in which students group-write a story starting 'When she saw the building for the first time she knew there was something wrong.'

A number of points can be made about this lesson plan. In the first place decisions were taken based on what students had been doing recently (recent work). It appears that students had not been doing much reading and that a lot of their oral work had been either in lockstep or was at best controlled practice output. There had not been many opportunities for students to express themselves, but the students had done some listening practice.

The record of recent work led to a number of decisions being taken, therefore. In the first place it was clearly time for some reading work. Secondly students needed involving in some communicative oral interaction. They did not appear to have been doing much vocabulary work, either, so this was a good time to work on some words.

These were the considerations that affected the pre-plan. The *plan* then allowed for a detailed response based not only on recent work, but also on what we wished to achieve. The lack of previous oral interaction is why the opening buzz group and the 'creating expectations' activity were used since they allow the students to use spontaneous speech. The reading text was appropriate here since we recognised the need for reading. Vocabulary work follows naturally from a reading so that slotted in nicely. Finally we used the preceding stages to build up to a piece of guided writing.

Note the 'additional possibilities' part of the plan. We realise that things may well go slower than planned, so any of these activities would be good alternatives to the writing preparation (for example) since they can be completed in less time. Alternatively the teacher might want to use (one of) them to liven up the class if either the reading process and/or the vocabulary study have been too 'heavy'.

**12.6
Conclusions**

In this chapter we have considered an approach to the planning of language classes. We have shown how an over-reliance on the textbook and the syllabus may well cause teachers to give classes which are not as motivating as they could be. We have stressed the need to choose appropriate activities for the class, highlighting the need for variety, flexibility and balance.

We have discussed what teachers need to know before making a plan. This includes a knowledge of how to teach – including ideas for different activities and a knowledge of useful techniques. Teachers should also be familiar with the (rules of the) institution they are working in. Most important, however, is a knowledge of the students; who they are and what needs they have.

We have looked at a pre-plan in which teachers make general decisions about what they are going to teach: these decisions are made on the basis of activities, language skills, language type and subject and content. We emphasised the fact that language type (the traditional syllabus) was only one of the necessary components of the pre-plan and that activities and subject and content were equally important since here teachers could base decisions on how the students were feeling and what they had been doing recently.

Finally we have looked at how an actual plan can be put together, stressing that experienced teachers seldom write plans in such detail but that to do so forces us to consider important aspects of planning (and will be useful if we are to be observed).

Discussion

1 If variety is the cornerstone of good planning, is it possible to have too much variety?

2 Do you think activities can (or should) last for a whole class period? Give examples to back up your opinions.

3 How important is it for teachers to know about their students? What else should they know apart from the things mentioned in 12.3.3?

4 What do you think of the specimen plan in 12.5.1? Would it be appropriate for the students you teach?

Exercises

1 Look at a unit in a textbook you are using (or are familiar with). What activities are there in the unit? Do you think you would have to include extra material when teaching the unit? Why?

2 Look at a unit in a textbook you are using (or are familiar with) and say what language skills and language type are included in the unit. Is the language for presentation or controlled practice or is there some provision for communicative interaction?

3 List the recent work that your/a class have been doing. Plan the next class.

4 Make a rough plan to cover the next six classes bearing in mind the need for variety, but keeping a coherent pattern.

References

1 For a memorable discussion on the value or otherwise of teaching materials see R Allwright (1981), who argued against their use, and the noted textbook writer R O'Neill (O'Neill 1982), who replied in defence of textbook use. The articles are reprinted in R Rossner and R Bolitho (1990). N Grant (1988) shows how teachers can adapt the textbook material they have to deal with, and S Deller (1990, Section 2) gives a graphic example of how stages of a unit in a textbook can be adapted and added onto with extra and more student-centred activities.

2 Not all textbooks expect the teacher to follow the written sequence, however. A notable exception is *The Sourcebook* (Shepherd and Cox, 1991) which provides teachers and students with a wealth of grammar, vocabulary and skills material which the teacher can select from only if and when it is appropriate.

3 For more on planning see M Underwood (1987) Chapter 6, P Hubbard et al. (1983) Chapter 4, S Hill (1986) and S McClennan (1987). J Harmer (1984) and in Rossner and Bolitho (1990) shows how a game-like activity can be used to make planning decisions over a series of classes.

4 M Underwood points out (Underwood 1987:7) that a perfect knowledge of English is not necessary for English teachers, even though such a state might be desirable: you need to know the language you are teaching (and more) but much of the most successful language teaching is done by people who are not native speakers but who are competent users of the target language (see Chapter 2).

5 For a detailed needs analysis see R Mackay (1978). P Shaw (1982) is probably a more useful model for the classroom teacher. A detailed and controversial approach in its time was J Munby (1978).

6 This specimen lesson plan is extremely detailed and contains a lot of material. Especially where they are being observed teachers sometimes try to include too much. In such situations it is probably better to cut down on the amount you actually plan to get through but have a number of additional possibilities up your sleeve.

Appendix: Evaluating materials[1]

At various stages of their professional lives teachers will be involved in the selection of material for their students. Sometimes these materials will be of a supplementary kind (e.g. to complement a coursebook) and sometimes they will be the coursebooks themselves.

There may be various reasons for looking closely at materials to see if they are appropriate for a group of students: the teacher may have seen exciting material at a teachers' meeting or convention. He or she may have seen enticing publicity about a new course, or heard about some successful materials from a colleague. Often the desire to look for new materials stems from a dissatisfaction with what is being currently used, and the teacher or course planner may want to compare a number of different alternatives.

Whatever the reasons for considering whether or not materials are appropriate for a group of students, the decision that a teacher or course planner takes is vital. It is vital because teachers will take at least some of their ideas from the textbook, and may even use it as the basic syllabus for a course (see 12.1). Where a number of teachers in an institution are using the same book it will have a powerful influence over what type of teaching takes place in that institution.

Before attempting to evaluate materials, however, the teacher must have come to some conclusions about the students and what their needs are. This knowledge is necessary for us to be able to judge the materials in the light of our knowledge of the students who may eventually use them. Once we have drawn up a profile of our students and their needs we can then go about evaluating materials that seem to be suitable for the students in two ways. One of these ways is to study the book and see how well it matches our students. The *materials evaluation form* (see pages 281–284) will be useful for doing this. Another is to *pilot* the course. This means that the book (or materials) is tried out on a small group of students in the school and the results measured before a decision is taken about whether all the classes will use the material. Once again, after such piloting, the materials evaluation form will be useful here.

There are two steps, then, in the evaluation of materials: the first is to have a profile of the students and their needs which leads you to conclusions about the type of material which would be appropriate for them, and the second, subsequent step, is to apply this knowledge to the completion of the materials evaluation form, which aims to measure how far the materials under consideration match up to student needs and the general methodological principles which the teacher holds.

The profile of student needs has three major components. In the first the teacher describes the students, saying who they are and what they bring to class (this is the same as the class planner, who also needs this information to take planning decisions – see 12.3.3); the second is to describe student needs in terms of when the students are likely to use English and what skills they should acquire in the language (see 12.3.3(c)). The third part of the student profile describes in general terms the type of material the teacher would like to see for these students. We can summarise the profile of students' needs in the following way:

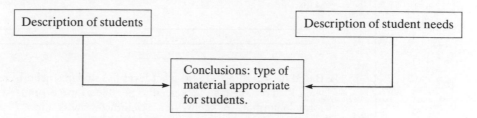

Figure 29 Profile of student needs for materials selection

The 'description of students' will answer questions in the following way:

DESCRIPTION OF STUDENTS

1 Age: _____
2 Sex: _____
3 Social/cultural background: _____
4 Occupation(s): _____
5 Motivation/attitude: _____
6 Educational background: _____
7 Knowledge (a) English level: _____
           (b) Of the world: _____
8 Interests and beliefs: _____

Based on the above, what conclusions can you draw about the kind of materials that would be suitable for your students?

_____
_____

We now have an idea of the kind of materials that would be appropriate for the students based on their personal characteristics. The second stage is to come to some kind of conclusion about what their needs are.

DESCRIPTION OF STUDENT NEEDS

1 What contexts and situations (if any) will your students probably use English in at some future date?

a _____
b _____
c _____

2 Give an order of priority for the different language skills (including sub-skills) that your students will need when using English.

a _____
b _____
c _____
d _____
e _____

3 Now say what percentage of class time should be spent on these various skills.

a _____   d _____
b _____   e _____
c _____

4 Based on the above say (a) what level the students need to reach and (b) what kind of language they need to be able to use or understand (e.g. formal/informal, spoken/written, scientific/business, etc.).

We now have a clearer idea about what our students' needs are and we can move to some conclusions about the type of material we wish to look at.

CONCLUSIONS: TYPE OF MATERIALS APPROPRIATE
FOR STUDENTS

Based on the description of students and their needs, say what type of materials you think would be most appropriate for these students.

_____
_____
_____
_____

These descriptions of students and their needs can be arrived at in a number of ways and may have more or less specific results depending on who the students are.

Finding out what the students' needs are may be done very formally (see for example R Mackay (1978)) especially where there is a clear demand for a high level ESP course. The needs analysis will take the form of questionnaires, interviews with students and their teachers and/or employers, and a study of the kind of English they will have to cope with. A more informal way of arriving at conclusions about student needs is teacher intuition together with conversations with the students concerned.

Where students have a very specific purpose for studying English the entries on the 'description of student needs' form will be precise. Where students are studying general English (particularly in a secondary school situation) the entries will clearly be less specific. Nevertheless, it will still be possible to come to informal (but informed) decisions about such things as priorities for certain skills. The fact that students are studying general English may mean that it is less easy to say that certain skills should predominate, but the mere fact of saying this will lead to decisions about the kind of materials the teacher wishes to use.

Armed with a knowledge about the students the teacher can now evaluate materials that seem to be more or less appropriate for the students. The evaluation of materials, however, should be as formal and principled as possible, and that is why there is a need for the materials evaluation form.

In the materials evaluation form questions are asked which demand the answer 'yes' or 'no' and an additional comment. After completing the form teachers are asked to say whether they recommend the course for their students: by the time they get to this point they will have already come to a number of decisions about the materials as a result of completing the form, and should therefore be in a position to make this decision.

The materials evaluation form has seven major headings: *practical considerations*, *layout and design*, *activities*, *skills*, *language type*, *subject and content* and *guidance*. Under *practical considerations* the teacher is asked to say whether the price of the materials is right for the students (it should be remembered that some coursebooks are very expensive) and if the integral parts of the course (e.g. tapes, teacher's book, etc.) are available. If the answer to these first two questions is 'no' then there is no need to complete the form since the teacher will have to decide not to use the materials.

Under *layout and design* the teacher is simply asked to judge whether the materials look attractive to the students. This does not necessarily mean full-colour photographs: for science students it is possible to argue that the design should be suitably scientific-looking in a clear and interesting way.

The next four headings refer to the concerns of course and lesson planning that we mentioned in 12.4. It is under these headings that we look at the content and methodology of the materials under consideration. The first concern is, as in 12.4, the range and balance of *activities* in the material. The teacher wants to be sure that there is a reasonable balance of the sort we discussed in 4.4. Particularly important is that there should be a substantial amount of language input and that there should be a variety of communicative activities. The teacher wants to be sure that the practice activities are useful and motivating and that presentation of language takes place in realistic and motivating contexts. Under *skills* the teacher measures whether the course answers the students' needs from the description of those needs that has been previously prepared. Thus the teacher asks whether the right skills are included and whether the balance between the different skills is appropriate for the group. He or she also answers a question about skill integration which we said was an important principle in methodology (see 5.5). In Chapters 6–10 we have seen many examples of how practice in using different skills can be integrated with the practice of other skills.

Under *language type* the materials evaluation form asks the teacher to consider whether the language in the materials is realistic (see, for example, our comments about questions and answers in 7.1.4) whether the language is at the right level for the students, whether it is of the right type (e.g. students studying English for medicine will probably not want materials with purely social English) and whether the progression of 'new' language is logical and appropriate for the students. This last point concerns how, and in what order, students are asked to produce new language. In general we would expect them to be able to build on what they already know so that there will be some connection between what they have just learnt and what they are learning now. The connection does not necessarily have to be grammatical only, however, and may concern situations in which language is used, or further extensions of an interaction. Perhaps what we are looking for here is a sequence that will be intelligible to the learner rather than unconnected items thrown into a course at random.

Under *subject and content* we analyse what topics, etc. are included in the course and whether they match up to our students' personalities, backgrounds and needs. We ask, therefore, if the subject and content is relevant to our students' needs, whether it is – at least sometimes – realistic, whether it is interesting for the students, and whether there is sufficient variety to sustain motivation. We assess whether the materials avoid harmful stereotypes while reflecting the multicultural nature of modern society.

Lastly the materials evaluation form asks whether there is sufficient *guidance* not only for the teacher, but for the students. In the former case we would expect clear explanations of how the material can be used to its maximum advantage. In the latter case we would expect the materials to be clear, easy to follow (in terms of instructions, etc.), and to have clearly stated objectives that both students and the teacher can understand.

When the teacher has finally completed the materials evaluation form she or he is asked to recommend whether the materials should (continue to) be used. We can now look at the complete materials evaluation form. After many of the questions, references will be given in brackets to various parts of this book so that readers can take up these references if in doubt about what exactly the questions mean or imply.

Materials evaluation form

NAME OF MATERIALS UNDER CONSIDERATION

_____

_____

AUTHORS(S) _____

PUBLISHER _____
LEVEL _____

A – Practical considerations

1 Is the price of the materials appropriate for your students?

Yes ☐ _No_ ☐ _Comment_ _____

_____

2 Are the integral parts of the materials (coursebook, tapes, teacher's book, etc.) available now?

Yes ☐ _No_ ☐ _Comment_ _____

_____

B – Layout and design

1 Is the layout and design of the materials appropriate for your students? (Refer to description of students/student needs.)

Yes ☐ _No_ ☐ _Comment_ _____

_____

C – Activities

1 Do the materials provide a balance of activities that is appropriate for your students? (See 4.4, 12.1 and 12.4(a).)

Yes ☐ _No_ ☐ _Comment_ _____

_____

(You may also want to refer to Exercise 1 on page 275.)

2 Is there a sufficient amount of communicative output in the materials under consideration? (See 4.3 and 5.3 for a description of what this means, and Chapter 8 for a large number of examples of this type of activity, both speaking and writing.)

Yes ☐ _No_ ☐ _Comment_ _____

_____

3 Do the materials provide enough roughly-tuned input for your students? (See 4.3.)

Yes ☐ _No_ ☐ _Comment_ _____

_____

4 Is 'new' language introduced in motivating and realistic contexts? (See Chapter 6, especially 6.1.1 and 6.1.2.)

Yes ☐ *No* ☐ *Comment* _____

_____

5 Where the materials encourage practice, is the practice motivating for your students? (See 5.4.2 and the many examples of practice activities in Chapter 7.)

Yes ☐ *No* ☐ *Comment* _____

_____

D – Skills

1 Do the materials include and practise the skills your students need? (See 2.5 and the description of student needs on page 278.)

Yes ☐ *No* ☐ *Comment* _____

_____

2 Do the materials have an appropriate balance of skills for your students? (See especially questions 2 and 3 in the description of student needs on page 278.)

Yes ☐ *No* ☐ *Comment* _____

_____

3 Is the practice of individual skills integrated into the practice of other skills? (See especially 5.5 and the many examples of skill integration in Chapters 6–10.)

Yes ☐ *No* ☐ *Comment* _____

_____

E – Language type

1 Is the language used in the materials realistic – i.e. like real-life English? (See, for example, 7.1.4 and 10.2.2.)

Yes ☐ *No* ☐ *Comment* _____

_____

2 Is the language used in the materials at the right level for your students? (Note that when a coursebook is advertised as intermediate, for example, this level is not necessarily the same as what the term 'intermediate' means for you.)

Yes ☐ *No* ☐ *Comment* _____

_____

3 Is the language in the materials the right type of language for your students? (See especially question 4(b) in the description of student needs on page 278 and the comments on page 280.)

Yes ☐ No ☐ Comment _____

_____

4 Is the progression of 'new' language appropriate for your students? (See the comments on page 280.)

Yes ☐ No ☐ Comment _____

_____

F – Subject and content

1 Is the subject and content of the materials relevant to the students' needs? (See especially question 1 in the description of student needs on page 278.)

Yes ☐ No ☐ Comment _____

_____

2 Is the subject and content of the materials realistic at least some of the time?

Yes ☐ No ☐ Comment _____

_____

3 Is the subject and content of the materials interesting for the students? (See 12.4(d).)

Yes ☐ No ☐ Comment _____

_____

4 Is there sufficient variety for your students in the subject and content of the materials?

Yes ☐ No ☐ Comment _____

_____

5 Do the materials avoid harmful stereotypes of different members of society (e.g. women, older people, men, etc.)?

Yes ☐ No ☐ Comment _____

_____

6 Do the materials avoid harmful stereotypes of different races and cultures? Do they reflect the multicultural nature of modern society?

Yes ☐ No ☐ Comment _____

_____

G – Guidance

1 Do the materials contain clear guidance for the teacher about how they can be used to the best advantage (for example in a teacher's book)?

Yes ☐ *No* ☐ *Comment* _____

_____

2 Are the materials clearly written for your students and are the objectives clearly stated for both students and teacher?

Yes ☐ *No* ☐ *Comment* _____

_____

H – Conclusion

1 Would you recommend adopting (or continuing with) these materials for your students?

Yes ☐ *No* ☐ *Comment* _____

_____

The materials evaluation form, then, is designed to get teachers to answer the central questions about what they need and expect from the materials which are under consideration. The teacher will complete the form on the basis of the previous student needs profile which tells him or her what kind of materials will be appropriate for the students. The issues raised in the materials evaluation form are precisely those which have formed the content of this book.

If the teacher is able to answer 'yes' to all the questions (which is unlikely) then it is probable that the conclusion will be to use the materials. Usually, however, there will be a number of 'no' answers as well. Particularly where two books or sets of materials are being compared, however, the answers to the questions on the materials evaluation form will be most revealing and will help to facilitate the choice between the two.

Exercise

Complete the student needs profile for a group of students you teach or are familiar with. On the basis of this profile use the materials evaluation form to assess the relative merits of two textbooks that might be appropriate for the students you have been considering.

References

1 Various different kinds of materials evaluation forms have been designed. See, for example, L Van Lier (1979), L Mariani (1980) and M Ellis (1986). N Grant (1987), Chapter 9 discusses methods of textbook evaluation, inventing the acronym CATALYST to embrace the questions that should be asked (is the book Communicative, are its Aims appropriate, is it Teachable, are the 'Add-ons' Available, is the Level right, is Your impression good, does it have Student interest and is the material and methodology Tried and Tested?)

Bibliography

ABBS, B and FREEBAIRN, I *Family Affair* (Longman 1985)

ABBS, B and FREEBAIRN, I *Discoveries: Students' Book 1* (Longman 1986)

ABBS, B and FREEBAIRN, I *Blueprint Intermediate* (Longman 1989); *Blueprint One* (Longman 1990)

ALEXANDER, L G 'To drill or not to drill' (*Practical English Teaching* 5/4 1985)

ALLAN, M *Teaching English with Video* (Longman 1985)

ALLWRIGHT, R 'Motivation – the teacher's responsibility?' (*ELT Journal* 31/4 1977a)

ALLWRIGHT, R 'Language Learning Through Communication Practice' (*ELT Documents* 76/3 1977b), reprinted in Brumfit and Johnson (eds.) (1979)

ALLWRIGHT, R 'What do we want teaching materials for?' (*ELT Journal* 36/1 1981), reprinted in Rossner and Bolitho (1990)

ASHER, J 'The Total Physical Approach to Second Language Learning' (*Modern Languages Journal* 53 1969)

ASHER, J 'Motivating children and adults to acquire another language' (*The Teacher Trainer* 1/3 1987)

ATKINSON, D 'The mother tongue in the classroom: a neglected resource?' (*ELT Journal* 41/3 1987)

ATKINSON, D '"Humanistic" approaches in the adult classroom: an affective reaction' (*ELT Journal* 43/4 1989)

BACHMAN, L *Fundamental Considerations in Language Testing* (Oxford University Press 1990)

BARTOLI, C 'Teaching the silent way' (*Practical English Teaching* 2/2 1981)

BERETTA, A and DAVIES, A 'Evaluation of the Bangalore project' (*ELT Journal* 39/2 1985)

BERTOLDI, E, KOLLAR, J and RICARD, E 'Learning how to learn English: from awareness to action' (*ELT Journal* 42/3 1988)

BLACK, V, MCNORTON, M, MALDEREZ, A and PARKER, S *Fast Forward 1* (Oxford University Press 1986)

BLANCHARD, K, ZIGARMI, P and ZIGARMI, D *Leadership and the One Minute Manager* (Fontana 1987)

BOLITHO, R 'But where's the teacher?' (*Practical English Teaching* 3/3 1983)

BOLITHO, R and TOMLINSON, B *Discover English* (Heinemann 1980)

BOYD, T *In their own words* (Thomas Nelson 1988)

BRAZIL, D, COULTHARD, M and JOHNS, C *Discourse Intonation and Language Teaching* (Longman 1980)

BRUMFIT, C 'Communicative language teaching: an assessment' in Strevens (ed.) *In Honour of A S Hornby* (Oxford University Press 1978)

BRUMFIT, C *Problems and Principles in English Teaching* (Pergamon Press 1980)

BRUMFIT, C 'Teaching the "general" student' (in Johnson and Morrow (eds.) (1981))

BRUMFIT, C 'The Bangalore procedural syllabus' (*ELT Journal* 38/4 1984)

BRUMFIT, C and JOHNSON, K (eds.) *The Communicative Approach to Language Teaching* (Oxford University Press 1979)

BYRNE, D *Teaching Oral English: New Edition* (Longman 1986)

BYRNE, D *Techniques for Classroom Interaction* (Longman 1987)

BYRNE, D *Teaching Writing Skills: New Edition* (Longman 1988)

BYRNE, D and HOLDEN, S *Follow it Through* (Longman 1978)

CANALE, M and SWAIN, M 'Theoretical bases of communicative approaches to second language teaching and testing' (*Applied Linguistics 1/1*)

CARTER, G and THOMAS, H '"Dear Brown Eyes . . .": Experiential learning in a project oriented approach' (*ELT Journal* 40/3 1986) reprinted in Rossner and Bolitho (eds.) (1990)

CARTER, R and MCCARTHY, M *Vocabulary and Language Teaching* (Longman 1988)

CELCE-MURCIA, M 'New methods in perspective' (*Practical English Teaching* 2/1 1981)

CHANNELL, J 'Psycholinguistic considerations in the study of L2 vocabulary acquisition' in Carter and McCarthy (eds.) (1988)

CHOMSKY, N 'Review of "Verbal Behaviour"' (*Language* 35 1959)

COE, N 'Comprehension inside and outside the classroom' (*Modern English Teacher* 6/1 1978)

COULTHARD, M *An Introduction to Discourse Analysis: New Edition* (Longman 1985)

CROUCH, C 'Performance teaching in ELT' (*ELT Journal* 43/2 1989)

CUNNINGHAM, G *Listening and the Cambridge exams* (Training folder prepared for the University of Cambridge Local Examinations Syndicate 1990)

CUREAU, J 'Harnessing the power of suggestion' (*Practical English Teaching* 2/3 1982)

CURRAN, C *Counseling-learning in Second Languages* (Apple River Press 1976)

DAVIES, E and WHITNEY, N *Reasons for Reading* (Heinemann 1979)

DAVIS, P and RINVOLUCRI, M *Dictation* (Cambridge University Press 1989)

DAVIS, P and RINVOLUCRI, M *The Confidence Book* (Longman 1990)

DE BONO, E *Think-Links* (De Bono Games 1982)

DELLER, S *Lessons from the Learner* (Longman 1990)

DOBLE, T 'Approaches to teaching children' (*Practical English Teaching* 5/1 1984)

DOFF, A, JONES, C and MITCHELL, K *Meanings into words: Intermediate Students' Book* (Cambridge University Press 1983)

DOFF, A, JONES, C and MITCHELL, K *Meanings into Words: Upper intermediate Students' Book* (Cambridge University Press 1984)

EDGE, J *Mistakes and Correction* (Longman 1989)

ELLIS, G and SINCLAIR, B *Learning to Learn English* (Cambridge University Press 1989)

ELLIS, M 'Choosing and using coursebooks' (*Practical English Teaching 6/3–4 1986*)

ELLIS, R 'Informal and formal approaches to communicative language teaching' (*ELT Journal 36/2 1982*)

ELLIS, R 'Review of Krashen S "Principles and Practice in Second Language Acquisition"' (*ELT Journal 37/3 1983*)

ELLIS, R *Understanding Second Language Acquisition* (Oxford University Press 1985)

ELLIS, R 'The role of practice in classroom learning' (*AILA review 5 1988*)

ELSWORTH, S *Meridian Plus: Workbook 3* (Longman 1988)

FLETCHER, C *Pronunciation Workbook* and cassette (to go with Wells 1989) (Longman 1990)

FRANK, C and RINVOLUCRI, M *Grammar in action* (Pergamon Press 1983)

FRIED-BOOTH, D 'Project work with advanced classes' (*ELT Journal 36/2 1982*)

FRIED-BOOTH, D *Project Work* (Oxford University Press 1986)

GAIRNS, R and REDMAN, S *Working with Words* (Cambridge University Press 1986)

GARDNER, R and LAMBERT, W *Attitudes and Motivation in Second Language Learning* (Newbury House 1972)

GATTEGNO, C *The Commonsense of Teaching Languages* (Educational Solutions inc. 1976)

GATTEGNO, C 'Talking shop' (*ELT Journal 36/4 1982*), reprinted in Rossner and Bolitho (eds.) (1990)

GEDDES, M and MCALPIN, J 'Communication games – 2' in Holden, S (ed.) *Visual Aids for Classroom Interaction* (Modern English Publications 1978)

GEDDES, M and STURTRIDGE, G 'Jigsaw listening' (*Modern English Teacher 6/1 1978*)

GEDDES, M and STURTRIDGE, G *Listening Links* (Heinemann 1979)

GIBLIN, K and SPALDING, E *Setting up a course involving self-directed learning* (The Bell Education Trust Academic Reports 1988)

GIRARD, D 'Motivation – the responsibility of the teacher' (*ELT Journal 31/2 1977*)

GOWER, R and WALTERS, S *Teaching Practice Handbook* (Heinemann 1983)

GRANT, N *Making the most of Your Textbook* (Longman 1987)

GREGG, K 'Krashen's monitor and Occam's razor' (*Applied Linguistics 5/2 1984*)

GRELLET, F *Developing reading skills* (Cambridge University Press 1981)

HAMP-LYONS, E 'Motivation for learning English as a world language: integrative and instrumental' (*World Language English 2/3 1983*)

HARMER, J 'What is communicative?' (*ELT Journal 36/3 1982*)

HARMER, J 'Krashen's input hypothesis and the teaching of EFL' (*World Language English 3/1 1983*)

HARMER, J 'Balancing Activities: a Unit-Planning Game' (*ELT Journal 38/2 1984*), reprinted in Rossner and Bolitho (eds.) (1990)

HARMER, J *Teaching and Learning Grammar* (Longman 1987)

HARMER J *Meridian Plus: Students' Book 1* (Longman 1988a); *Meridian Plus: Students' Book 2* (Longman 1988b)

HARMER, J *Language Issues and the Cambridge Exams* (Training folder prepared for the University of Cambridge Local Examinations Syndicate 1990)

HARMER, J and ELSWORTH, S *Meridian Plus: Students' Book 3* (Longman 1988)

HARMER, J and ELSWORTH, S *The Listening File* (Longman 1989)

HARMER, J and ROSSNER, R *More than Words: Book 1* (Longman 1991)

HARMER, J and SURGUINE, H *Coast to Coast: Students' Book 3* (Longman 1988)

HELGESON, M, BROWN, S and VENNING, R *Firsthand Access* (Longman Lingual House 1990)

HICKS, D, POTE, M, ESNOL, A and WRIGHT, D *A Case for English* (Cambridge University Press 1979)

HILL, S 'Lesson planning in TEFL: a proposal' (*Modern English Teacher 13/2–3 1986*)

HINDMARSH, R *Cambridge English Lexicon* (Cambridge University Press 1980)

HOADLEY-MAIDMENT, E 'The motivation of students studying English in London' (*ELT Journal 31/3 1977*)

HUBBARD, P, JONES, H, THORNTON, B and WHEELER, R *A Training Course for TEFL* (Oxford University Press 1983)

HUTCHINSON, T *Project English* (Oxford University Press 1985)

HUTCHINSON, T and WATERS, A 'How communicative is ESP?' (*ELT Journal 38/2 1984*)

IANTORNO, G and PAPA, M *Turning Points 2* (Addison-Wesley 1986)

ILSON, R (ed.) *Dictionaries, Lexicography and Language Learning* (ELT Documents 120. The British Council/Pergamon Press 1985)

JACOBS, G 'Co-operative goal structure: a way to improve group activities' (*ELT Journal 42/2 1988*)

JOHNSON, K 'The Deep-end strategy in communicative language teaching' (*Mextesol Journal 4/2 1980*) and in Johnson (1982)

JOHNSON, K 'Two practical problems: a response' (*Modern English Teacher 8/2 1980*) and in Johnson (1982)

JOHNSON, K 'Some background, some key terms and some definitions' (in Johnson and Morrow (eds.) (1981)

JOHNSON, K *Communicative Syllabus Design and Methodology* (Pergamon Press 1982)

JOHNSON, K and MORROW, K (eds.) *Functional Materials and the Classroom Teacher* (Centre for Applied Language Studies, University of Reading 1978)

JOHNSON, K and MORROW, K *Communication in the classroom* (Longman 1981)

JONES, C and FORTESCUE, S *Using Computers in the Language Classroom* (Longman 1987)

JONES, K *Simulations in Language Teaching* (Cambridge University Press 1982)

KACHRU, B (ed.) *The Other Tongue* (Pergamon Press 1983)

KENNEDY, C and BOLITHO, R *English for Specific Purposes* (Macmillan Press 1984)

KENWORTHY, J *Teaching English Pronunciation* (Longman 1987)

KERR, J *Picture Cue Cards* (Evans 1979)

KRASHEN, S *Second Language Acquisition and Second Language Learning* (Pergamon Press 1981)

KRASHEN, S 'Acquiring a second language' (*World Language English* 1/2 1982)

KRASHEN, S 'The Input Hypothesis' in Alatis, J (ed.) *The Georgetown Round Table on Language and Linguistics* (Georgetown University Press 1982), also in Krashen (1984)

KRASHEN, S *The Input Hypothesis* (Longman 1984)

KRASHEN, S and TERELL, T *The Natural Approach* (Pergamon Press 1982)

LAWLOR, M 'The inner track method of successful teaching' (*Practical English Teaching* 6/3 1986)

LEE, W *Language Teaching Games and Contests: New Edition* (Oxford University Press 1980)

LITTLEJOHN, A 'Using groupwork with large classes' (*Practical English Teaching* 7/3 1987)

LITTLEWOOD, W *Communicative Language Teaching – an introduction* (Cambridge University Press 1981)

LONERGAN, J *Video in Language Teaching* (Cambridge University Press 1984)

LONG, M 'Groupwork in the teaching and learning of English as a foreign language – problems and potential' (*ELT Journal* 31/4 1977)

LONON BLANTON, L 'Reshaping ESL students' perceptions of writing' (*ELT Journal* 41/2 1987)

LOWE, T 'Making teacher-talking-time worthwhile' (*Modern English Teacher* 12/1 1985)

LOWE, T 'An experiment in role reversal: teachers as language learners' (*ELT Journal* 41/2 1987)

LYONS, J *Chomsky* (Fontana 1970)

MACKAY, R 'Identifying the nature of the learners' needs' in Mackay and Mountford (eds.) (1978)

MACKAY, R and MOUNTFORD, A 'The teaching of English for Specific Purposes: theory and practice' in Mackay and Mountford (eds.) (1978)

MACKAY, R and MOUNTFORD, A *English for Specific Purposes* (Longman 1978)

MALEY, A and DUFF, A *Sounds Interesting* (Cambridge University Press 1977)

MANUEL CUENCA, C 'What makes an activity truly communicative?' (*Modern English Teacher* 17/1 and 2 1990)

MAPLE, R *New Wave: Students' Book 1* (Longman 1988)

MARIANI, L 'Evaluating coursebooks' (*Modern English Teacher* 8/1 1980)

MARKSTEIN, L and GRUNBAUM, D *What's the Story?* (Longman 1981)

MATTHEWS, A and READ, C *Tandem* (Evans 1981)

MAULE, D '"Sorry, but if he comes, I go": teaching conditionals' (*ELT Journal* 42/2 1988)

MCALPIN, J *The Longman Dictionary Skills Handbook* (Longman 1989)

MCCARTHY, M *Vocabulary* (Oxford University Press 1991)

MCCLENNAN, S 'Integrating lesson planning and class management' (*ELT Journal* 41/1 1987)

MCGOVERN, J (ed.) *Video applications in English language teaching* (ELT Documents 114. The British Council/Pergamon Press 1983)

MCLEAN, A 'Destroying the teacher: The need for learner-centred teaching' (*Forum* 18/3 1980)

MEDGYES, P 'Queries from a communicative teacher' (*ELT Journal* 40/2 1986).

MOOIJAM, J and VAN DEN BOS, J 'Total physical response' (*Practical English Teaching* 4/3 1984)

MOOIJAM, J and VAN DEN BOS, J 'Total physical response in action in the classroom' (*Practical English Teaching* 7/1 1986)

MORGAN, J and RINVOLUCRI, M *Vocabulary* (Oxford University Press 1986)

MORROW, K 'Teaching the functions of language' (*ELT Journal* 32/1 1977)

MORROW, K 'Principles of communicative methodology' in Johnson and Morrow (eds.) (1981)

MOSCOWITZ, G *Caring and Sharing in the Foreign Language Classroom* (Newbury House 1978)

MUNBY, J *Communicative Syllabus Design* (Cambridge University Press 1978)

MUNRO, L and PARKER, S 'Teaching advanced learners' (*Modern English Teacher* 13/1 1985)

NATION, P and COADY, J 'Vocabulary and reading' in Carter and McCarthy (eds.) (1988)

NAUNTON, J *Think First Certificate* (Longman 1989)

NORMAN, S 'Using Cuisenaire rods' (*Practical English Teaching* 2/2 1981)

NORRISH, J *Language Learners and their Errors* (Macmillan Press 1983)

O'NEILL, R *English in Situations* (Oxford University Press 1970)

O'NEILL, R 'Why use textbooks?' (*ELT Journal* 36/2 1982), reprinted in Rossner and Bolitho (eds.) (1990)

O'NEILL, R and MUGGLESTONE, P *Third Dimension* (Longman 1989a)

O'NEILL, R and MUGGLESTONE, P *Fourth Dimension* (Longman 1989b)

PIPER, A 'Helping learners to write: a role for the wordprocessor' (*ELT Journal* 41/2 1982)

PLUMB, W 'An Analysis of classroom discourse' (*Mextesol Journal* 3/1 1978)

PLUMB, W 'Are short answers a help or a hindrance?' (Paper presented at the 5th Mextesol convention 1979)

PRABHU, N S *Second Language Pedagogy* (Oxford University Press 1987)

PUJALS, M 'Tackling monotony at the Intermediate level' (*Practical English Teaching* 6/3 1986).

RAMPTON, M 'Displacing the "native speaker": expertise, affiliation, and inheritance' (*ELT Journal* 44/2 1990)

REDMAN, S and ELLIS, R *A Way with Words 1* (Cambridge University Press 1989)

REID, J 'The Learning style preferences of ESL students' (*TESOL Quarterly* 21/1 1987)

RICHARDS, J 'Answers to yes/no questions' (*ELT Journal* 31/2 1977)

RICHARDS, J, HULL, J and PROCTOR, S *Interchange: Students' Book 1* (Cambridge University Press 1990)

RINVOLUCRI, M 'Writing to your students' (*ELT Journal* 37/1 1983)

RINVOLUCRI, M *Grammar Games* (Cambridge University Press 1985)

ROBERTS, J 'Teaching functional materials: two problems' (*Modern English Teacher* 8/2 1980 and in Johnson (1982))

ROBERTS, J 'Teaching with functional materials: The problem of stress and intonation' (*ELT Journal* 37/3 1983)

ROSSNER, R Review of 'Working with Words' (*ELT Journal* 41/4 1987)

ROSSNER, R *The Whole Story* (Longman 1988)

ROSSNER, R and BOLITHO, R (eds.) *Currents of Change in English Language Teaching* (Oxford University Press 1990)

ROSSNER, R, SHAW, P, SHEPHERD, J and TAYLOR, J *Contemporary English Students' Book 1* (Macmillan Press 1979a)

ROSSNER, R, SHAW, P, SHEPHERD, J and TAYLOR, J *Contemporary English Book 2* (Macmillan Press 1979b)

ROSSNER, R, SHAW, P, SHEPHERD, J and TAYLOR J *Contemporary English Book 6* (Macmillan Press 1980)

SANO, M 'How to incorporate total physical response into the English programme' (*ELT Journal* 40/4 1986)

SCOTT, M, CARIONI, L, ZANATTA, M, BAYER, E and QUINTANILHA, T 'Using a "standard exercise" in teaching reading comprehension' (ELT Journal 38/2 1984)

SCOTT, W and YTREBERG, L *Teaching English to Children* (Longman 1990)

SEAL, B *Vocabulary Builder 1* (Longman 1987)

SHARWOOD-SMITH, M 'Consciousness-raising and the second language learner' (*Applied Linguistics* 1/1 1981)

SHAW, P 'Ad hoc needs analysis' (*Modern English Teacher* 10/1 1982)

SHEPHERD, J and COX, F *The Sourcebook* (Longman 1991)

SINCLAIR, J (ed.) *Collins COBUILD English Language Dictionary* (William Collins 1984)

SKINNER, B *Verbal Behavior* (Appleton-Century-Crofts 1957)

SOARS, J and SOARS, L *Headway Intermediate* (Oxford University Press 1986)

SOARS, J and SOARS, L *Headway Upper Intermediate* (Oxford University Press 1987)

STEVICK, E *Memory, Meaning and Method* (Newbury House 1976)

STEVICK, E *Teaching and Learning Languages* (Cambridge University Press 1982)

STREVENS, P *New Orientations in the Teaching of English* (Oxford University Press (1977)

STURTRIDGE, G 'Role play and simulations' in Johnson and Morrow (eds.) (1981)

SUAREZ J 'Reading comprehension' (*Modern English Teacher* 6/6 1979)

SWAN, M 'A critical look at the communicative approach 1 and 2' (*ELT Journal* 39/1–2 1985).

SWAN, M and WALTER, C *The Cambridge English Course: Students' Book 1* (Cambridge University Press 1984); *The Cambridge English Course: Students' Book 3* (Cambridge University Press 1987)

TENCH, P *Pronunciation Skills* (Macmillan Press 1981)

THOMAS, H 'Developing the stylistic and lexical awareness of advanced students' (*ELT Journal* 38/3 1984)

TOMSCHA, T 'Using TPR communicatively' (*Practical English Teaching* 5/1 1984)

UNDERHILL, A *Use your dictionary* (Oxford University Press 1980)

UNDERHILL, A 'Working with Monolingual Dictionaries' in Ilson (ed.) 1985

UNDERWOOD, M *Effective Class Management* (Longman 1987)

UNDERWOOD, M *Teaching Listening* (Longman 1989)

UR, P *Discussions that work* (Cambridge University Press 1981)

UR, P *Teaching Listening Comprehension* (Cambridge University Press 1984)

UR, P *Grammar Practice Activities* (Cambridge University Press 1988)

VAN LIER, L 'Choosing a new EFL course' (*Mextesol Journal* 3/3 1979)

VARELA, M 'The disadvantage of the functional approach' (*Mextesol Journal* 4/4 1980)

WATCYN-JONES, P *Pair Work: Activities for Effective Communication* (Penguin 1981)

WATSON, J B and RAYNOR, R 'Conditioned emotional reactions' (*Journal of Experimental Psychology* 3/1 1920)

WELLMAN, G *The Heinemann English Wordbuilder* (Heinemann 1989)

WELLS, J C *Longman Pronunciation Dictionary* (Longman 1989)

WEST, M P *A General Service List of English Words* (Longman 1953)

WHITCUT, J 'Using your dictionary more effectively' (*Practical English Teaching* 5/1 1984)

WHITE, R V *Teaching Written English* (Heinemann 1980)

WIDDOWSON, H 'The teaching of English as communication' (*ELT Journal* 27/7 1972)

WIDDOWSON, H *Teaching Language as Communication* (Oxford University Press 1978)

WIDDOWSON, H 'The communicative approach and its application' in Widdowson, H *Explorations in Applied Linguistics* (Oxford University Press 1979)

WIDDOWSON, H 'Against dogma: a reply to Michael Swan' (*ELT Journal* 39/3 1985), reprinted in Rossner and Bolitho (eds.) (1990)

WIDDOWSON, H 'The roles of teacher and learner' (*ELT Journal* 41/2 1987)

WIDDOWSON, H 'Knowledge of language and ability for use' (*Applied Linguistics* 10/2 1989)

WILKINS, D A *Linguistics in Language Teaching* (Edward Arnold 1972)

WILKINS, D A *Notional Syllabuses* (Oxford University Press 1976)

WILLIAMS, R '"Top ten" principles for teaching reading' (*ELT Journal* 40/1 1986)

WILLIS, D and WILLIS, J *The Cobuild English Course* (William Collins 1988)

WILLIS, J *Teaching English Through English* (Longman 1981)

WRIGHT, A *Roles of teachers and learners* (Oxford University Press 1987)

WRIGHT, A, BUCKBY, M and BETTERIDGE, D *Games for Language Learning: New Edition* (Cambridge University Press 1984)

Index

289